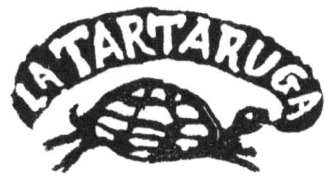

La Tartaruga. The Story of a Gallery
by Ilaria Bernardi

© 2022 Postmedia Srl, Milano

translated from:
La Tartaruga. Storia di una galleria
di Ilaria Bernardi

© 2018 Postmedia Srl, Milano

The photographs included in this book are held at the Archivio di Stato Latina, and are published here courtesy of the Ministry of Cultural Heritage and Activities (Concessione n. 0001686/2022) prohibiting any further reproduction.

Translated from the Italian: Sylvia Notini
Book design: Alessandra Mancini

www.postmediabooks.it
ISBN 9798359268622 (english edition)
ISBN 9788874901920 (italian edition)

LA TARTARUGA

THE STORY OF A GALLERY

Ilaria Bernardi

postmedia ● books

7		**INTRODUCTION**
		The Reasons for This Study
13	**I.**	**PLINIO DE MARTIIS**
		The Man, the Photographer, the Gallerist
17	**II.**	**1954 – 1962**
		VIA DEL BABUINO no.196

17	1954: The Gallery Opens
20	1955-1956: The Conflict Between Figuration and Abstraction
25	1957: The Echoes of American Abstract Expressionism and European Informal Art
29	1958: The Relationship with the United States Intensifies
35	1958-1959: Interest in the Publishing World
37	1960: An Eye on the Younger Generation
39	1961: The Making of a 'School'
43	1961-1962: Toward the Relocation of the Venue

INDEX

49 III. 1963 – 1968
PIAZZA DEL POPOLO no. 3

49	1963: The Gallery's New Venue
54	1964: American Invasion
61	1965: The Practice of the Environment
73	1966: Upholding Rome's Independence from New York
75	1967-1968: Spilling over into Action May 6-31,
87	1968: The Teatro delle Mostre June-October
93	1968: Toward the Closing of the Gallery

99 CONCLUSION
The Main Events from 1969 to 2004

103 APPENDIX
1954-2004 Chronology

INTRODUCTION

THE REASONS FOR THIS STUDY

In the wake of the ever-growing interest in 1960s and 1970s Italian art, in recent years there has been an increasing number of exhibitions and publications dedicated to the most important artists, movements, and exhibition events from those decades. Nonetheless, only rarely do we come across monographic texts that focus on a careful and in-depth reconstruction of the private Italian exhibition spaces (the art galleries) that hosted those artists, those movements, and those events. Moreover, most of them correspond to catalogues or books published on the occasion of exhibitions,[1] while publications for research purposes are instead few and far between.[2] The idea of publishing a book that scientifically retraces the events of a gallery – the Galleria La Tartaruga – that was essential to the development of Italian art during the second postwar period is based on the belief that the artists' output and in particular the conception of some of the exhibitions held in those years are more easily understood if contextualized within the activity carried out by the gallerist promoting them.

Founded in Rome in February 1954 by Plinio De Martiis and managed by him with the constant help of his wife Maria Antonietta Pirandello (known as Ninì), from the very start La Tartaruga was the favorite meeting place of artists, literati, critics, gallerists, and both Italian and foreign intellectuals. After having determined, in 1957, that the avant-garde was the specific direction that should be followed when choosing the artists it intended to promote, and after having hosted the first solo shows in Europe of the works of Franz Kline and Cy Twombly, as well as important Robert Rauschenberg, Salvatore Scarpitta, and Ettore Colla exhibitions, in the early 1960s La Tartaruga was the first private exhibition space to promote research into Pop Art in Rome, thus becoming the point of reference for that group of young artists destined to be a part of the so-called 'Pop italiana,' better defined as the 'Scuola di Piazza del Popolo.' Included were Franco Angeli, Mario Ceroli, Tano Festa, Giosetta Fioroni, Renato Mambor, Mario Schifano, and Cesare Tacchi. During those same years, it also promoted the debuts of Jannis Kounellis and Eliseo Mattiacci; it hosted the first solo show of the work of Gerhard Richter in Italy; and it organized significant exhibitions of Alberto Burri, Mimmo Rotella, Enrico Castellani, Piero Manzoni, Pino Pascali, and Fabio Mauri. La Tartaruga's importance also lies in the numerous collaborations that, especially in the 1960s, it undertook with Italian galleries (like the Apollinaire, l'Ariete, L'Attico, Blu, de' Foscherari, Lambert, Marconi, Naviglio, and Schwarz) and ones abroad (including Iris Clert in Paris; Martha Jackson and Sonnabend in New York; Anne Abels in Cologne). Of fundamental importance was the close relationship with the New York gallery owned by Leo Castelli which guaranteed the constant renewal of Italian art vis-à-vis what was present across the ocean, and vice versa. Capable of intercepting the most recent trends in avant-garde research, in the second half of the 1960s La Tartaruga was among the first exhibition spaces to propose the transition from the traditional art of the painting and sculpture to the ephemeral action and to the site-specific installation, welcoming and supporting these types of research until 1968, the year of the event titled *Teatro delle Mostre* that was specifically devoted to them. It was also after the death, also in 1968, of Lucio Fontana, Pino Pascali, and Marcel Duchamp, that De Martiis brought his activity in the gallery's Piazza del Popolo location to an end as a sign of the end of a unique era, undeniably influenced by those three artists. From 1969 onwards De Martiis would reopen his gallery in a series of venues, but without ever achieving the success of the previous years. After his wife passed away in 1971, he focused his activity on theater, cinema, music, visual poetry, while from the late 1970s to 1985 he supported the group of the so-called Anacronisti, after which, until 1995, he chose to devote most of his time to art publishing. That was the year when he opened a new location for the gallery in Castelluccio di Pienza (Siena), which remained active until 2000.

The activity of La Tartaruga from 1969 to 2000, in addition to being discontinuous, was no doubt less far-sighted, purposeful, and incisive with respect to the first fifteen years, as himself De Martiis admits: "The real gallery was short-lived; it began in 1957 and continued until 1968, ending with *Teatro delle Mostre*; then, in the 1970s I did things that I could also do today, without painters, which was the case of the IIa Tartaruga, while the IIIa Tartaruga can be described as an unrealistic, nebulous return to painting."[3] For these very reasons, this monographic text focuses on the "real gallery," that is, on the period from when it opened on Via del Babuino to the closing in 1968 of its second location in Piazza del Popolo. Chapters I and III center on the activity at the gallery from 1954 to 1968; their subchapters instead focus not so much on analyzing the individual exhibitions and works of the artists over the period of a single year, or of a specific period examined each time, but on identifying for the first time ever the junctures, the reasons, the common threads, and what was unique about the relative scheduling. The last, conclusive chapter instead sums up the exhibition activity post-1969. Lastly, the appendix offers the first chronological reconstruction of all the events promoted by De Martiis, from 1954 to his passing in 2004. Further, included with the chronology relating to the first and most important period of exhibition activity from 1954 to 1968, is an anthology of extracts from the respective invitations, brochures, and catalogues, or from reviews published at the time.

By consulting the publications released in memory of La Tartaruga and mentioned on various occasions in the notes to this book, we realize how they are limited to homages to the figure of De Martiis, or analyses relative to the 'Scuola di Piazza del Popolo' of which he was the mentor, without ever accurately describing the history of the gallery based on a study of its archive. This monographic text aims to provide an accurate and documented reconstruction of the exhibitions, the publishing experiences, the relationships and events of La Tartaruga, based on meticulous research conducted in the De Martiis archive, currently preserved at the Archivio di Stato di Latina and made available to scholars at the behest of the gallerist himself.

Indeed, as early as 1999, De Martiis had suggested that the Istituto della Grafica - Calcografia Nazionale di Roma purchase the part of the archive that included the signs-posters made by the artists for the gallery exhibitions, the cartoons, pastels, and oils by the various authors, as well as the photographic archive made up of around 5,000 photos and negatives. However, the negotiations fell through and the Istituto della Grafica acquired only the signs-posters. Hence, the papers for the acquisition of the remaining part of the archive were handed over to the Direzione Generale per l'Arte Contemporanea, then to the Direzione Generale per gli Archivi, and finally to the Sovrintendenza archivistica per il Lazio, which in August 2003 declared it to be of considerable historical interest, thus advising that the Administration acquire it. When De Martiis passed away, in July 2004, his daughters Caterina and Paola advanced the matter of said acquisition, managing to achieve this goal. The archive of La Tartaruga, which entered the Archivio Centrale di Stato di Roma that soon afterwards transferred it to the Archivio di Stato di Latina, essentially includes: correspondence with artists, critics, art historians, literati; catalogues, posters of various kinds and brochures relative to the gallery exhibitions; various types of printed materials and publications; and lastly, the whole photographic archive.[4]

Here I have chosen to reconstruct the history of La Tartaruga by providing images and materials taken solely from its archive for the purpose of showing just what De Martiis was not able to bring to term, but in view of which he had rearranged the entire archive fond before deciding to sell it: "the last obsession of his life," reveals Ottaviano Del Turco, was "the drafting of a book-cum-document meant to be a mirror of his identity and, at the same time, a Penelope's shroud that could never, in his lifetime, be finished."[5] The book is dedicated to the history of his gallery, focused on the years from 1954 to 1968, and based on documents and photographs that are a part of his archive.

The intention to fulfill the gallerist's desire cannot however overlook a preliminary study of De Martiis' personality (in chapter one here); one that encouraged him, as early as the 1950s, to abandon the traditional task of the art dealer and instead take on the role of the 'director' of a coherent exhibition plan in so far as it was based on his ability to carefully guide the artists, working alongside them and even suggesting exhibition-related solutions to them. For this reason, De Martiis can retrospectively be considered a curator *ante litteram*. Reconstructing the history of La Tartaruga in its "original years"[6] thus involves a parallel reflection on how the figure of the curator has developed in today's capitalist society. In other words, it means asking oneself whether the profession of the curator that De Martiis, albeit unknowingly, foreshadowed, and that in his case corresponded to incentivizing the development of an avant-garde art that was high in quality, in time has instead become functional to the capitalistic need to conceive art as a consumer product, assessed on the basis of revenues and the number of visitors, rather than on the significance of the specific contents.

This book would not have been possible without the precious help of so many people it would be impossible to name them all here. In any case, I wish to express my heartfelt thanks to Caterina and Paola De Martiis for their help and the materials they provided me with, as well as to all the staff of the Archivio di Stato di Latina for having made available to me the gallery archive and for having given me all the photographic reproductions published here.

1. Mentioned are: Sargentini F. - Lambarelli R. - Masina L. V. (eds.), *L'Attico, 1957-1987. 30 anni di pittura, scultura, musica, danza, performance, video*, catalogue of the exhibition (Spoleto, Church of San Nicolò, July 1 - August 30, 1987), Mondadori, Milan - De Luca, Rome 1987; Lancioni Daniela (ed.), *Gian Tomaso Liverani. Un disegno dell'arte. La Galleria La salita dal 1957 al 1998*, U. Allemandi, Turin 1998, volume published on the occasion of the eponymous exhibition (Rome, Spazio per l'Arte Contemporanea Tor Bella Monaca, December 2, 1998 - January 10, 1999); Manno Tolu R. - Messina M. G. (eds.), *Fiamma Vigo e "numero." Una vita per l'arte*, exhibition catalogue (Florence, Archivio di Stato, October 7 - December 20, 2003), Centro Di, Florence 2003; Giovannetti Tatiana (ed.), *2 dicembre 1963: nasce una nuova galleria. Opere e testimonianze*, exhibition catalogue (Rome, Studio Arco d'Alibert, December 14, 2006 - February 24, 2007), Gangemi, Rome 2006; Maubant J. L. - Jarauta F. (eds.), *Collezione Christian Stein. Una storia dell'arte italiana*, exhibition catalogue (Valencia, IVAM Institut Valencià d'Art Modern, October 7, 2010 - January 23, 2011; Lugano, Museo Cantonale d'arte, March 12 - May 15, 2011), Electa, Milan 2010; Barbero L. M. - Pola F., (eds.), *Macroradici del contemporaneo: L'attico di Fabio Sargentini, 1966-1978*, exhibition catalogue (Rome, MACRO - Museo d'Arte Contemporanea Roma, October 26, 2010 - June 12, 2011), MACRO - Museo d'Arte Contemporanea Roma, Roma - Electa, Milan 2010; Viliani Andrea (ed.), *Lucio Amelio. Dalla Modern Art Agency alla genesi di* Terrae Motus *(1965-1982). Documenti, opere, una storia…*, exhibition catalogue (Naples, Museo d'Arte Contemporanea Donnaregina - Madre, November 22, 2014 - April 6, 2015), Electa, Milan 2014.

2. Reference is made in particular to the following two volumes: Monola A. - Mundici M. C. - Poli F. - Roberto M. T. (eds.), *Gian Enzo Sperone. Torino, Roma, New York. 35 anni di mostre tra Europa e America*, Hopefulmonster, Turin 2000; Bandini M. - Mundici M. C. - Roberto M. T., *Luciano Pistoi: inseguo un mio disegno*, Hopefulmonster, Turin 2008.

3. Plinio De Martiis in conversation with Chiara Criconia, in Criconia Chiara, *La Tartaruga*, graduation thesis 2003-2004, Università Ca' Foscari, Venice, p. 22.

4. For more on the acquisition of the archive of La Tartaruga see "Breve storia della galleria La Tartaruga," in *Engrammi*, July 14, 2011: http://engrammi.blogspot.it/2011/07/breve-storia-della-galleria-la.html.

5. Del Turco Ottaviano, "Il libro non finito di Casa De Martiis," in Savinio A. - Antonini F. - de Feo G. C. (eds.), *La Tartaruga. Privato. Plinio De Martiis. Marzo 2006*, Il Segno, Rome 2006, p. 10.

6. It was De Martiis himself who defined the "original years" the ones related to his exhibition activity until "1968 (De Martiis Plinio, "Gli anni originali", in *La Tartaruga. Quaderni d'Arte e Letteratura* 5-6, De Luca, Rome 1989).

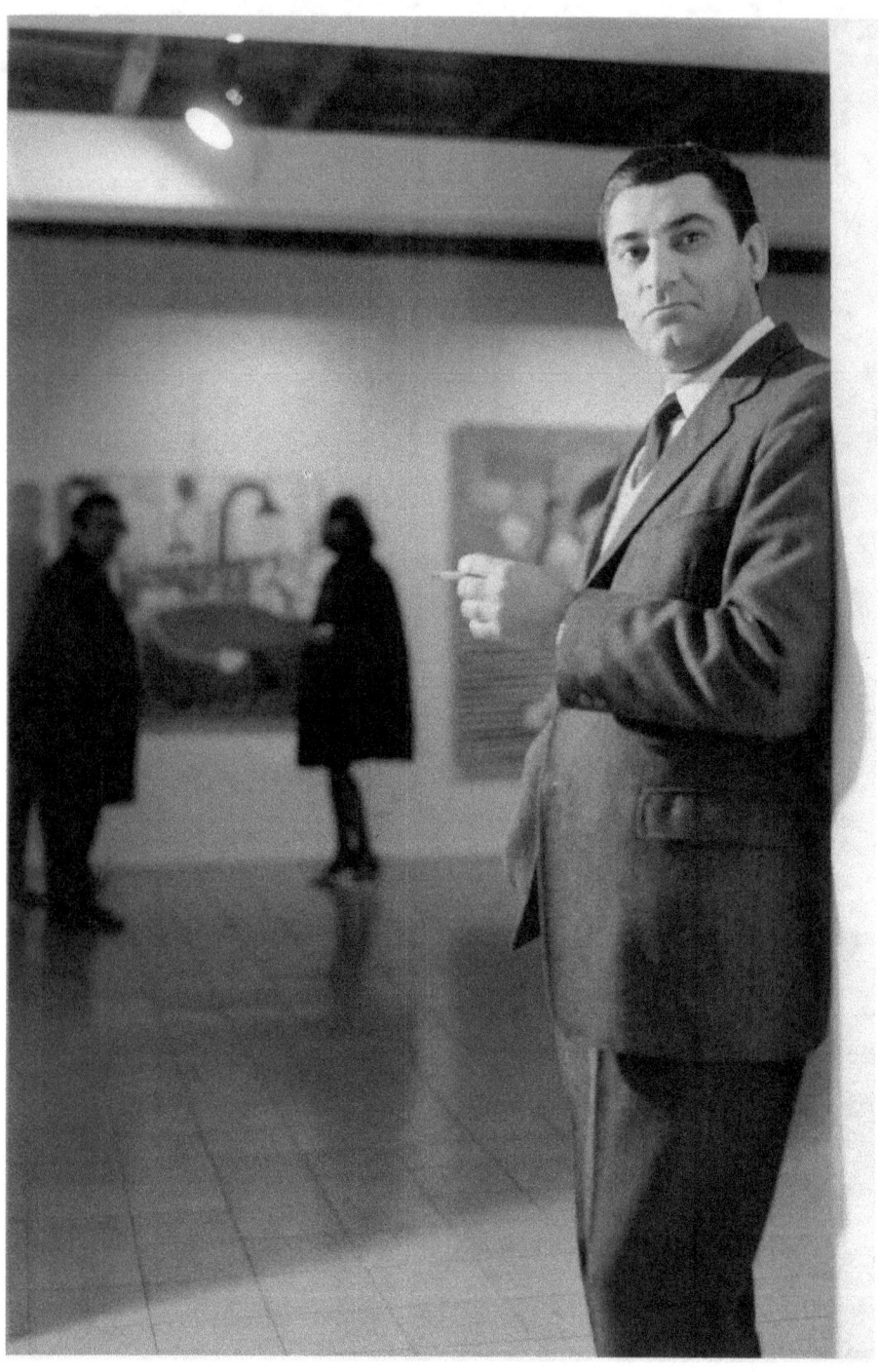

PLINIO DE MARTIIS ON THE OCCASION OF THE
PETER SAUL EXHIBITION AT LA TARTARUGA,
ROME, DECEMBER 21, 1963
PH.: PLINIO DE MARTIIS

PLINIO DE MARTIIS

THE MAN,
THE PHOTOGRAPHER,
THE GALLERIST

"I don't want to represent myself. I'm filled with doubts. I'm not 'finalized.' Even now I still don't know what I'm going to do in my life."[1] This is how Plinio De Martiis described himself, one of the figures who contributed most of all to the development of Italian art in the 1950s and 1960s. Born in Giulianova, in the province of Teramo, on October 30, 1920, the firstborn child of Guido De Martiis and Olga Barnabei, when he was still a boy his family, including him and one of his younger sisters (his other sister had died at a tender age) moved to Rome. When the Second World War began he was called to arms, but one evening in 1942 he got off the streetcar headed to the barracks in Pietralata where he should have resumed his military service and decided never to return. Now that he was a deserter he joined an anti-fascist cell that included among its members the artists Giulio Turcato, Emilio Vedova, Mario Mafai, and Renato Guttuso. A highly committed and anti-fascist militant Communist, he devoted himself heart and soul to the organization. He lived in hiding, moving from one place to another to avoid being arrested, until June 4, 1944, when Rome was liberated by the United States Army and the world war started to come to an end.

The lively Roman climate that developed in the postwar period allowed him to develop several of his interests, including photography, cinema, and, most of all, theater. On the night between December 31, 1945 and January 1, 1946, De Martiis founded and inaugurated the cabaret of the "Teatro dell'Arlecchino" (currently Teatro Flaiano), with performances by Franca Valeri, Alberto Bonucci, and Vittorio Caprioli, among others. The name "L'Arlecchino" was suggested to him by his friend the painter Mafai, who also created the sign for the venue: a collage made with the Am-lire distributed by the Americans in Rome right after the war.[2] Situated on Via Santo Stefano del Cacco, "L'Arlecchino" immediately became a place where artists and intellectuals like Giorgio de Chirico, Palma Bucarelli, Luchino Visconti, Anna Magnani, Vittorio Gassman, Bice Valori, and Alberto Moravia would meet. Almost a clue to his future profession as a gallerist was the evening when De Martiis organized a spectacular event ahead of its time there: a competition between Roman artists that involved decorating to music, and in just four minutes, the section of the wall they had chosen before starting.[3]

Although it was an important experimental and avant-garde theater, "L'Arlecchino" closed just two years after it had first opened. The reason for this was of an administrative nature that had nothing to do with Plinio, who in the meantime, in 1946, had married Marina Antonietta Pirandello (nicknamed Ninnì). She was the daughter of the writer Stefano (nom de plume Stefano Landi) and granddaughter of the Sicilian playwright Luigi. The couple had met at the "L'Arlecchino" where Ninnì had worked as a dancer and actress. Soon afterwards Plinio became interested in photography, his first real work experience.

De Martiis developed this interest thanks to the photographer who was living in the apartment opposite to the one where he had gone to live with his new wife. After purchasing a Rolleicord and choosing as his masters Cartier Bresson, the American photographers of *Life*, and the Magnum Agency, and Mario Garrubba, in a short period of time De Martiis became a professional photographer and from 1949 to 1954 began working for national newspapers like *L'Unità* and *Il Mondo*.[4] In 1951, tasked with creating the image for the cover of the book *Die Perlmutterfarbe* (Little White Lies) by the German writer Anna Maria Jokl, he chose to portray a child who was almost seven years old, Duccio Trombadori, and who would later become his friend.[5] At the same time he worked for the weekly *Vie Nuove* and for the monthly *Noi Donne*, and eventually joined the Agenzia dei Fotografi Associati along with Mario Garrubba, Franco Pinna, Pablo Volta, and Nicola Sansone. Photography would continue to accompany him even when he became a gallerist, in that he himself would take on the job of documenting all the events he organized. His shots were always without posing, filled with details captured at an angle thanks to the "mordi e fuggi" (cut and run) method of the news reporter, but at the same time slightly built up in order to "capture the metaphysical immobility of the subject."[6] His subjects were mostly friends and acquaintances according to the belief that in-depth knowledge alone would allow a photographer to choose the right moment to take a picture.[7]

The project to open an art gallery in the location that he had rented at Via del Babuino no. 196, near Piazza del Popolo, was not De Martiis' own idea, as he instead wanted to open a photography studio with Tonino Cervi; it was his painter friends, including Mario Mafai, Achille Perilli, and Francesco Menzio in particular, who convinced him to "do what Nadar did,"[8] that is, devote himself to photography and at the same time host art shows, investing the eleven thousand lire he had at his disposal in a gallery that could be used as a venue for artists and intellectuals, and that, most importantly, would introduce avant-garde artistic research to the capital. Even though he had already seen to installing a partition between the space used for posing from the darkroom, he decided to follow his friends' advice: he left the partition in place and turned the space for posing into a gallery and the photography studio into an office. From that moment onwards he would forever abandon photography as a profession, and instead use it as a tool with which to document the events held at the gallery.

His inclination to move suddenly from one interest to another, from politics to theater, to photography, and now art, was also reflected in his activity as a gallerist, for which his wife Ninnì provided him with indispensable and constant support. The Baron Giorgio Franchetti, who was soon to become his biggest client and financial supporter, described the series of exhibitions at La Tartaruga as being the fruit of a "mente fulminante" (lightning-speed mind),[9] capable of leading to the success of young artists, of capturing the most innovative strands in contemporary artistic research, of heeding other disciplines with respect to traditional painting and sculpture, and, above all, of offering artists a panoply of fundamental inputs for the success of each of the shows. De Martiis "was not an art dealer," Mario Ceroli confirmed, "he was an artist/gallerist: his instructions to the artists were so precise it was impossible to go wrong! [...] when he wanted to organize an exhibition, he would go see the artist's work, bring it to the gallery, and then as he was about to install it there was a risk of the show being canceled or of everything having to be changed right away."[10] "Plinio was truly a *deus ex machina*," Giosetta Fioroni would say: "a *unicum* [...] a director-actor [...] a Duchampian figure because of the possibilities, insights, provocations he produced along with the artists."[11]

De Martiis' role as a director-cum-artist probably stemmed from his activity as an impresario at "L'Arlecchino," and from his interest in theater, which he began developing when he was an adolescent: "I have always had theater as a model," he would declare. "I would always go to the Teatro delle Arti to see Antonio Giulio Bragaglia rehearsing and so that was always a model for me, my readings of these books by Bragaglia on the Teatro degli Indipendenti about the exhibitions themselves."[12] Indeed, the Teatro degli Indipendenti, which remained active in Rome until 1930, offered cycles of concerts, exhibitions, and avant-garde performances based on the notion of the "theatrical theater"; that is, an activity in which the central element was the introduction of a director conceived as the new "coràgo," the coordinator and harmonizer of all the elements of the *mise-en-scène*. De Martiis' choice is probably based on this: from the opening of the gallery acting as a director-cum-actor capable of turning each exhibition into a work in itself, but at the same time a link in the chain or a passage between the previous event and the one that followed. It would be this way of working, together with his multifaceted personality and the cultural climate in Rome during the two decades of the 1950s and 1960s, characterized by a constant osmosis of ideas between poets, directors, writers, and artists, that made La Tartaruga a *unicum* in the Italian exhibition scene, and not just that.

---

1. Trombadori Duccio, *Quel centesimo di secondo*, in *Archivio - Fotografie di Plinio De Martiis*, exhibition catalogue (Rome, Galleria Netta Vespignani, November 1993), Rome 1993, p. 14.
2. Cf. Mughini Giampiero, "Un fotografo che somigliava a Dustin Hoffman," in Id., *Che belle le ragazze di via Margutta*, Mondadori, Milan 2004, p. 159. Am-lira (acronym for Allied Military Currency) was the currency that the American military organ assigned to the administration of the territories occupied by the Allies during World War II (the AMGOT) put in circulation in Italy after the first landing in Sicily that took place on the night between July 9 and 10, 1943.
3. Cf. "Incontri/Plinio De Martiis," in *L'Espresso Sera* 8, May 28, 1967.
4. Cf. Trombadori Duccio, *Quel centesimo di secondo*, *op. cit.*, p. 11.
5. Cf. "Plinio de Martiis gli scatti del tempo," in *La Repubblica*, November 19, 2001.
6. Cf. Trombadori Duccio, *Quel centesimo di secondo*, *op. cit.*, p. 12.
7. Cf. Plinio De Martiis, in Mirolla Miriam, *L'arte c'est moi*, Avagliano Editore, Rome 2006, p. 103.
8. Trombadori Duccio, *Quel centesimo di secondo*, *op. cit.*, p. 10.
9. Giorgio Franchetti, in Tugnoli Andrea, *La scuola di Piazza del Popolo*, Maschietto editore, Florence 2004, p. 121.
10. Mario Ceroli in conversation with Ilaria Bernardi, Rome, December 1, 2009, in Bernardi Ilaria, *Teatro delle Mostre, Roma, maggio 1968*, Scalpendi editore, Milan 2014, p. 187.
11. Giosetta Fioroni in conversation with Ilaria Bernardi, Rome, December 6, 2009, *ivi*, p. 175.
12. Plinio De Martiis in conversation with Arabella Natalini, in Natalini Arabella, *Roma e l'esperienza della Pop Art: 1954-1964*, graduation thesis 1994/1995, Università degli Studi di Firenze, p. 121.

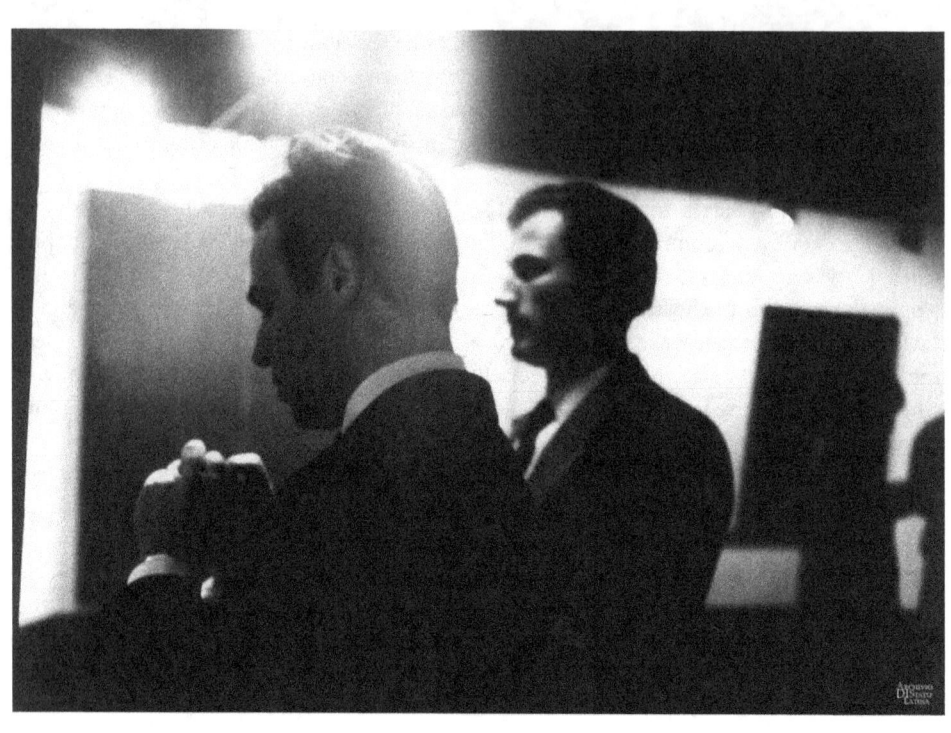

MARIO SCHIFANO AND PLINIO DE MARTIIS AT
THE *MARIO SCHIFANO* EXHIBITION
PH.: PLINIO DE MARTIIS

II 1954 – 1962
VIA DEL BABUINO no. 196

1954: The Gallery Opens

The birth of the Galleria La Tartaruga is in some ways linked to chance. During an evening with friends, De Martiis, his wife Ninì, Mino Maccari, Mario Mafai, and the intellectual Nicola Ciarletta decided to put forward, each on a single slip of paper, a possible name to attribute to the future exhibition space. After placing the five options inside Mafai's hat, they proceeded to extract one of them. The slip that was drawn by chance read "La Tartaruga": it was the name chosen by Maccari who thought it would be good luck to name a gallery like an animal that is famous for being slow, but synonymous with always getting to where it wants to go. After the name was chosen, it was up to Mafai to design the logo, which depicted a more or less stylized turtle: in the first version the turtle floated surrounded by a starry sky, while in the second and final one it appeared suspended against a white background in what seemed like a self-introduction thanks to the addition of a sort of cartoon that read "LA TARTARUGA."[1]

By that time, everything was ready for the opening of the gallery. Thursday, February 25, 1954, the exhibition space on Via Babuino no. 196 was inaugurated, presenting the exhibition *Cosacchi da ridere* as its first event. On display were forty lithographs representing the same number of caricatures made by the French artists Honoré Daumier, Cham (Amédée de Noé), and Charles Vernier, part of the eponymous book published by Le Chiavari (Paris). The lithographs arrived in Rome from Paris by way of the judge Gigi Pepe, a friend of De Martiis, but the reason for their exhibition probably derives from Maccari's influence on the gallerist, someone who had always been interested in graphic art. (On November 10 of that same year Maccari held his own solo show at La Tartaruga.) Perhaps for the same reason, on May 8, 1954 De Martiis dedicated a second exhibition to graphic art, presenting the lithographs of the French artist Jean-Louis Forain, accompanied by prints by Goya, Gericault, Daumier, Delacroix, Manet, Renoir, Sisley, Morisot, Cézanne, and Picasso.

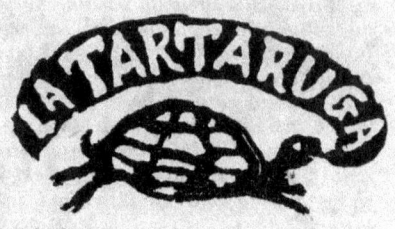

LA TARTARUGA

BOLLETTINO DELLA GALLERIA
Novembre 1954

MERCOLEDÌ 10 ALLE ORE 18
*Inaugurazione della mostra
di incisioni e disegni di*

MINO MACCARI

Galleria "La Tartaruga"
Roma, Via del Babuino 196
Tel. 61611

UNA TESTIMONIANZA DI NICOLA CIARLETTA

Dove le parole diventano segni, e i segni parole

*V*edete Maccari nelle vignette del «Mondo», nei frontespizi dei numeri unici, nei cul-de-lamp delle riviste letterarie, sulle tovaglie delle trattorie; dovunque potete vedere tracce del suo ingegno. Ma difficilmente vi riesce di vedere la sua mano, libera come un pesce, disegnare per chilometri e chilometri senza staccarsi mai dal foglio.

Se ciò vi capitasse, mettereste a fuoco il suo genio industre e leggero, scanzonato e fertilissimo, più scaltro che sentimentale, più loico che lirico, più incline all'infinito della grandezza che a quello della piccolezza: un genio che, maturando sovra un suolo strettissimo e sotto un cielo immenso, preferisce tenere le basi nell'empireo e guardare la terra. Se Maccari potesse disegnare senza interrompersi sull'intera superficie del globo, lo vedremmo quale realmente è: un topo che partorisce una montagna e non l'opposto come alcuni spiriti raffinatissimi.

Maccari è l'esempio più spontaneo e coerente della confusione odierna tra pittura e letteratura. Il suo amore dei pennini e degli inchiostri è amore della scrittura. Tracciare una figura sulla carta è come tracciare delle lettere. Infatti nelle figure di Maccari si intuiscono varie grafie: ora corsive, ora diritte, qua piegano a sinistra come la scrittura di certe donne esagitate, là si gonfiano come certi caratteri ampollosi; talvolta precipitano dal rigo come la grafia dei depressi, talaltra se ne levano giubilanti come dittatori.

Nello stesso tempo la scrittura di una lettera è come il disegno di una figura. Un'a può essere un disegno floreale; una u, un disegno espressionista: l'i è ironico; l'o è bonario. Malgrado il suo impersonale decoro, un vocabolario può mutarsi in un teatro amenissimo. E se pure il mondo di Maccari raggiunge talora le soglie di una estrema raffinatezza, ben altrimenti il suo impulso na-

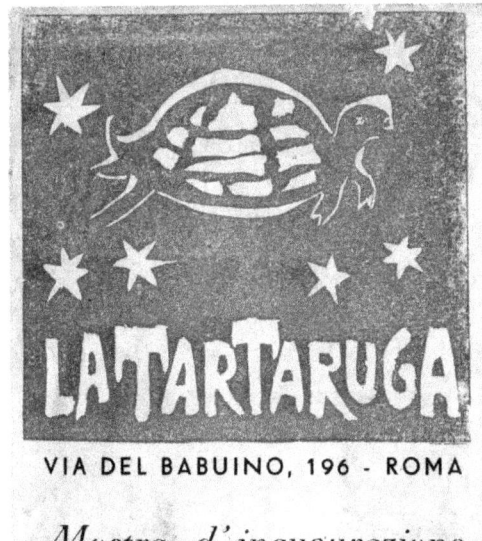

INVITATION TO THE INAUGURAL EXHIBITION OF THE FIRST GALLERY VENUE *"COSACCHI DA RIDERE" LITOGRAFIE DI DAUMIER CHAM & VERNIER*, FEBRUARY 25, 1954

The exhibitions dedicated to the artists in the Roman milieu were instead the result of Mafai's influence on the gallerist. Most of the artists in the group were linked to the 'Scuola Romana' of expressionist inclination, of which Mafai was the initiator in 1929 (*Giovanni Omiccioli*, March 10; *Piero Sadun*, April 13), or to the Associazione Artistica Nazionale on Via Margutta where he had shown his work in 1927 (*Eva Fischer*, March 20; *Pierluigi Sonetti*, April 1).

At the same time, the suggestions made by his friend Turcato could have favored both the solo show of Antonio Vangelli (April 26) with whom he had displayed his work in 1943 at the exhibition *La pittura cambia pelle* hosted by the Galleria Campana di Roma, and the solo show of Sante Monachesi (May 29) with whom, in 1946, he had shared the group exhibition *Corpora, Fazzini, Guttuso, Monachesi, Turcato* at the Galleria del Secolo in Rome.

The first group show hosted by La Tartaruga (December 11), with works by Mafai, Turcato, and by painters close to them (Birolli, Consagra, Corpora, Fazzini, Franchina, Gentilini, Guttuso, Leoncillo, Pirandello, Raphael), confirms the great influence that Mafai and Turcato had on De Martiis' exhibition choices. In the early years of his activity, the gallerist let his artist friends guide him, which resulted in his having a very heterogeneous program, not to mention the importance of an identity specific to the gallery, which solely supported the most recent avant-garde research.

His previous profession as a photojournalist and therefore time he spent in the publishing environment, resulted, however, in his paying closer attention to communication than his Roman colleagues. This led him to make sure that the events held in the gallery were always accompanied and publicized by specific publications. It was on the occasion of the above-

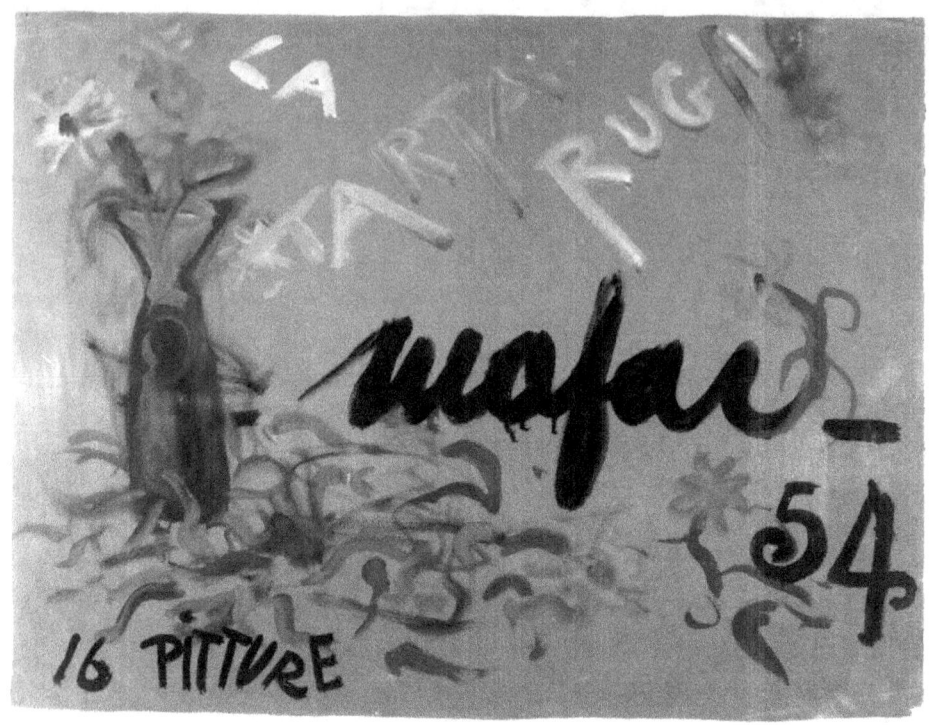

MARIO MAFAI, SIGN-POSTER OF ONE OF HIS SOLO SHOWS
SCHEDULED FOR 1954 AT LA TARTARUGA

mentioned solo show of Maccari's work, which opened after the ones dedicated to Henry Inlander (May 19), Eva Llorens (June 10), and Detomi (June 24), that the *Bollettino della galleria* was published: it was a sort of brochure printed by the Istituto Grafico Tiberino di Roma, whose four pages (a single sheet of cardboard folded in half lengthwise) were filled with the writings of the most important art critics and intellectuals who were not just from Rome. The first issues provided further information about the exhibitions held in the gallery each time, and included at the end was a newsletter about the most important artistic and cultural events underway in Italy. It was starting from the solo show of the work of Luigi De Angelis (December 30, 1954), instead, that the *Bollettino* came to resemble more of a catalogue, eliminating the newsletter, and dedicating more room to the criticism of the exhibitions, commissioned from art historians, intellectuals and poets, and often accompanied by the biographies and bibliographies of the artists showcased. Proof of De Martiis' close attention to Italian criticism is the long text by Maurizio Calvesi published in the *Bollettino* for the solo show of the work of Armando Buratti (November 24, 1954): the essay also marked Calvesi's joining of La Tartaruga's entourage as a critic, along with Cesare Vivaldi.

Included among the communication tools that favored the knowledge and dissemination of the gallery's exhibition activity was the sign that, in 1954, the gallerist asked Mafai to make, perhaps on the occasion of a personal visit planned for that year but that never took place. From that moment until 1962, all the exhibitions at the La Tartaruga were marked by

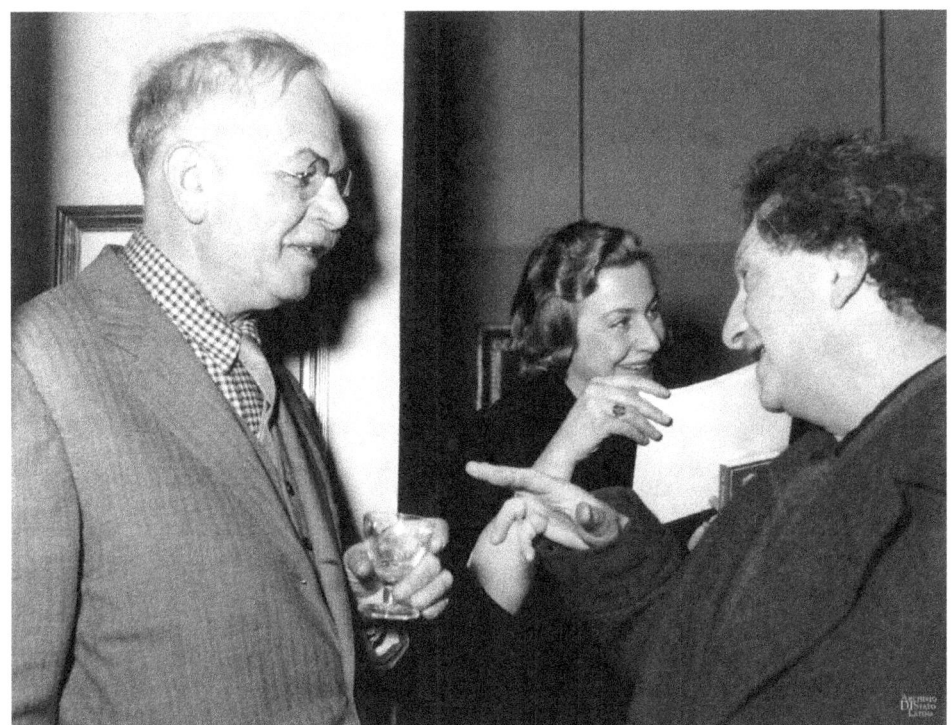

BEN SHAHN, LISA SPAGNOLI AND CARLO LEVI ON THE OCCASION OF THE *BEN SHAHN* EXHIBITION, APRIL 4, 1955
PH: PLINIO DE MARTIIS

so-called 'signs': average-sized sheets measuring 500 x 600 mm, made by each of the artists invited to show their work. The idea above all derived from the need to endow the gallery with something that could be viewed from the street, as the entrance was in the space beyond the front door of the building where it was located. At the same time, the posters were seen as tools capable of instantly registering in an immediately recognizable sign the complex style of the artist currently on display.[2] This underpinned the idea of the exhibition as a work in itself, a unitary and coherent one, that would always be supported and put into practice by De Martiis in the years that followed.

1955-1956: The Conflict Between Figuration and Abstraction

From 1955 onwards, La Tartaruga's program revealed a first openness toward artists from English-speaking countries. In fact, on January 18, 1955, the Englishman John Bratby showed his work, which was influenced by the realism of the painter Walter Sickert, and was characterized by the crude details and the vigorous brushwork used to depict conventional and everyday places and objects.

Nevertheless, in the first half of the 1950s Rome wasn't ready to accept this type of research just yet: the most successful exhibitions in the eyes of the critics were in fact the solo shows of

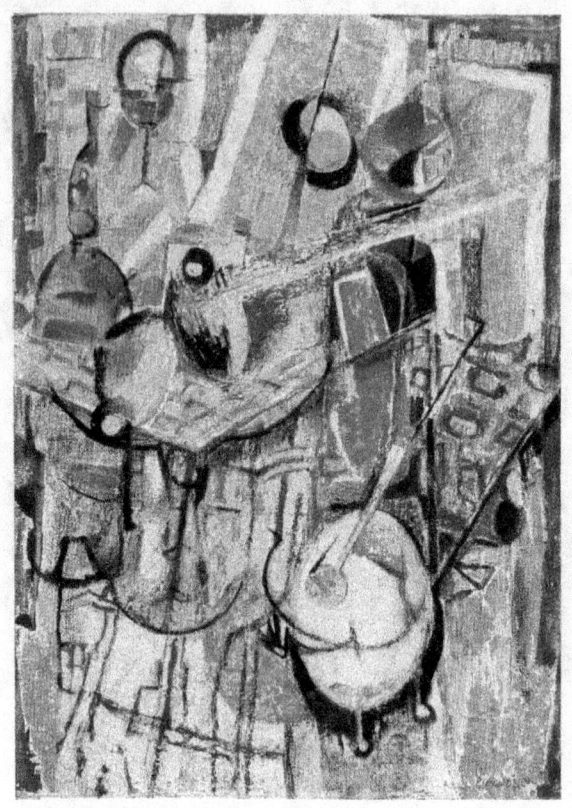

THE FIRST BROCHURE PUBLISHED BY LA
TARTARUGA ON THE OCCASION OF THE
FAUSTO PIRANDELLO EXHIBITION

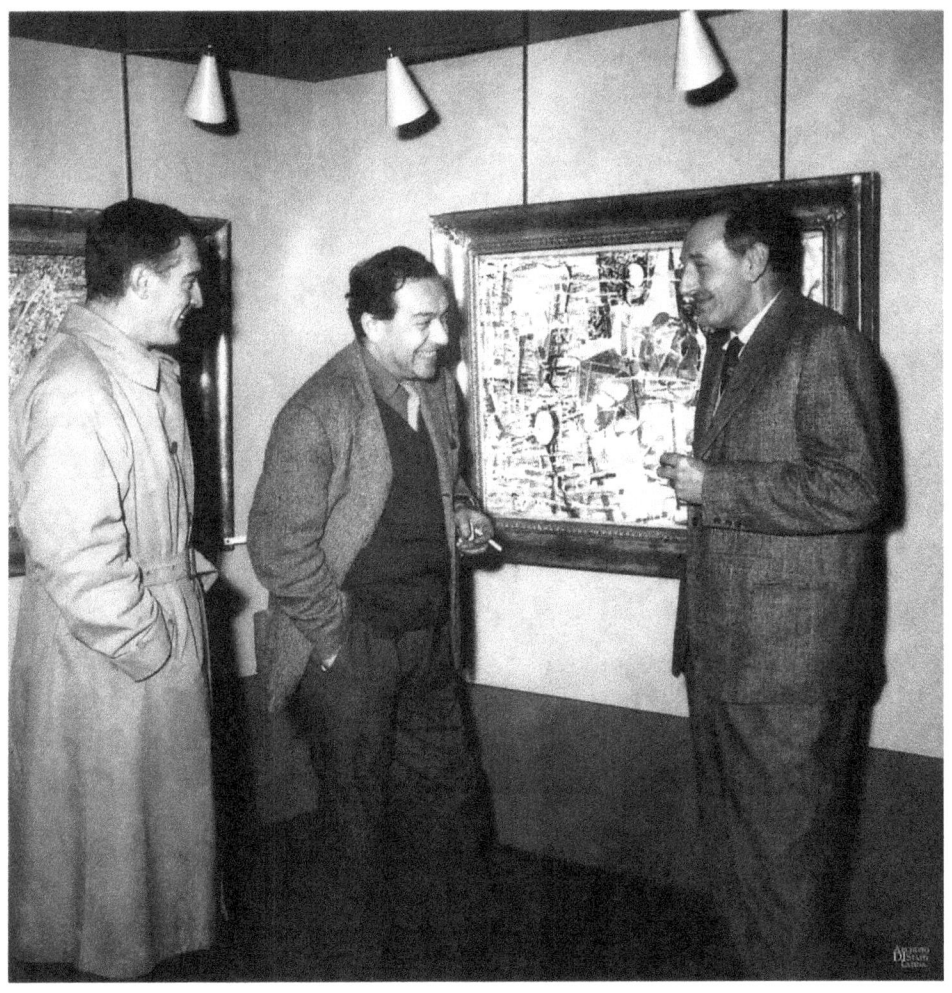

RENATO GUTTUSO (CENTER) AT THE *FAUSTO PIRANDELLO* EXHIBITION, NOVEMBER 8, 1956
PH.: PLINIO DE MARTIIS

artists in the Roman milieu, including Francesco Trombadori (February 3, 1955), Mario Mafai (February 21, 1955), and Giulio Turcato (March 11, 1955). For this reason as well, the gallery's activity for 1955, but also for 1956, was conceived by De Martiis to be a part of the wholly Italian debate between figuration and abstraction; foreshadowed right after the war by the opposition between Socialist Realism and Formalism, this debate had especially developed following the presence of the Abstract Expressionism of Willem De Kooning, Arshile Gorky, and Jackson Pollock at the United States Pavlion at the 1950 Venice Biennale.[3] Understanding the importance of this debate, De Martiis chose to act as a go-between: on the one hand, he paid attention to figurative art, while, on the other, he favored the dissemination of abstract art. The former intent saw exhibitions dedicated to Antonio Scordia (March 23, 1955), Ben Shahn (April 4, 1955), Antonietta Raphael Mafai (May 12, 1955), Antonio Cardile (May 28, 1955), Piero Sadun (November 12, 1955), Giuseppe Macrì (December 20, 1955), Riccardo Francalancia

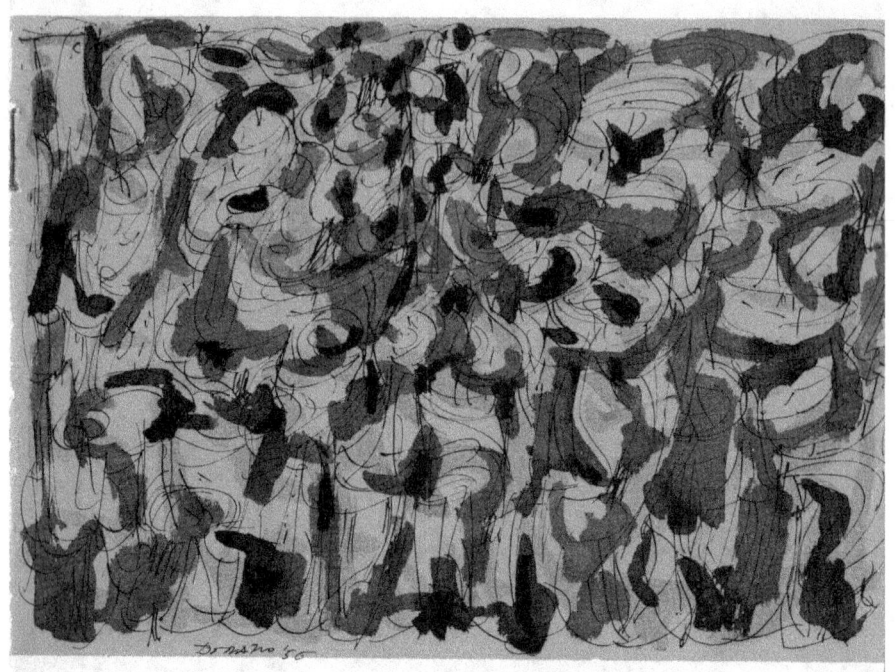

PIERO DORAZIO

GALLERIA LA TARTARUGA

THE FIRST CATALOG PUBLISHED BY LA TARTARUGA
ON THE OCCASION OF THE *PIERO DORAZIO*
EXHIBITION, JANUARY 24, 1957

(January 24, 1956), and Corrado Cagli (April 11, 1956); the latter intent instead involved the solo shows of Titina Maselli (April 16, 1955), Salvatore Scarpitta (April 30, 1955), Maria Petrucci (January 10, 1956), as well as of the artists Giacomo Balla, Filippo De Pisis, Mario Mafai, Giovanni Omiccioli, Mario Sironi, Renzo Vespignani all of whom included in the group show of December 30, 1955. However, the exhibition that more than any other paved the way for a fully-fledged 'conflict' between figuration and abstraction was *Sette pittori romani*, which opened on March 20, 1956. Facing each other on the gallery walls were the still figurative works of Vespignani and Muccini, and the abstract ones of Perilli, Dorazio, and Scarpitta. The *Bollettino* itself was designed to be 'conflictual': after a short introduction, the texts in which the participants explained their working method were paged so that a figurative artist alternated with an abstract one, as though they were engaged in a virtual debate on paper.

Until late 1956 La Tartaruga continued to reflect on the figuration-abstraction debate without ever taking a clear stance, however, to the extent that, on the occasion of a group show of Umbrian artists (De Gregorio, Marignoli, Raspi, Toscano, on April 28, 1956), the text written by Leoncillo in the *Bollettino* put forward the idea of a compromised dialectic between the two research strands as the path that should be taken. It was when the exhibition of the anti-realist works of Ugo Attardi (May 14, 1956) was held that De Martiis began to defend abstraction, presenting, later that same year, the paintings of Fausto Pirandello (November 8) and of Afro, Birolli, Corpora, Mafai, Moreni, Pirandello, Santomaso, Turcato, and Vedova (October 20).

1957: The Echoes of American Abstract Expressionism and European Informal Art

The final exhibition in 1956 included lithographs by Adam, Braque, Chagall, Hartung, Léger, Mirò, Picasso, Singier, Soulages. The choice was probably based on economic reasons rather than an interest in graphic art and French art. Inaugurated close to the Christmas season, it offered well-known names on the international scene, and more affordable and therefore more sellable art as compared with painting and sculpture.

After all, the appreciation that De Martiis showed for France's artistic research from the earliest days of the gallery had in the meantime declined in favor of a clear interest in the experiments being conducted across the Atlantic, first and foremost American Abstract Expressionism, in line with the new direction that had been taken over the past few years in Italy's artistic context. From the second half of the 1950s, in fact, in Italy there was a reinforcement of the axis with the United States, which had been constituted right after the war, thanks to numerous exhibition events.[4] It was in 1957, in particular, that the relationship between Rome and America became more intense: Cy Twombly arrived in the capital settling there permanently in 1960, while McCann founded the Rome-New York Art Foundation headquartered on Isola Tiberina, inaugurating it with an exhibition in which the works of Pollock, De Kooning, Kline, Sam Francis, Tobey, and Marca-Relli were placed side by side with the Italian ones of Capogrossi, Burri, Accardi, and Colla. Later, the first Pollock retrospective in Europe, hosted in March 1958 by Palma Bucarelli at the Galleria Nazionale d'Arte Moderna in Rome, would further strengthen the Rome-New York axis, whose constitution De Martiis would perceive from the year before.[5]

In 1957, in fact, after an exhibition dedicated to the abstract painting of the Turin artist Mario Lattes (January 9), and before the presentation of the lithographs and drawings of Antonio Scordia (February 7), on January 24, La Tartaruga welcomed for the first time the

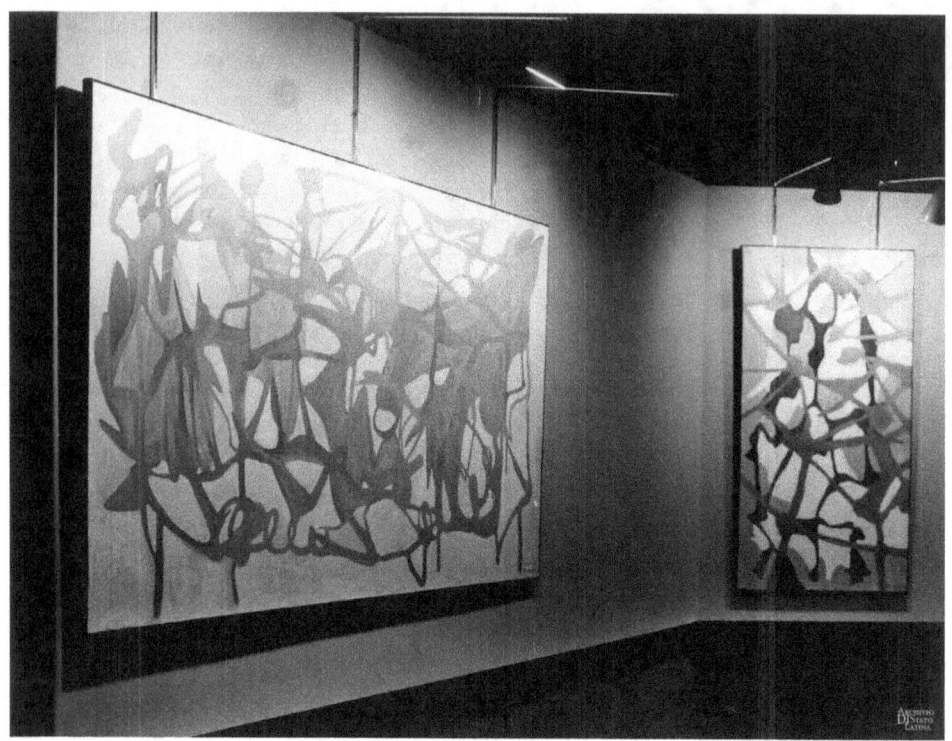

trends in American artistic research through the work of a Roman artist, Piero Dorazio, who five years earlier had moved to the United States where he had met De Kooning, Rothko, Pollock, Newman, and the critic Clement Greenberg, and later showed his work in New York at both the Stable Gallery and the Rose Fried Gallery.[6] Thanks to his first relationships with artistic research in the United States, from 1957, and especially from 1958, De Martiis bestowed on his gallery a precise identity, establishing it as an exhibition space for the promotion of avant-garde American art and especially art that was 'pro-American.'

On February 19, 1957, De Martiis dedicated a group show to Afro, Burri, and Scialoja. Three artists who had felt the need to look from close-up at the most recent research across the Atlantic. Afro had gone to New York in 1950 to show his work at the Catherine Viviano Gallery, with exhibitions held almost yearly until 1960: he had thus become an important link in Rome-US relations, introducing to America his friends Birolli, Morlotti, and Vedova, and organizing a solo show of Gorky's work at the Galleria L'Obelisco in Rome.[7] Burri had been sent to a prisoner-of-war camp in Texas and it was there that he began painting in 1943. After returning to Italy, he was chosen, in 1953, along with Capogrossi, to participate in the traveling exhibition *Younger European Painters: A Selection*. Moreover, upon receiving an invitation from the then-director of the Guggenheim Museum in New York, he went back to the United States where he showed his work at the Frumkin Gallery in Chicago, at the Stable Gallery in 1955, where he had a solo show, and at a group show that same year titled *The New Decade: 22 European Painters and Sculptors* at the Museum of Modern

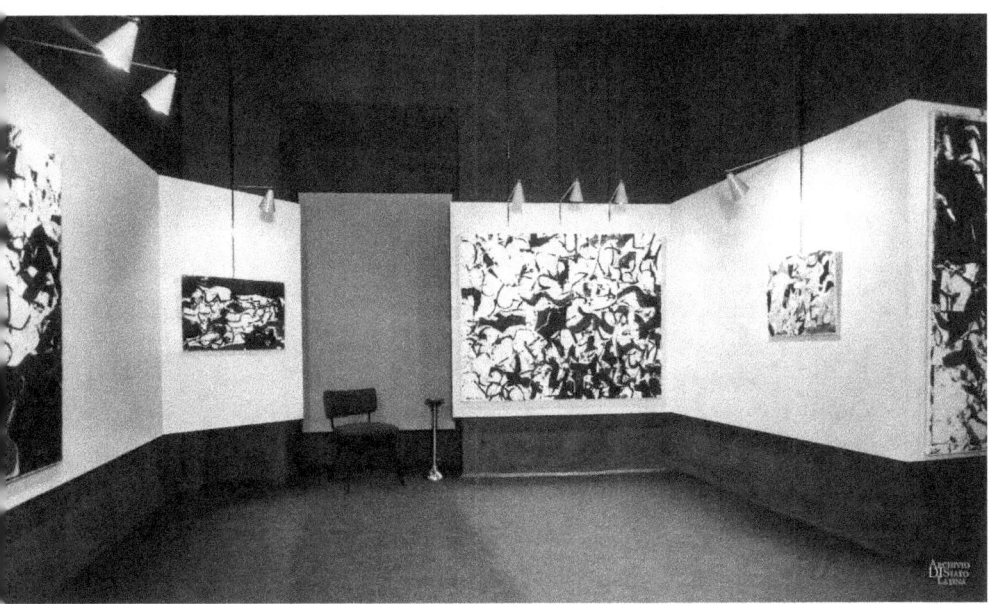

EXHIBITION VIEW OF *MARCA-RELLI.*
COLLAGES PAINTINGS, OCTOBER 19, 1957
PH.: PLINIO DE MARTIIS

LEFT: EXHIBITION VIEW OF *TURCATO*,
APRIL 24, 1957
PH.: PLINIO DE MARTIIS

Art.[8] Lastly, Scialoja was among the first to learn the lessons of Abstract Expressionism and Action Painting thanks to his spending time in America with Rothko, De Kooning, and Guston. After doing a show at the Catherine Viviano Gallery in 1956, he returned to Rome bringing with him some large drawings by Rauschenberg that he showed to his students at the Fine Arts Academy to encourage them to reflect on the New-Dada.[9] Of seminal importance in this sense was the exhibition that Scialoja himself inaugurated at La Tartaruga on June 16, 1959 where the cycle *Impronte* was displayed, consisting of signs repeated at times with a few small variations, where you the influence of the research that was being done across the Atlantic was clear to see.

In 1957, the echo of American Abstract Expressionism and American culture also reached La Tartaruga thanks to Salvatore Scarpitta and Conrad Marca-Relli, whose solo shows (on May 27 and October 19, respectively) followed the first Roman solo show of the Dutch artist Karel Appel (June 14) and the group show with works by Dorazio, Nuvolo, Perilli, Sterpini, and Scarpitta himself (October 7). While Scarpitta helped De Martiis to establish a relationship with the United States, since he had been born there in 1919 and lived there until 1936, Marca-Relli brought to Italy the tangible example not only of Abstract Expressionist research, but also of American culture. Born in Boston in 1913 to Italian parents, in 1948 he went to Rome for the first time, where he met Burri and Afro, and where he returned in 1951 and in 1957, after becoming a part of the group of Abstract Expressionists once they had returned to New York in 1949.

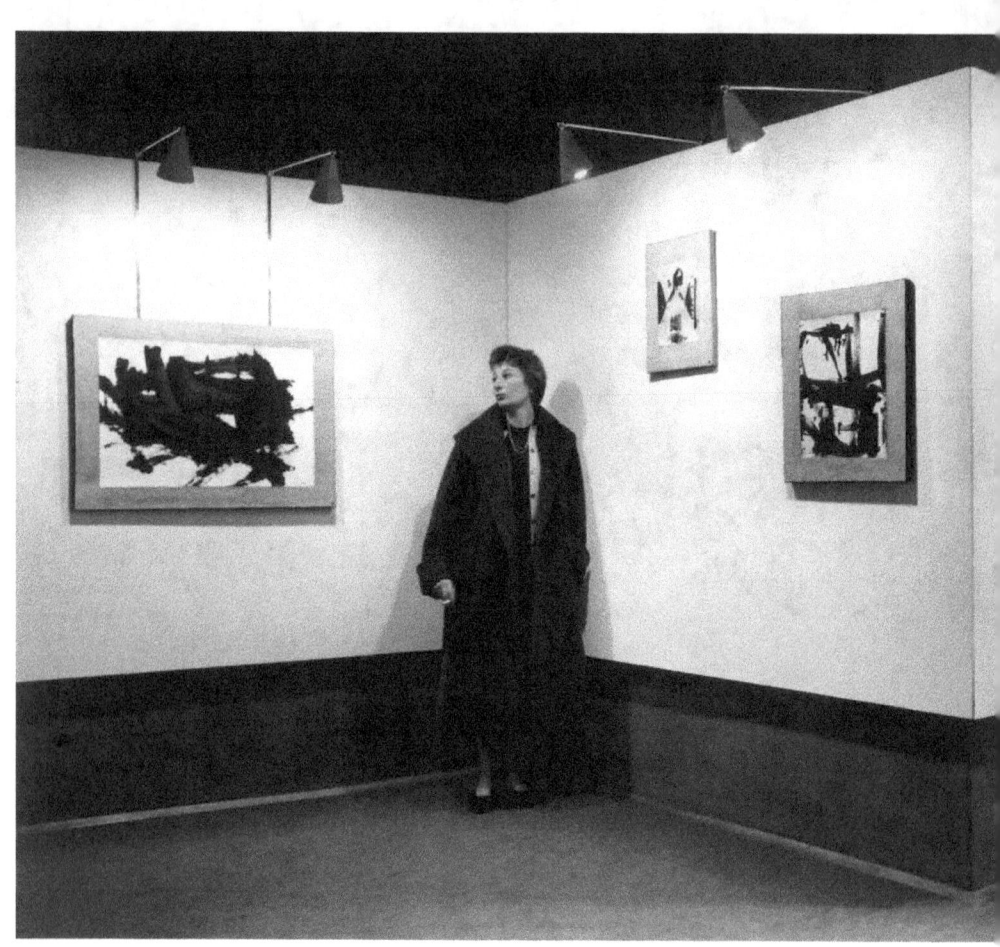

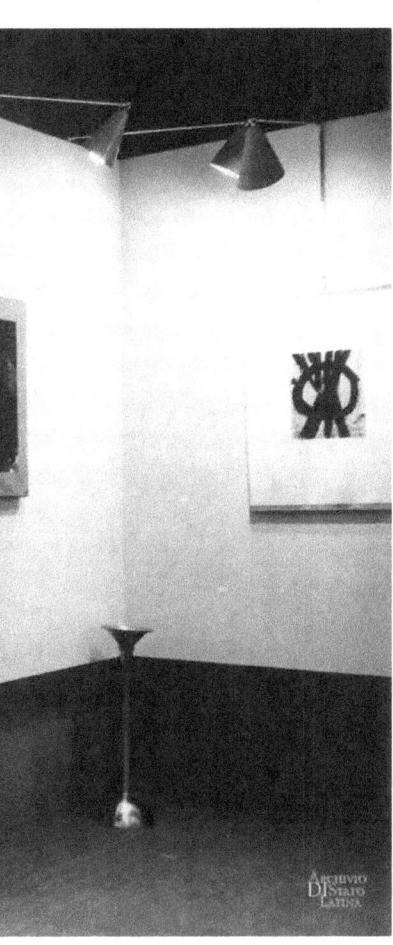

NINNÌ PIRANDELLO ON THE OCCASION OF
THE *KLINE* EXHIBITION, FEBRUARY 27, 1958
PH.: PLINIO DE MARTIIS

From 1956-1957 to the late 1950s, Dorazio, Afro, Burri, Scialoja, Scarpitta, and Marca-Relli were the main links between La Tartaruga and the research that was going on in the United States, but if, on the one hand, it was through them that De Martiis opened up to American Abstract Expressionism, on the other, he supported the informal research that was being done in Europe. It should come as no surprise that the solo show dedicated to Leoncillo's 'textural' informal art (March 4) was followed by a show dedicated to the abstract-concrete painting of Corpora (March 18), an artist who belonged to the Gruppo degli Otto and was therefore close to Turcato. The latter artist, on April 24, showed works that were midway between the two strands of informal art at the time, that of the sign and that of the material. Interest in the informal art of the sign likewise characterized the exhibition dedicated to Perilli (May 11), while the works presented at the Mafai solo show (April 3) were an example of painting that was dominated by the vibration of the chromatic material. Informal research later returned to La Tartaruga on the occasion of both the first solo show of the work of Ettore Colla titled *Ferri Legni* (November 18) and the group show *4 pittori contemporanei. Afro, Burri, Capogrossi, Matta* (December 5). Eleven months later, it was instead the foreign side of this research to be documented in a solo show dedicated to the German artist Wols (November 22, 1958), celebrated that same year by a retrospective at the Venice Biennale. However, it is worthwhile pointing out that unlike the convinced and heartfelt promotion of American Abstract Impressionism, De Martiis' support of the gestural, textural painting of informal art seems to have derived not so much from a real interest in this type of research – which he unsurprisingly referred to as "stifling academia"[10] – but rather from the willingness to stage the 'debate' between the two major trends at that moment in time. De Martiis had done the same thing in 1954 when he became the voice of the conflict between figuration and abstraction. From 1958 onwards this willingness would disappear entirely.

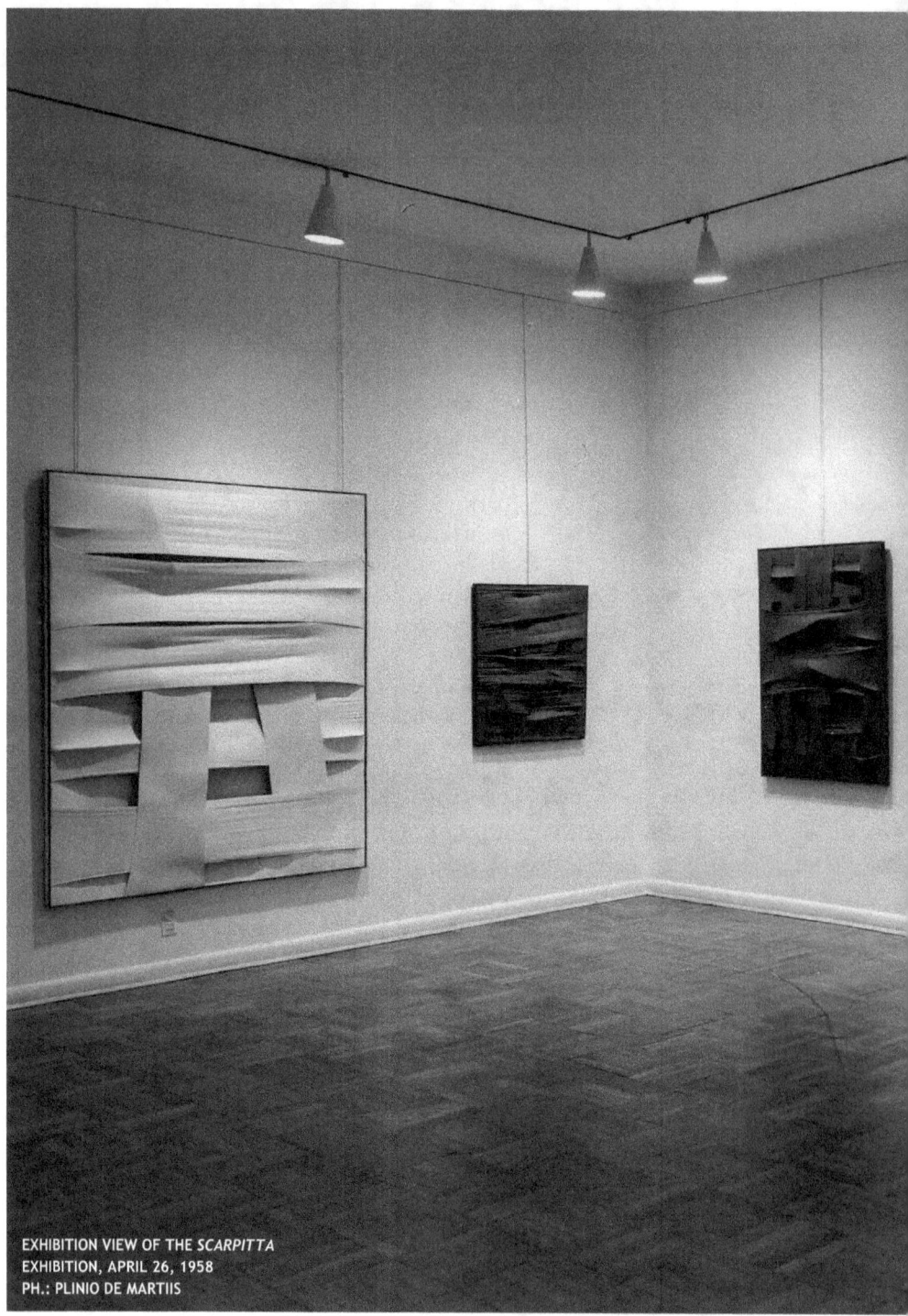

EXHIBITION VIEW OF THE *SCARPITTA* EXHIBITION, APRIL 26, 1958
PH.: PLINIO DE MARTIIS

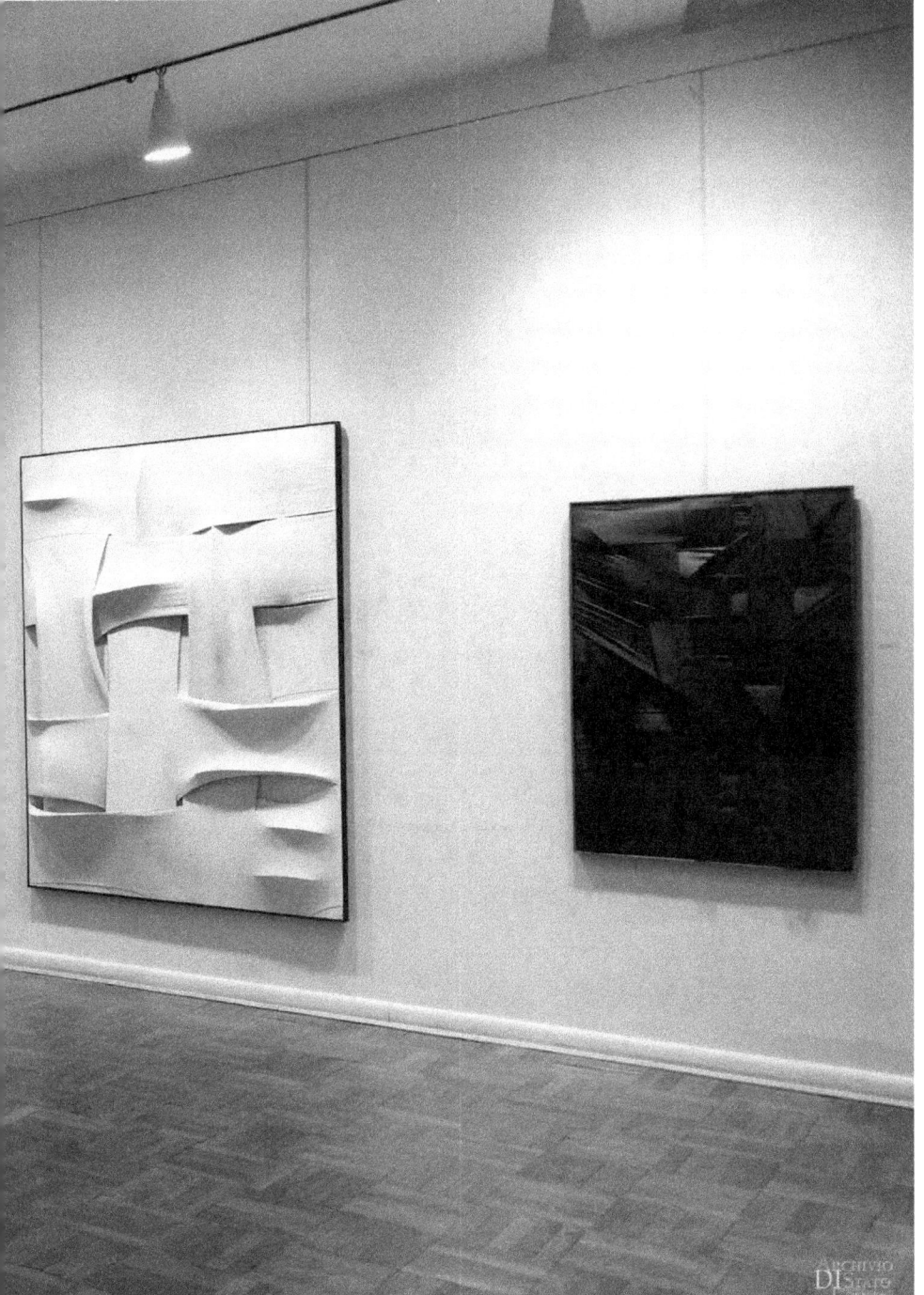

luglio ottobre **1958**

GALLERIA LA TARTARUGA

Roma

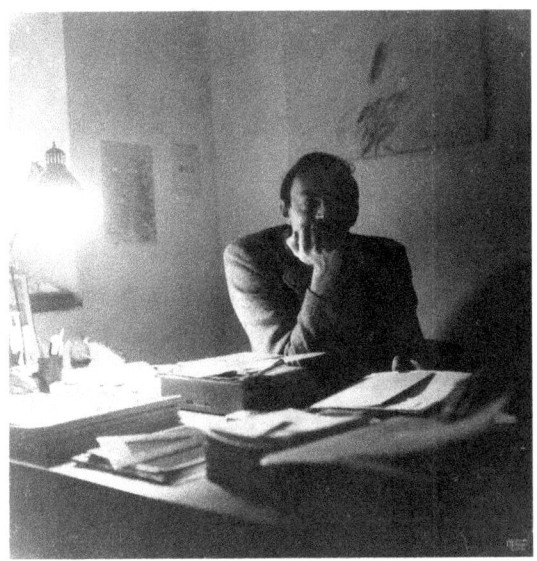

CY TWOMBY AT THE GALLERIA LA TARTARUGA,
AROUND NOVEMBER 1958
PH.: PLINIO DE MARTIIS

LEFT: CARD OF THE EXHIBITION IN TWO VENUES
*AFRO, CAPOGROSSI, CONSAGRA, DE KOONING,
KLINE, MARCA-RELLI, MATTA E BROOKS, DONATI,
OKADA,* JULY AND OCTOBER 4, 1958

1958: The Relationship with the United States Intensifies

The group show *Micro Salon* which was held for purely commercial reasons (December 18, 1957), organized in collaboration with the Paris gallery Iris Clert and consisting of the works of around one hundred artists, small-scale ones that were thus easier to sell, marked the end of the exhibition activity in 1957. But not just that: along with the first exhibitions in 1958 dedicated to the architect-painter Miguel Ocampo (January 7), to the informal artists Corpora, Scialoja, and Turcato (January 25), and to Gianni Bertini (February 8), it also marked the end of La Tartaruga's 'germinal' period. Starting in 1958, in fact, rather than providing an up-to-date spectrum of the artistic research underway and proposing the works of artist friends or of artists close to them, De Martiis chose the art and culture of the United States as a common thread of the exhibition program. He thus convinced the Baron Giorgio Franchetti, the descendant of a very rich Venetian family and one of the people financing the gallery, to go to the United States to get to know the American artists and their research from close-up. "You wouldn't believe how hard I'm working," wrote Franchetti from New York," I'm taking advantage of every connection, every small gust of wind that is to our advantage."[11] While in America the Baron attended galleries, museums, studios, and bought paintings by Kline, De Kooning, and Rothko. This led to Kline's first solo show in Europe: opening at La Tartaruga on February 27, it consisted of the canvases brought to Rome by Franchetti thanks to Marca-Relli, who managed to "convince a group of painters [...] to each send a few paintings to Rome, to La Tartaruga [...]. He was also successful in the Klein maneuver."[12] It is instead likely that the idea for the show had come up before the Baron's departure for the United States, because De Martiis had no doubt seen Kline's works at the 1956 Venice Biennale and at the first group show that had been organized the following year by the Rome-New York Art Foundation.

8 PAGINE - L. 100   GIOVEDÌ 15 MAGGIO 1958

artecronaca

NUMERO UNICO a cura di Plinio De Martiis   Roma - Via del Babuino, 196 Telef. 61611

Cronaca d'arte

GALLERIA NAZIONALE D'ARTE MODERNA
MOSTRE ★ ATTIVITÀ DIDATTICA ★ CONFERENZE ★ DAL 1945 AD OGGI

Articolo di Cesare Vivaldi

Quaranta gallerie d'arte moderna si popolano ogni sera a Roma di un pubblico interessato e vivace. Le inaugurazioni delle mostre sono sempre più affollate e una fitta rete di interessi culturali e commerciali si è stabilmente intrecciata tra le gallerie, i pittori e i collezionisti romani. Tre mercanti del Nord hanno aperto succursali o si sono definitivamente trasferiti a Roma: Pogliani da Torino con la Bussola, Zanini dal Veneto, e Cardazzo da Venezia e Milano si è affiancato alla Selecta.

Tre gallerie sono state aperte da tre cittadini americani: la Schneider, la Odyssia e l'88. La signora Mc Cann ha allestito all'Isola Tiberina la Rome New York Art Foundation. Gallerie come l'Obelisco, La Tartaruga, la Salita, il Segno, la Medusa e l'Attico, offrono al pubblico romano un panorama artistico internazionale molto prossimo a quello di New York e di Parigi. Roma è oggi il terzo centro artistico mondiale.

A questo fatto nuovo e importantissimo di cronaca cronaca manca totalmente il cronista. La stampa romana non informa, nè sembra essersi accorta del fatto a giudicare dall'opacità degli scarsi e arretrati servizi che vengono dedicati a tutto ciò che riguarda l'arte figurativa in Roma.

Siamo certi che nella vecchia redazione del quotidiano romano c'è ancora l'idea del pittore con pizzo e basco che beve il cappuccino al Caffè Greco. Siamo certi che per molti redattori la vita artistica della Capitale è ancora ferma all'immagine folkloristica della Fiera di Via Margutta. Non si capisce come il cronista d'arte dei quotidiani possa decidere (da solo) di aprire tale l'esistenza storica, e quindi almeno cronachistica, di tutta una vasta e ormai consacrata corrente dell'arte moderna internazionale.

Forse perchè fra i « critici » c'è chi ha passato il limite di età, o chi è legato a superate ortodossie politiche di partito, o chi ancora non ha mai mosso dall'Italia, o, caso limite, è anche egli stesso pittore.

Questo numero unico esce come primo tentativo di una cronaca che registri l'interessante e folta attività di cronaca e di vita artistica delle gallerie romane. Abbiamo voluto soltanto ed esclusivamente informare seguendo un criterio prospettico non privato, ma internazionale.

Abbiamo cercato di usare un linguaggio chiaro e semplice. Ci siamo riusciti solo in parte poichè, comprensibilmente, è difficile muoversi ed uscire dalla ragnatela di una critica misteriosa (unica eccezione Lionello Venturi) alla quale siamo stati abituati.

Possiamo considerare questo numero unico come un saggio di un giornale di cronaca artistica che abbiamo in programma di far uscire, mensilmente e puntualmente, a partire dal mese prossimo.

★ ★ ★

QUANDO, TRE ANNI fa o giù di lì, Paolo Monelli ebbe il coraggio di scrivere che Roma era una città « provinciale », tranne che per il programma e l'attività della Galleria Nazionale d'Arte Moderna, l'affermazione parve a molti (e naturalmente a tutti i « romanisti ») blasfema ed assurda, e destò polemiche, rimbrotti e scalpore a non finire. Polemì che che in verità ebbero una ragione, poichè proprio in quel periodo si iniziava, nella vita artistica della capitale, un processo di rinnovamento e svecchiamento, oggi in pieno corso e sviluppo, che ha mutato radicalmente il panorama locale (e nazionale), e che ha trasformato Roma in un ambiente vivo, anzi vivissimo, ricco di succhi e di fermenti; una città in cui sono sorte nuove e moderne gallerie private, in cui si affermano nuovi artisti (mentre i migliori di quelli già conosciuti si sono a loro volta rinnovati), in cui gli scambi internazionali sono diventati fittissimi: per dirla tutta, l'atmosfera chiusa della provincia si è quasi totalmente dissolta, la vecchia « scuola » ha ceduto il posto ad un centro pulsante e dinamico, a livello internazionale.

Ma, e qui occorre dar ragione a Monelli, se tutto ciò è avvenuto lo si deve in gran parte per merito della Galleria d'Arte Moderna e della sua Soprintendente Palma Bucarelli. Quanto la Galleria ha fatto per la diffusione della cultura figurativa mondiale contemporanea non è stato ancora, ci sembra, giustamente apprezzato; eppure le sue iniziative hanno un merito enorme. In un'epoca di « cultura di massa » come la presente, non è più pensabile che lo annuale « viaggio a Parigi » di alcuni singoli artisti possa bastare a « svecchiare » un ambiente; occorre invece un'opera di diffusione e, se vogliamo, « volgarizzazione » larga e disinteressata, che deve costituire la base per la creazione di una cultura autonoma ed insieme « inserita » nella cultura mondiale. E proprio questa opera di diffusione (e insieme di aggiornamento audace, anche spregiudicato, non solo vantaggio di ristrette élites ma di un pubblico vasto) Palma Bucarelli è riuscita prima ad impostare e ad imporre, e quindi a svolgere.

PICASSO

Un esame, anche sommario, dell'attività svolta dalla Galleria d'Arte Moderna dal 1945-1946 ad oggi sarà più che sufficiente a dimostrare quanto sin qui abbiamo asserito.

Nella stagione 1945-1946 la Galleria, dati i tempi, non ha potuto che organizzare una sola « Arte inglese contemporanea », e così pure avvenne nella stagione 1946-47, in cui fu presentata al pubblico romano un'espo-

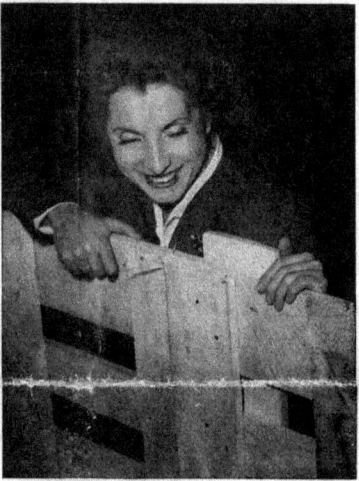

LA SOPRAINTENDENTE ALLA GALLERIA D'ARTE MODERNA, DOTT. PALMA BUCARELLI, SORRIDE ALL'ARRIVO DELLE OPERE DI KANDINSKY

sizione di « Pittura francese d'oggi » che sollevò (come tutti ricorderanno) interesse grandissimo. Dal 1947-48 in poi, il calendario si è infatti però sempre più folto. Appunto nella stagione 1947-48 si ebbe una « Mostra di quadri moderni della Tate Gallery di Londra », una Mostra degli « Artisti dell'Università e Accademie di Belle Arti », la « III Mostra d'Arte ispirata allo sport », ed una di « Arte ungherese contemporanea ». In quella 1948-49 si ebbe la « III Mostra dell'Art Club », una di « Incisori polacchi », la Mostra didattica del disegno nell'arte e nella tecnica », la Mostra di « Architettura svizzera contemporanea ». In quella 1949-1950 si ebbe, organizzata dall'Art Club la « Jeune Peinture Belge » e « Austria, Belgio, Stati Uniti, Sud Africa », la Mostra dell'Istituto Solidarietà Artistica, la Mostra dei « Bronzi nuragici », la Mostra d'« Arte moderna sarda », la « IV Mostra dell'Art Club », la Mostra delle « Olimpiadi della Gioventù », una « Mostra d'artigianato artistico ».

Le tre stagioni dal 1950-51 al 1952-53 sono state, dopo questi primi anni diciamo così « di preparazione », caratterizzate da una scelta sempre più decisa in favore dell'arte moderna. Proprio in queste stagioni si è delineato il ruolo e della Galleria e la sua insostituibile funzione didattica. La enorme successo della grande Mostra di Picasso che chiuse la stagione 1952-53, oltre che alla Soprintendente per un prestigio nazionale ed internazionale

ben meritato. La Mostra di Picasso allineava centosessantasette quadri, quaranta incisioni e trentanove ceramiche, fu visitata da sessantatremila visitatori in due mesi (5 maggio-5 luglio 1953), ed ebbe un catalogo stampato in tre edizioni tutte rapidamente esaurite. Ma precedentemente all'esposizione picassiana vi era stato: nel 1950-51 la Mostra del « Concorso per la illustrazione del libro », la « V Mostra dell'Art Club », una Mostra di « Arte Popolare polacca », una Mostra di « Pittori astrattisti americani », una organizzata dall'Art Club e dall'Age d'or » di « Arte Astratta e Concreta in Italia », la Mostra di « L'Allegoria nei secoli XVI e XVII », nel 1951-52 una Mostra fotografica di « Architettura Belge », la « VI Mostra dell'Art Club », una Mostra di « Incisioni di Fattori », una commemorativa di Alberto Savinio; nel 1952-53 la « II Mostra delle Olimpiadi della Gioventù », la « II Mostra internazionale del disegno per ragazzi », la « Mostra di Previati », « Pittura ellenica contemporanea », « Arte astratta italiana e francese », « Monumenti medioevali della Sardegna ».

MOSTRE ESTERE

L'attività della Galleria, dal 1953-54 ad oggi, ha seguito una linea « ascensionale ». Le Mostre si sono fatte sempre meglio scelte e sempre più rappresentative, ed alcune di esse sono state tali da porre la Galleria su di un piano di assoluta avanguardia rispetto al-

le altre capitali europee (basti pensare alla mostra di Pollock, che Roma ha visto per prima). Nel 1953-54 si son viste sei Mostre, di cui tre (« Pittura americana dell'800 », « Architettura brasiliana » e « Scipione ») di notevole importanza; nel 1954-55 se ne son viste nove, di cui almeno cinque del massimo interesse (« Pittura brasiliana contemporanea », « Arte moderna d'Israele », « Disegni e incisioni austriache moderne », « Giovani pittori », « Arti Plastiche e civiltà meccaniche ») per non parlare delle Mostre di disegni di Celentano e Morelli, e della Mostra annuale dell'Art Club. Nel 1955-56 le Mostre sono state solo quattro, di cui però tre notevolissime (« Arte italiana contemporanea », « Gino Rossi », e « I Macchiaioli »).

MONDRIAN E POLLOCK

L'anno scorso e quest'anno, infine, si sono viste esposizioni di enorme importanza (« Mondrian », « Grafici tunisini », « La collezione Cavellini », « Burle Marx », « Scultura italiana del XX secolo », « Capolavori del Museo Solomon Guggenheim » (Mostra tra l'altro molto discussa per motivi più o meno politici, che ha avuto ventimila visitatori), « Jackson Pollock »; e inoltre: « Arte Jugoslava contemporanea », « Acquarelli inglesi dell'800 », « Roberto Melli » ecc. ecc. Nè la stagione è finita, ma anzi sono annunciate esposizioni di Modigliani e Morandi, ed una sceltissima Mostra di Kandinsky che si inaugura in questi giorni (e questo punto vorremmo permetterci di suggerire alla Soprintendenza l'opportunità di una retrospettiva di Giacomo Balla, che renda onore al Maestro scomparso così recentemente).

MOSTRE DIDATTICHE

Ma oltre alle Mostre vere e proprie, la Galleria d'Arte Moderna può vantare ancora una lunga serie di iniziative, queste più propriamente didattiche. Ci sono le ben note Mostre di riproduzioni (chiamate appunto « Mostre didattiche »), le Conferenze, le proiezioni di documentari, ecc. ecc. Dal 1945 ad oggi abbiamo avuto, tra le « Mostre didattiche », « Capolavori della pittura moderna », « Van Gogh », « Cézanne », « Renoir », « Matisse », « Gli espressionisti », « L'Impressionismo », « Degas », « Braque », e tante altre; tra le Conferenze: « Il Neoclassicismo », « Il Romanticismo », « Il Divisionismo », « Il Futurismo », « Il Verismo », « Daumier », « Fattori », « La scuola romana », « L'astrattismo », « Il Novecento », « La pittura metafisica », « Medardo Rosso », « Gauguin », « Modigliani », « Scipione », « Arturo Martini », « Morandi », « Moore », « Sant'Elia », « Rouault », « L'Impressionismo », « Manet »,

(continua a pag. 8)

In 1958, a second connection between La Tartaruga and the United States coincided with the Scarpitta exhibition that opened on April 26, after several less important exhibitions like *Jorn* (March 15), *Nuvolo* (March 27), and the group show *Gruppo 11* with works by Birò, Kirchberger, Pfahler, and Sieber (April 12). Scarpitta did not attend the opening, however, because he was in New York, invited by Leo Castelli to join the artists in his gallery.

This invitation stemmed from the relationship between De Martiis and Castelli, which began in 1956 when Dorazio introduced them, and was reinforced two years later with the fully-fledged constitution of an 'agreement.' On August 19, 1958, in fact, Castelli wrote to De Martiis asking him to help him organize an exhibition to be held in his gallery in New York and at La Tartaruga, dedicated to the Spanish artists Millares and Saura, whom he had met at the Venice Biennale that year. But not just that: "we could perhaps give a *coup de main* not just for the Spaniards, but for painters from other countries as well." Castelli also wrote to De Martiis: "I arranged with Cardazzo [...] that she do the Jasper Johns show in Rome. Cardazzo wants it for February. So you could have it in March. As for Rauschenberg, which date would be convenient? Perhaps as soon as possible if you can then circulate it in Germany or elsewhere."[13] Whereas the exhibitions of the Spanish artists and Johns were never actually held at La Tartaruga, the project for the Rauschenberg solo show was successful. Already in May 1958, De Martiis had shown that he was willing to allow the American gallerist to replicate Scarpitta's *Le Bende* exhibition, which had opened on April 26, on the condition that Rauschenberg's solo show *Combine-Paintings*, held at the Galleria Castelli from March 4 to 29, was transferred, after it closed, to the exhibition space on Via del Babuino. Rauschenberg's solo show was not held in Rome until the following year, on May 30, 1959, after Castelli managed to send to De Martiis "with Miss Silvana Aliatis, fourteen of Rauschenberg's watercolors."[14]

Nevertheless, the American artist's show did not receive a single line of criticism, and none of the *Combined-Drawings* displayed were sold, confirming how Italy in the late 1950s was still not ready for research that was so avant-garde. However, it is interesting to note how this exhibition was held just a few days after the Alberto Burri solo show at La Tartaruga (May 13, 1959). De Martiis had no doubt learned that in 1953 Rauschenberg had stayed in Rome for almost eight months, that he had visited Burri's studio, and that the two artists had given each other one of their works. He also knew that after returning to the United States, Rauschenberg had visited the Italian artist's solo exhibition at the Stable Gallery in New York, sending him an exhibition view to keep him up to date.[15] So it is not unlikely that the gallerist from La Tartaruga had suggested the Burri solo show just before Rauschenberg's in order to imply that the former influenced the latter.

However, Rauschenberg's arrival in Rome was just as important as the arrival of another American artist, Cy Twombly, whom De Martiis had met thanks to Franchetti and whose first solo show he organized for May 17, 1958, seeking at the same time to promote him in New York, insisting that Castelli organize a solo show in his gallery.[16] After arriving in Rome – where he settled permanently soon afterwards –, Twombly immediately became integrated with the young local artists teaching them from closer up about the art and culture of the United States.

**THE SINGLE ISSUE OF *ARTECRONACA*,
EDITED BY PLINIO DE MARTIIS, ROME,
MAY 15, 1958**

ROMA BABUINO 196 GALLERIA LA TARTARUGA TELEFONO 61611 SI APRE NEL POMERIGGIO DALLE ORE 4 ALLE 8 MARTEDI 16 GIUGNO 1959

BACK OF THE *SCIALOJA* EXHIBITION POSTER WITH INFORMATION ON GALLERY OPENING HOURS

Wanting to promote the American research that was underway, De Martiis cut down on the number of solo shows of the works of his artist friends (*Mafai*, December 3, 1959) or of artists close to them (*Consagra*, May 31, 1958 and January 31, 1959). He also reduced the number of exhibitions dedicated to artists from the Roman milieu (*Scarpitta, Perilli, Novelli, Accardi, Sanfilippo, Bignardi, Rotella, Marotta, Nuvolo, Buggiani*, February 10, 1959) as well as exhibitions of works from the gallery's collection (July and October 1958). By so doing, in 1958-1959 the exhibition space at La Tartaruga began to impose itself on the national and international scene as the "bearer of a great epic myth, that of America."[17]

1958-1959: Interest in the Publishing World

De Martiis' farsightedness in wanting to weave relations with the American artistic milieu went hand in hand with the farsightedness he showed during those same years as concerned publishing. After setting in motion the periodical publication of the *Bollettino della galleria*, in May 1958 he published the single issue of *Artecronaca*: a magazine-cum-document whose purpose was to account for the exhibition activity conducted in the previous two months by the Roman galleries, to which, according to De Martiis, the critics and journalists had always paid very little attention.[18] *Artecronaca* also dedicated a great deal of space to the most important international events. It contained interviews with some of the major critics, gallerists, and artists, and there were also the prices and valuations of the works on the market. All this was offered to the readers in clear and direct language, the goal being to "emerge from the spider's web of mysterious and *parolibera* criticism"[19] that, the gallerist said, with its overly complex reasoning based on refined formal constructions and high-sounding words, had never done anything to help the dissemination of avant-garde art.

The interest in art publishing as an informative tool for the most recent experiments in the field was developed further in 1959 both with the creation of the series *Quaderni di Arte Attuale*, which included two monographs dedicated to Scialoja and Scarpitta, respectively, and with the idea, a foreshadowing of the most recent advertising strategies, of organizing in the gallery, on January 13 , an exhibition for the purpose of presenting and handing out the book *Pittori italiani d'oggi* written by Lionello Venturi and released one year earlier by the publisher De Luca.

In 1959 De Martiis also conceived a new type of foldout for the exhibitions which the gallery would start using from 1960. It was a large-format poster that when folded into four parts became a small invitation. What made it unique was the absence of critical texts. The omission from the foldout of the traditional in-depth essay stemmed from the desire to abolish critical interpretation in favor of documenting the works themselves, which it was believed were capable on their own of channeling their contents. The gallerist is thus credited with having anticipated by a few years the debate that developed in the first half of the 1960s, which called into question the role of art criticism and supported the need for new means of interpretation.

De Martiis' awareness of having breathed life into many such avant-garde publishing experiences led him to publish, in 1960, *Album: raccolta dei cataloghi 1957-1960*, a monographic text dedicated to the catalogues he published and the photographs he took in the gallery during the period of time referred to in the title.

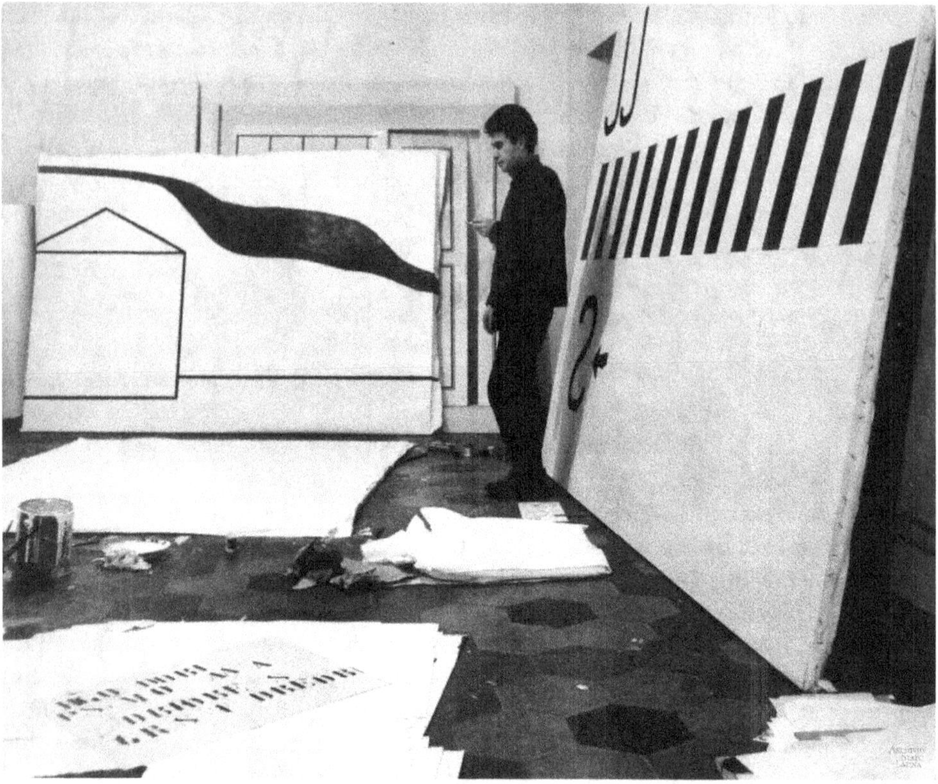

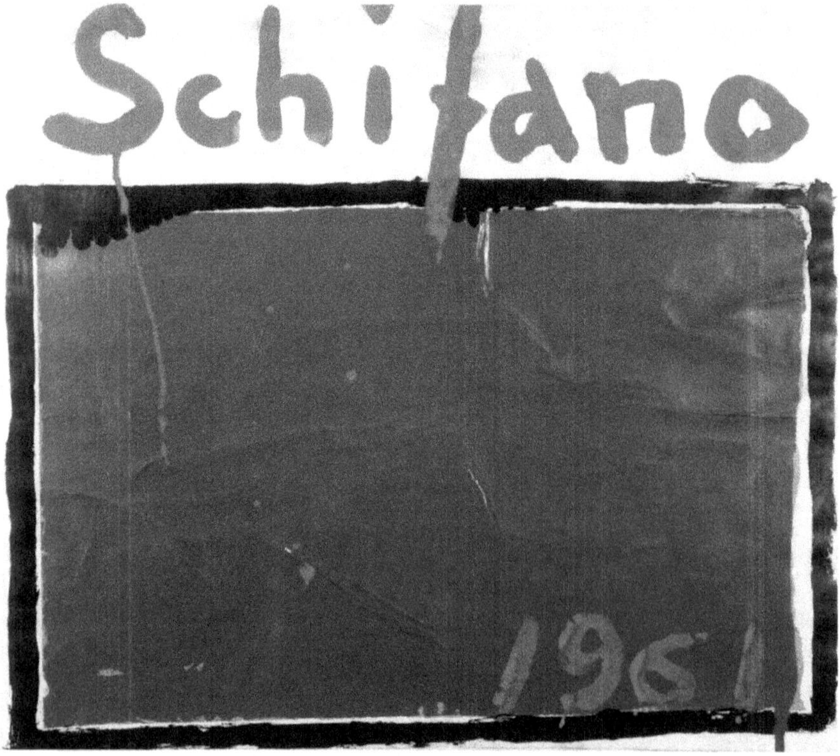

1960: An Eye on the Younger Generation

In 1960 La Tartaruga confirmed its attention toward international art by planning, with the help of the critic Pierre Restany, a solo show of the work of Arman, which never came to fruition, however,[20] and by hosting the first solo show in Rome of the German artist Peter Brüning (March 23), but also an exhibition by the Greek artist Caniaris (April 4), as well as three events dedicated to the research that was being conducted in the United States or that was influenced by it: a solo show by Wood (October 8); a group show that, alongside the Italians Burri and Consagra, included works by De Kooning, Matta, and Rothko (November 3); and an exhibition of forty drawings and gouaches by the Italian artist Afro (February 23) who had been among the first to go to New York, collaborating since 1950 with the Catherine Viviano Gallery and participating in 1955 in the exhibition *The New Decade: 22 European Painters and Sculptors* at the Museum of Modern Art.[21] De Martiis' desire to weave an ever stronger relationship between Italy and the United States also arose on the back of the direction that was being taken by the Italian cultural context at the time. Also in 1960, the Premio del Ministero della Pubblica Istruzione of the 30th Venice Biennale was awarded to Kline, and the Galleria Nazionale d'Arte Moderna in Rome proposed an anthological exhibition of Rothko's woks, as well as the group show *Arte italiana del XX secolo da collezioni americane*, whose goal was to demonstrate the strong relationship between the artistic spheres in Italy and in America.[22] Leaving aside two relatively insignificant shows (the solo exhibition of the Friuli-born Dino Basaldella, on May 14, and the traditional group show at the end of the year for commercial purposes as it was dedicated to *Opere di piccolo formato*, small-scale works, on December 3), 1960 was an important year for La Tartaruga, not only because of its greater support for the research that was being conducted across the ocean. Indeed, on the one hand, De Martiis began backing artists who wished to renew their artistic language via the creation of an innovative rapport between the image and the word (see the exhibitions *Novelli*, January 12; *Perilli*, January 30; *Cy Twombly*, April 26); on the other, there was an opening up to the younger generation of Roman artists. The interest in promoting the latter may have been influenced by the need to make La Tartaruga competitive vis-à-vis the Galleria L'Attico. Opened in Piazza di Spagna on November 25 1957 by Bruno and Fabio Sargentini, its goal from the start was to be an avant-garde space of excellence, thanks also to the owner's substantial financial resources. It was perhaps in response to the group show *Possibilità di relazione* held in May 1960, where L'attico presented the research of young members of the Nuova Figurazione movement (Aricò, Bendini, Dova, Pozzati), that on June 4 De Martiis organized the first exhibition of the still unknown Jannis Kounellis, Greek by birth but a pupil of Toti Scialoja at the Fine Arts Academy in Rome. Kounellis showed a series of unprimed canvases with enlarged black—painted typographical symbols. Underlying it was no doubt the textural nature of the work of Burri and the spatialism of Fontana, but here such elements were used to create a new linguistic code, one capable of superseding the informal gestural automatism connected to the release of interior impulses, as well as of opening the work up to the flow of collective communication and fruition. The linguistic fragments of these *Alfabeti* that floated on the surface of the canvas and in themselves were devoid of meaning were thus submitted to a rationally arranged structure, reminiscent of Constructivist syntaxes.

LEFT: JANNIS KOUNELLIS IN HIS STUDIO A FEW MONTHS BEFORE HIS SOLO SHOW AT LA TARTARUGA, JUNE 4, 1960
PH.: PLINIO DE MARTIIS

MARIO SCHIFANO, SIGN-POSTER OF HIS FIRST SOLO SHOW AT LA TARTARUGA, MARCH 23, 1961

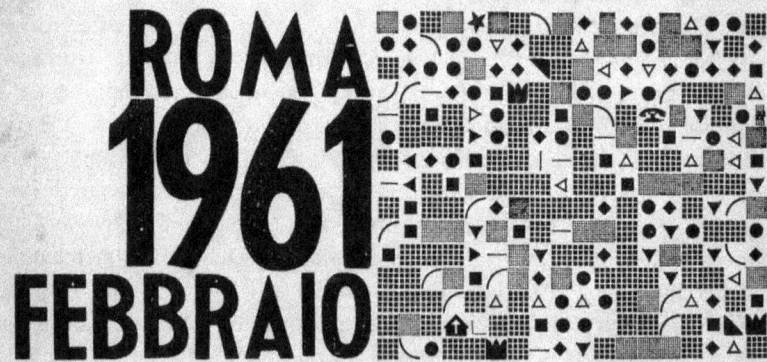

COVER OF THE FIRST AND ONLY ISSUE OF
QUADERNI DELLA TARTARUGA,
CURATED BY PLINIO DE MARTIIS

As De Martiis himself emphasized, these were works "'beyond' painting [...] born without a stretcher, closer to mural paintings, banners, in short, something that no longer had to do with traditional painting."[23] It was not long before La Tartaruga became a venue for environmental and performance art.

1961: The Making of a 'School'

Despite its high quality Kounellis's solo show was not well received by all. Some of the artists who were habitués of the gallery, like Pirelli and Novelli, went to the opening but left in protest because they were against the works that, in their opinion, couldn't even be defined "painting."[24] However, De Martiis was not dissuaded from the yearning to discover the young Roman talents capable of transcending the dimension of traditional painting and sculpture in favor of art that was more all-encompassing and unexpected. And so in 1961 he welcomed into the fold Mario Schifano, offering him a solo show (March 23) and the chance to show his works in two group shows (in November and in December). Born in Libya in 1934, Schifano had moved to Rome where he had begun to paint informal works collaborating with his father who was an archaeologist and a conservator at the Museo Etrusco di Valle Giulia. In 1959 Schifano had had his first solo show at the Galleria Appia Antica after which he had participated in a group show at the Galleria La Salita. After abandoning his experience in informal art, in 1960 he had made a series of monochrome papers glued to the canvas, which were then followed (in 1961) by works with painted signs, letters, and marks, on the one hand, in line with the more recent American Pop Art, and, on the other, original and free with respect to them.

The same originality and freedom regarding research in Pop Art in the United States can also be found in the works of the young Roman artist Giosetta Fioroni, whom De Martiis invited to show her work alongside that of the Bolognese Umberto Bignardi. The double solo show was planned for March 11, 1961. A pupil of Toti Scialoja at the Fine Arts Academy in Rome, in 1955 Fioroni had had a show at the 7th Quadriennale in Rome, and the following year at the 18th Venice Biennale. On display at La Tartaruga were canvases made with industrial colors, aluminum and gold, in which she cooled off the existential values typical of informal art by way of a technique that, albeit resembling the results of the 'Pop Artists,' showed a greater manipulation of the images and the pictorial material.

Actually, the same can be said of the works of all the young Roman artists whom De Martiis would soon intercept, and would end up being defined by Cesare Vivaldi "La giovane scuola di Roma"[25] by Maurizio Calvesi "Reportage,"[26] by Maurizio Fagiolo Dell'Arco "La figurazione 'novissima,'"[27] and, lastly, by Alberto Arbasino the "Scuola di Piazza del Popolo."[28] The emphasis was thus on the passing of the baton from the old 'Scuola romana di via Cavour' to the new research centering around La Tartaruga after it has relocated, in 1963, to Piazza del Popolo. The artists who were the members of this new 'school' shared their social extraction, young age, and, most importantly, desire to renew painting, going beyond the informal expression of the Self, by way of an art that was aimed at "once again accounting for the external, visual appearances of the world with all their weight, without any allusiveness or exclusiveness, objectifying them to the greatest extent possible."[29] Although what they had in common with American Pop Art was the desire to objectify reality and in particular the economic boom that was currently underway, the Romans differed based on two factors. The

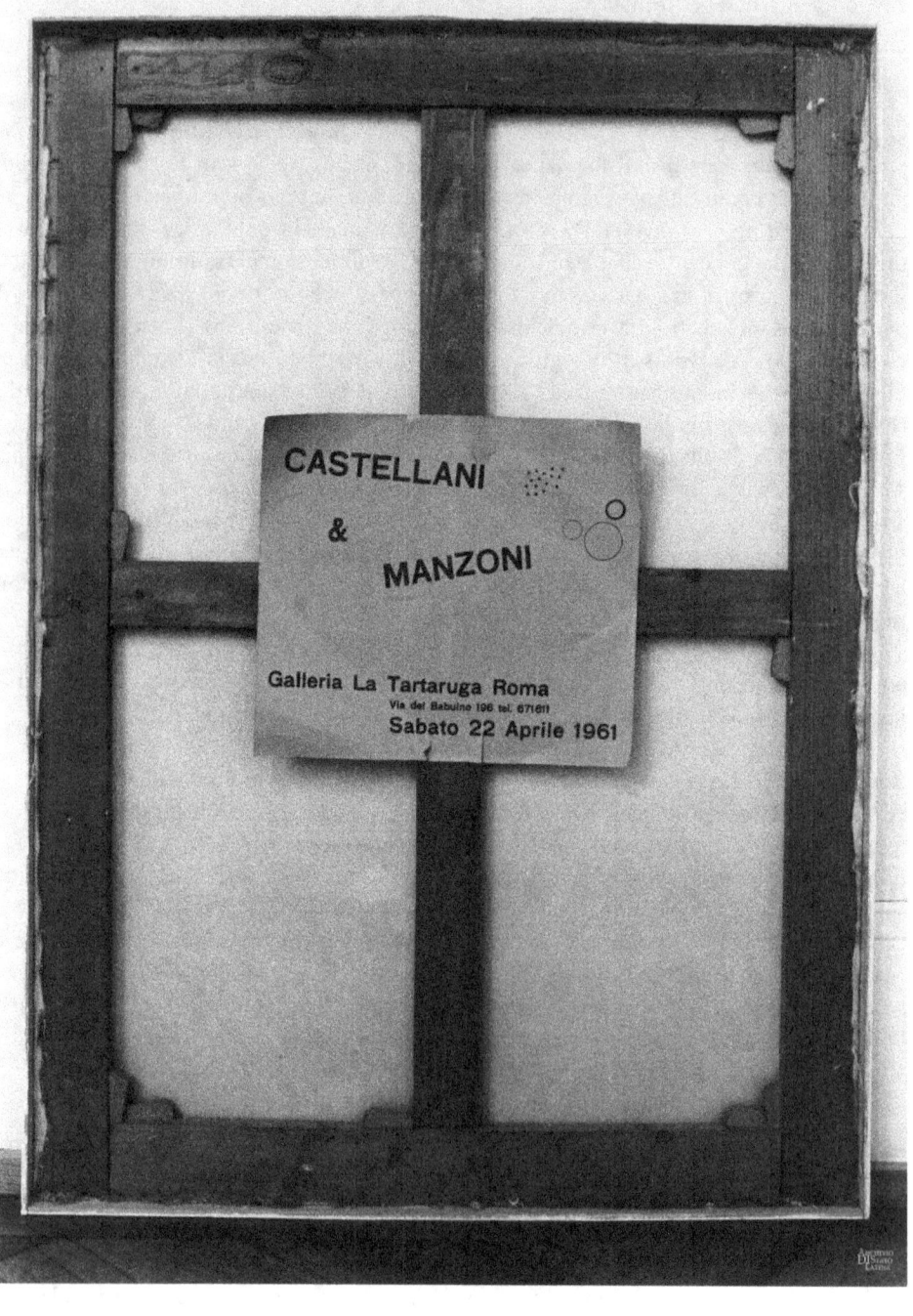

THE VERSO OF THE CANVAS WITH THE POSTER IN THE CENTER, DURING THE
ACCROCHAGE OF THE *CASTELLANI AND MANZONI* EXHIBITION, APRIL 22, 1961
PH.: PLINIO DE MARTIIS

first of these consisted in their strong 'artisanal' and manual intervention. Their paintings were made using the same subjective technique, rather than an aseptic and mechanical one. The second factor was based on their choice to work on cultural stereotypes, and not so much on consumer products channeled by the tools of mass communication. It was precisely the difference between the Roman 'school' and the American one that soon imposed the need for a stronger partnership and reciprocal encounter. As early as 1959 Castelli had written the following to De Martiis: "I have lots of plans for the upcoming season, and La Tartaruga will play an important role in these plans."[30] A few months later Castelli specified further: "I would like you to be able to do in Rome what I do here, that is to say: exhibit Jasper Johns, Rauschenberg (major canvases) a new painter whom I find sensational, Frank Stella." Castelli also announced that "my wife, Ileana, intends to go to Rome in around ten days and you can discuss all these things with her, which is easier than doing so by writing."[31] But the most important encounter with Ileana Sonnabend took place in 1961 when the far-sighted gallerist arrived in Rome with a plan to open an exhibition space there in collaboration with De Martiis. Despite her saying that her intention was to create a space where American and Italian art could be compared and support each other, Sonnabend's real motivation was to find for herself a 'window' (La Tartaruga) where she could introduce and impose on Rome the American Pop artists that she and her husband Castelli supported. After succeeding in stipulating a contract with Schifano, however, the project folded. When De Martiis realized her real motivations, he refused to collaborate.[32]

1961-1962: Toward the Relocation of the Venue

The year 1961 for La Tartaruga marked the beginning of the creation of a 'school,' which was later dubbed 'di Piazza del Popolo' (of Piazza del Popolo). But not just that. On the one hand, it was the year of the publication of the first issue of the avant-garde magazine *Quaderni della Tartaruga*, where texts by Cesare Vivaldi, Mario Diacono, and James Joyce conversed with the reproductions of works by Giosetta Fioroni, Mimmo Rotella, Mario Schifano, Jannis Kounellis, Salvatore Scarpitta, and Cy Twombly, to whom the gallery also dedicated a monographic text written by Vivaldi. On the other hand, it was the year that De Martiis embraced the more recent Milanese research, thanks also to the relationship he had in the meantime developed with Carlo Cardazzo, the owner of the Galleria Il Milione, and with Pierre Restany, the gallery's critic of reference. De Martiis thus invited two of their artists to show their work in a double solo show: Enrico Castellani and Piero Manzoni. The exhibition, which opened on April 22 was anticipated in a letter in which Manzoni stated as follows: "I am considering showing two works stitched with a sewing machine, 3 lines, 4-5 eggs, some fingerprints, a polystyrene surface, a small phosphorescent, and a painting of variable color. For the opening I could place my signature on a few people. To all those whom I sign I will give a special certificate of authentication, a card guaranteeing that they are genuine works of art... Castellani has five paintings ready and is preparing others."[33] Castellani presented several extroflexed monochrome surface exemplifying the zeroing of painting that was underway in Milan, while Manzoni proposed a new type of research that was very close to theater. In the wake of the Duchampian process of the readymade, the day of the inauguration Manzoni did indeed sign the bodies of several models and of some of the visitors, bestowing them, thanks to his autograph, with the status of work of art, or rather *Sculture viventi* (Living Sculptures). Each 'sculpture' was then given a certificate of authenticity, which the artist stamped in red (if the person/sculpture was a whole and everlasting work of art) or yellow (if the new status was to be considered limited to certain parts of the body); the stamp could also be green (if restricted by certain activities, like sleeping or running), or purple (if the body's artistic nature had been purchased). Convinced that art is not the bearer of a message and that the artwork does not exist as a concrete object that can be sold, Manzoni declared with his *Sculture viventi* that the public cannot remain confined in its passive role as spectator, but must instead intervene in the artwork.[34] By bringing performance art to La Tartaruga for the first time, Manzoni also foreshadowed the theatricalization of art that De Martiis would start supporting in 1965.

After the Castellani and Manzoni double show had ended, until late 1962 the scheduling on Via del Babuino saw the quantity and quality of the events organized diminish. These were limited to a small solo show of Garrubba's photographs (June 30, 1961) and a group show of the works of Appel, Brooks, Marca-Relli, Matta (January 1962), followed by a Giulio Turcato solo show (March 8, 1962), an exhibition dedicated to the Gutai artist Kazuo Shiraga (April 3, 1962), a group show titled *La materia a Roma* (May 1962) with works by Marotta, Rotella, Scarpitta, Burri along with Festa, Angeli, Schifano, and, lastly, a show dedicated to Fontana, Twombly, and Sam Francis (December 1962). The decline in exhibition activity was no doubt dictated by the need for the gallery to save its economic resources and leave Via del Babuino to open a new venue. In a letter he wrote to Manzoni as early as 1961 De Martiis considered the idea of opening a gallery in Milan, seeking the support of the collector Enrico Pizzi through Manzoni himself: "I spoke to Pizzi: […] he said he would be happy to help you, but before making any moves he needs to be sure of your intentions: he says he's happy to help you but he has the impression that for now you're not ready to move. […] he doesn't want to seem like someone who is insisting you open the gallery here. […] We hope you really do manage to open this gallery."[35] Castelli as well seemed to know about the possible move, and in September 1961 he asked De Martiis: "How are your plans for the new gallery going? Is it ready?"[36] The truth of the matter is that La Tartaruga's gallerist did not exploit the chance to open a branch in Milan, but instead chose to remain in Rome, where he did open a new venue just a stone's throw away from the previous one, right in the artistic and cultural heart of Rome: Piazza del Popolo.

1. Cf. Pegoraro Silvia (ed.), *L'arte e la Tartaruga: omaggio a Plinio De Martiis. Da Rauschenberg a Warhol, da Burri a Schifano*, exhibition catalogue (Pescara, Museo d'Arte Moderna Vittoria Colonna, March 3 – May 20, 2007), Skira, Geneva - Milan 2007, p. 152.

2. Cf. Ficacci Luigi (ed.), *Le collezioni: arte contemporanea per l'Istituto Nazionale per la grafica*, exhibition catalogue (Rome, Istituto Nazionale per la Grafica, June 3 – July 3, 2003), Hopefulmonster, Turin 2003, p. 19.

3. Cf. Crescentini Manuela, "L'ambiente romano. Principi di una rinascita: 1944-1949 (tra astrazione e realismo)," in Pirovano Carlo (ed.), *La pittura in Italia*, Il Novecento/2, vol. 1, Electa, Milan 1993, pp. 505-510.

4. Let us recall: the exhibition of Peggy Guggenheim's collection of works by American artists at the 1948 Venice Biennale; the exhibition *Twentieth-Century Italian Art* held in 1949 at the Museum of Modern Art in New York with works by Fontana, Scialoja, and Afro, among others; the first Rauschenberg solo show in Italy in 1953 at the Galleria L'Obelisco in Rome; the arrival in Rome in 1950 of the photographer Milton Gendel who, in *Art News*, described Rotella's first decollages exhibited after the *Arte attuale* show curated in May 1955 by Emilio Villa on an anchored boat in the Tiber; the group show *The New Decade: 22 European Painters and Sculptors* curated by Ritchie from May 10 to August 7, 1955 at the Museum of Modern Art in New York with the contribution of the Italian artists Afro, Burri, Capogrossi, and Mirko; the Calder solo show at the Galleria L'Obelisco in Rome in early 1956; the United States Pavilion *American Artists Paint the City* at the Venice Biennale that same year, with works by De Kooning, Pollock, and Kline on display; Scialoja's and Gabriella Drudi's departure for New York in October 1956 following in the footsteps of Afro, who had left for the United States in 1950.

5. Cf. D'Amico Fabrizio, "Pittura a Roma negli anni Cinquanta: tracce di un tempo felice. Roma-New York," in Castagnoli Pier Giovanni (ed.), *Pittura degli anni '50 in Italia*, exhibition catalogue (Turin, GAM-Galleria Civica d'Arte Moderna e Contemporanea, May 29 – August 31, 2003), Ed. GAM-Galleria Civica d'Arte Moderna e Contemporanea, Turin 2003, pp. 14-16 and Crescentini Manuela, "L'ambiente romano," *op. cit.*, pp. 513-514.

6. For further information see especially *Piero Dorazio: antologica 1947-1970*, exhibition catalogue (Turin, Galleria MartanoDue, February 1970), Turin 1970.

7. Cf. Zevi Adachiara, "L'Informale italiano: continuità o rottura?" in Id., *Peripezie del dopoguerra nell'arte italiana*, Giulio Einaudi Editore, Turin 2005, pp. 111-114.

8. Cf. Zevi Adachiara, "Il bilico tra pittura e materia: Alberto Burri," *ivi*, pp. 30-33.

9. Cf. Crescentini Manuela, "L'ambiente romano," *op. cit.*, p. 515.

10. De Martiis Plinio, [no title] in *Una vita a 100 all'ora*, exhibition catalogue (Piove di Sacco, Centro di Arte e Cultura, October 30 – November 22, 2015), Padua 2015, n. pag.

11. Franchetti Giorgio, letter to Plinio De Martiis, New York, January 20, 1958 (Archivio di Stato di Latina, Fondo La Tartaruga, busta 14/1).

12. Ibid.

13. Castelli Leo, letter to Plinio De Martiis, Switzerland, August 19, 1958 (Archivio di Stato di Latina, Fondo La Tartaruga, busta 5).

14. Castelli Leo, letter to Plinio De Martiis, New York, February 3, 1959 (Archivio di Stato di Latina, Fondo La Tartaruga, busta 5).

15. Cf. Messina Maria Grazia, "Il collage negli anni cinquanta. Una storia americana (o quasi)," in Lamberti M. M. – Messina M. M. (eds.), *Collage/Collages dal Cubismo al New Dada*, exhibition catalogue (Turin, GAM-Galleria Civica d'Arte Moderna e Contemporanea, October 9, 2007 – January 6, 2008), Electa, Milan 2007, pp. 300-321.

16. Cf. Castelli Leo, letter to Plinio De Martiis, New York, 1959-1961 (Archivio di Stato di Latina, Fondo La Tartaruga, busta 5). Let us also recall the major group shows organized by La Tartaruga that included Twombly (April 9 and July 2, 1959; November and December 1961) and the exhibition with works by

Perilli, Novelli, and Twombly as well, held from November 14 to 28, 1959, at the Palais Des Beaux Arts in Brussels, thanks to the support of the Galerie Aujourd'hui. On June 11, 1962, moreover, the Galleria del Leone in Venice dedicated a solo show to the artist produced in collaboration with De Martiis.

17. Lombardo Sergio, "Ricordando Plinio," in Pegoraro Silvia (ed.), *L'arte e la Tartaruga, op. cit.*, p. 35.

18. De Martiis Plinio, [no title], in *Artecronaca*, single issue, Rome, May 15, 1958.

19. Ibid.

20. Arman, letter to Plinio De Martiis, Nice, February 18, 1960 (Archivio di Stato di Latina, Fondo La Tartaruga, busta 21).

21. Zevi Adachiara, "L'Informale italiano," *op. cit.*, pp. 111-114.

22. Pancotto Pier Paolo, "Arte in Italia tra il 1947 e il 1960," in Castagnoli Pier Giovanni (ed.), *Pittura degli anni '50 in Italia, op. cit.*, p. 153.

23. Plinio De Martiis, in Mirolla Miriam, *L'arte c'est moi*, Avagliano Editore, Rome 2006, p. 106.

24. Cf. ibid.

25. Vivaldi Cesare, "La giovane scuola di Roma," in *Il Verri* 12, 1963, pp. 101-105.

26. Calvesi Maurizio, "Ricognizione e Reportage," in *Collage. Dialoghi di cultura* 1, 1963 [republished in Id., *Le due avanguardie. Dal Futurismo alla Pop Art* (1966), Laterza, Bari 2008, pp. 280-294].

27. Fagiolo Dell'Arco Maurizio, "La figurazione 'novissima,'" in Id., *Rapporto '60: le arti oggi in Italia*, Bulzoni Editore, Rome 1966, pp. 20-26.

28. Whether Arbasino invented the definition is uncertain, as underscored in: Vagheggi Paolo, "Giosetta Fioroni, l'arte come vita," in *La Repubblica*, March 17, 2003.

29. Vivaldi Cesare, "La giovane scuola di Roma," *op. cit.*, p. 102.

30. Castelli Leo, letter to Plinio De Martiis, New York, May 6, 1959 (Archivio di Stato di Latina, Fondo La Tartaruga, busta 5).

31. Castelli Leo, letter to Plinio De Martiis, New York, November 5, 1959 (Archivio di Stato di Latina, Fondo La Tartaruga, busta 5).

32. Cf. Pirani Federica, "Intervista a Plinio De Martiis," in Calvesi M. – Siligato R. (ed.), *Roma anni '60. Al di là della pittura*, exhibition catalogue (Rome, Palazzo delle Esposizioni, December 20, 1990 – February 15, 1991), Edizioni Carte Segrete, Rome 1990, p. 339.

33. Manzoni Piero, letter to Plinio De Martiis, Milan 1961 (Archivio di Stato di Latina, Fondo La Tartaruga, busta 25).

34. For further information about Manzoni's work see especially Gualdoni F. – Pasqualino di Marineo R. (eds.), *Piero Manzoni: 1933-1963*, exhibition catalogue (Milan, Palazzo Reale, March 26 – June 2, 2014), Skira, Milan 2014.

35. Manzoni Piero, letter to Plinio De Martiis, Milan 1961 (Archivio di Stato di Latina, Fondo La Tartaruga, busta 25).

36. Castelli Leo, letter to Plinio De Martiis, New York, September 23, 1961 (Archivio di Stato di Latina, Fondo La Tartaruga, busta 5).

13 Pittori a Roma La Tartaruga

*nuova sede
Piazza del Popolo 3
9 febbraio 1963*

INVITATION TO THE INAUGURAL
EXHIBITION, *13 PITTORI A ROMA*,
OF THE NEW GALLERY VENUE,
FEBRUARY 9, 1963

III 1963 – 1968
PIAZZA DEL POPOLO no.3

1963: The Gallery's New Venue

Early in 1963 La Tartaruga relocated to Piazza del Popolo, to the first floor of a building whose outside door was located in between the entrance areas of two of the most popular venues in Rome's artistic and cultural milieu: Caffè Rosati and the Dal Bolognese restaurant. From the very first days after it opened, the new venue, which was constantly attended by critics, intellectuals, directors, musicians, actors, and artists, lay the foundation for what De Martiis would describe as "a dense and fertile season experienced by those artists who knew how to absorb the remarkable climate of the city while creating a style. A style that was poised between the artwork and behavior, between material and images, between engagement and nihilism."[1] The artists he was referring to were those very young Romans who, from the relocation of La Tartaruga onwards, would begin to be associated under the name of 'Scuola di Piazza del Popolo.' The first exhibition held in the new location was dedicated to them, titled *13 Pittori a Roma* (February 9): along with the artists whom De Martiis had always supported (Novelli, Perilli, Rotella, Saul, and Twombly), also showing their works were Angeli, Bignardi, Festa, Fioroni, Kounellis, Mambor, Mauri, and Tacchi. For the occasion a catalogue was published featuring reproductions of the paintings accompanied by extracts from texts by Gillo Dorfles, Umberto Eco, Cesare Vivaldi, and from poems by Nanni Balestrini, Alfredo Giuliani, Elio Pagliarani, Antonio Porta, Edoardo Sanguineti. The aim was to foster an interdisciplinary exchange between artistic research and literary experimentation.

After a solo show dedicated to Twombly (March 6), a group exhibition was held of the works of Lombardo, Mambor, and Tacchi (April 8). Aware of the need to go *Oltre l'informale* (beyond the informal),[2] and to establish an objective relationship with reality, the three artists reproduced the 'reified' condition taken on by humans in mass society, that is, the loss of individual features in favor of the automatism of standardized behavior. Hence, Tacchi's *Tappezzerie*, representing individuals or their details outlined in a stylized way on quilted fabrics; or Mambor's *Timbri*, which consisted of the kind of silhouette that was used in statistics, repeated on the canvas with rubber stamp; there were also Lombardo's *Gesti*

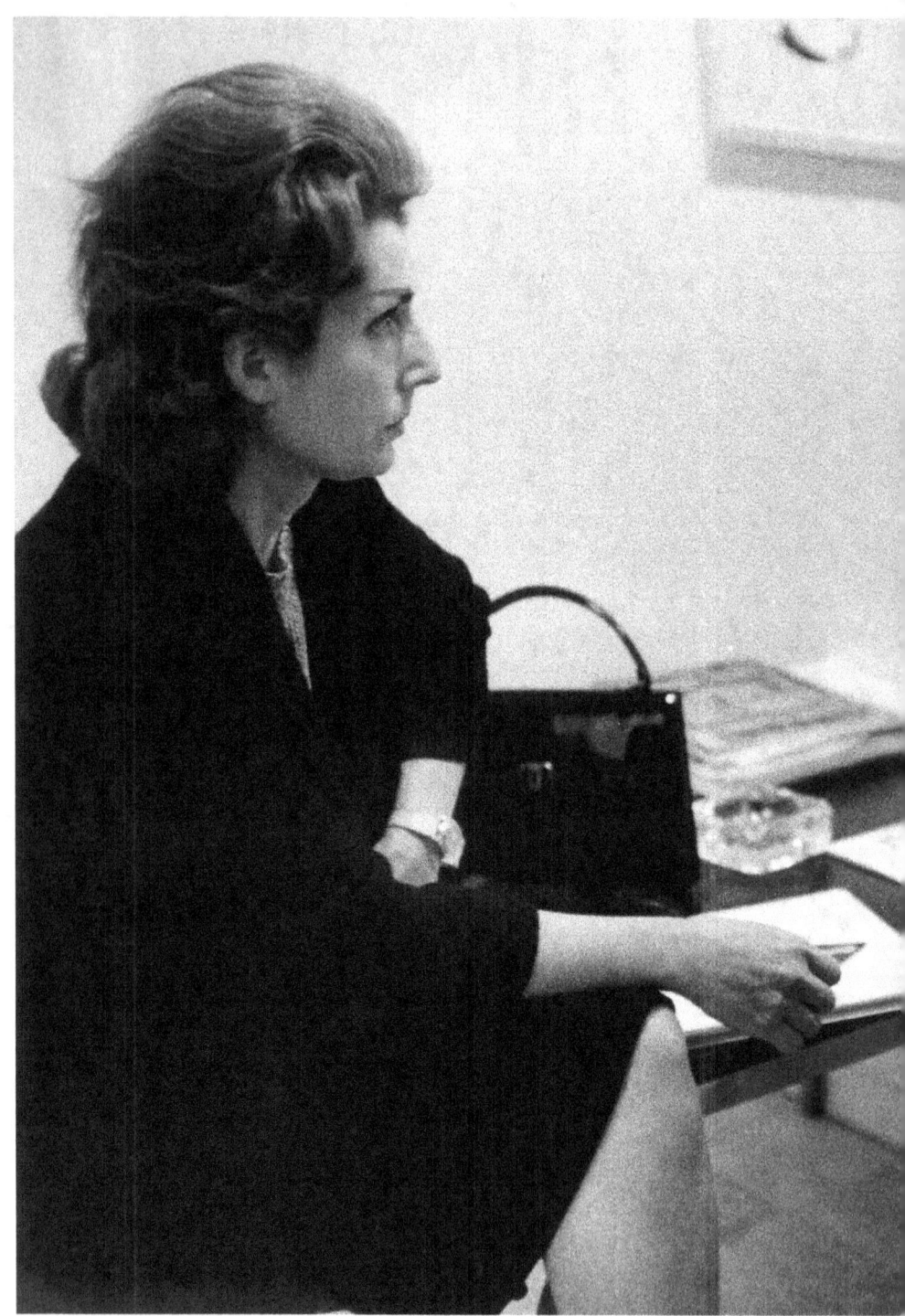

PALMA BUCARELLI AND MARCEL DUCHAMP ON THE OCCASION
OF THE *BARUCHELLO* EXHIBITION, MAY 20, 1963
PH.: PLINIO DE MARTIIS

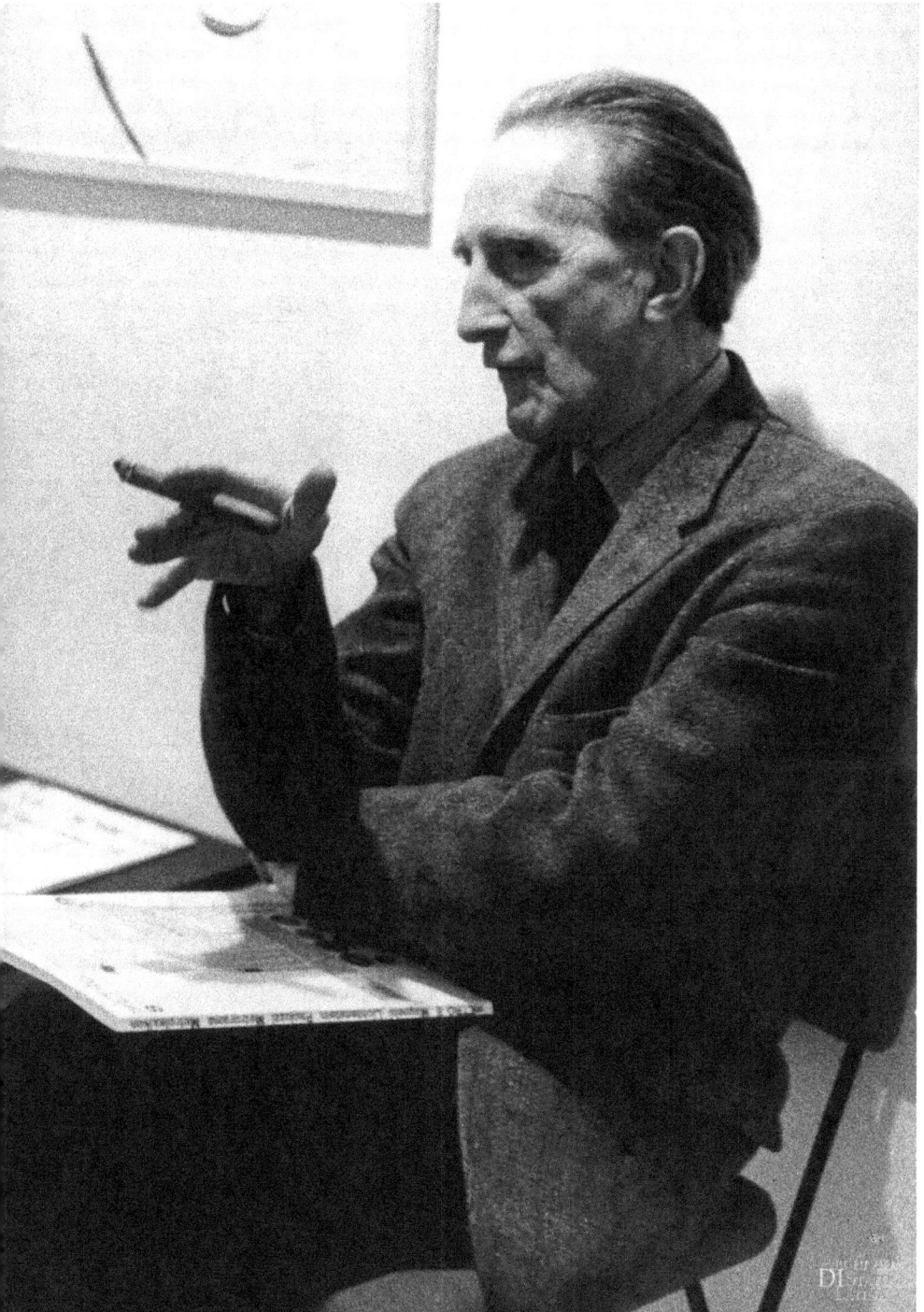

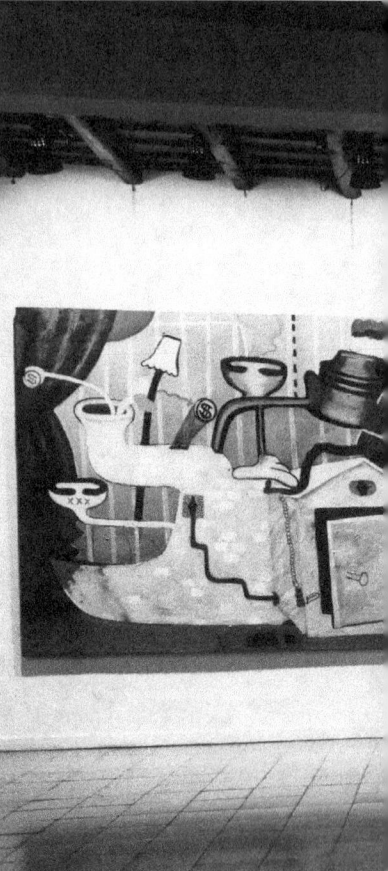

EXHIBITION VIEW OF *PETER SAUL*, DECEMBER 21, 1963
PH.: PLINIO DE MARTIIS

tipici, that is, black-painted shapes on canvas, most of them taken from the photographs of politicians caught during rhetorical gestures during their rallies.

A similar 'reification' of reality was also put forward by the solo show of the work of Umberto Bignardi (April 24) evoking homologating mass society through large collages on canvas where images borrowed from the repertory of communication are identifiable.

Nonetheless, the most important event in 1963 was no doubt the Tano Festa solo show (May 6). Born in 1938 and after writing poetry, he had approached painting that was influenced by the American research of Matta, De Kooning, Pollock, and Rothko. After showing his work at the Galleria La Salita in 1961, between 1962 and 1963 he had begun a different kind of experimentation, producing the first works in the *Persiane, Porte, Finestre, Specchi,* and *Obelischi* series. Whereas *Persiane, Porte, Finestre,* and *Specchi* reflect Duchamp's influence (suffice it to recall *Le Grand Verre*, 1915-1923 and *Fres. Widow*, 1920), the *Obelischi* instead stem more than from what the artist felt before the obelisk in Piazza del Popolo, from his reaction to the monument dedicated to Nelson that he had viewed during a period spent in London in 1963. "I arrived in London last night," wrote the artist: "I crossed [...] Trafalgar Square where there's a monument to Nelson. I was very impressed. [...] So I thought of obelisks, and I told myself that this theme has not been exhausted; quite the contrary, some wonderful stuff can be made out of them. On Monday I'm going to buy lots of postcards of the monument to Nelson, and if I manage to find one, a small bronze cast (like the ones of the Colosseum in Rome). When I return to Rome I will use this material for a large sculpture titled 'In the memorie of London.'"[3] This London inspiration was undoubtedly combined with Festa's great admiration for de Chrico's Metaphysical paintings; admiration which he himself had expressed a few months earlier in a letter from Paris addressed to De Martiis, in which he described with enthusiasm having discovered an edition of the novel *Les Gommes* by Alain Robbe-Grillet with an image of de Chirico's *Piazza d'Italia* on the cover.[4]

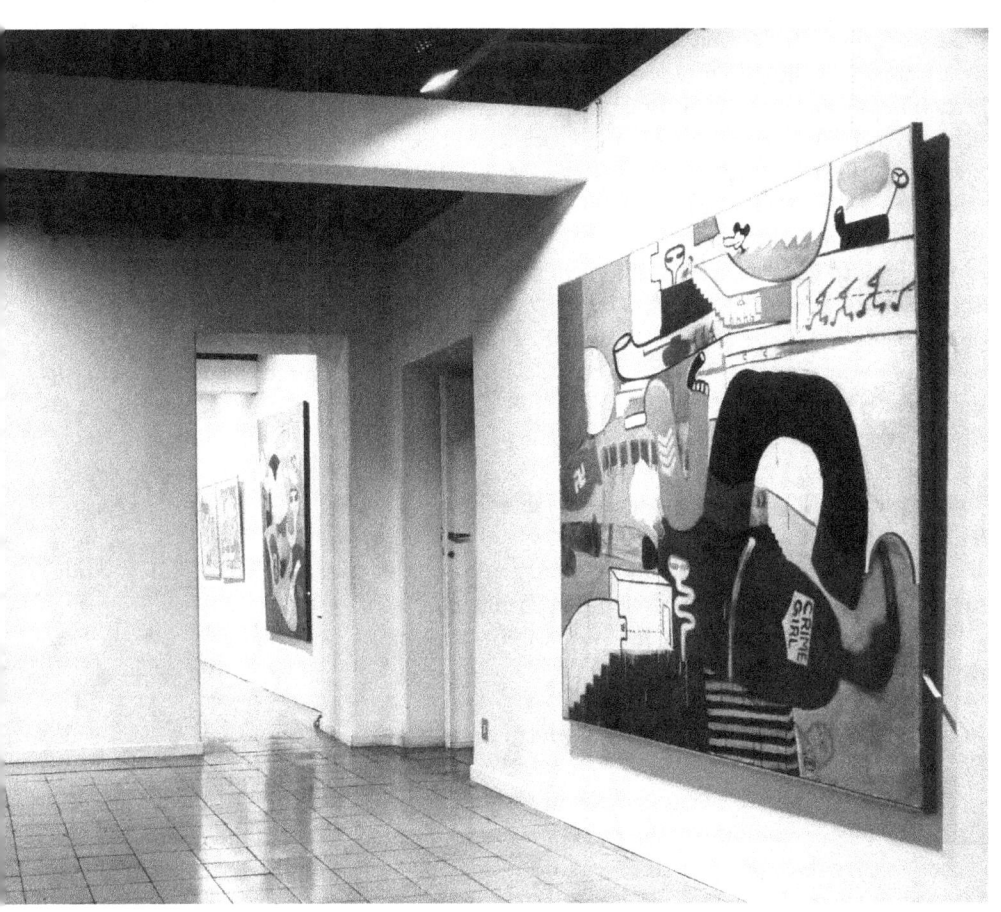

A similar Metaphysical ascendancy also characterized the works on display at La Tartaruga by the Livorno artist Gianfranco Baruchello on the occasion of his solo show, held on May 20, 1963. The founder, between 1949 and 1955, of the chemical-biological research and production company Società Biomedica, from 1959 Baruchello had decided to devote himself completely to art influenced by Matta and Duchamp. He then moved to New York, where he came face-to-face with the work of John Cage, Abstract Expressionism, and Pop Art. This led to the works he presented in Piazza del Popolo, characterized by fragmented and miniaturized painting made on large white surfaces, harkening back to the symbols of the consumer and television society, aimed at proposing another reality, however.

This underlying anti-capitalism was shared in the works of Franco Angeli included in the solo show held on June 6. Born in Rome in 1935 to a family that was traditionally socialist and anti-fascist, Angeli was a self-taught painter who became active in 1957 after the death of his mother and the bombing of the Roman quarter of San Lorenzo where he lived. The gauze and the dark red color he used in his early output refer to the dressings of those wounded and the human blood he had seen during the attack. Also inspired by the angst the experience had caused are the black surfaces with elements of paper and fabric that he produced in the late 1950s; in particular, the work *Elementi negativi* (1960), consisting of silhouettes of torn women's stockings covered by a thick gray veil. In 1963, for La Tartaruga the artist instead presented a new series of works where swastikas, Roman she-wolves, eagles, and dollars, veiled by a transparent diaphragm, invaded his canvases as the symbols of American capitalism, Nazi violence, and Roman history, the aim being to demonstrate their loss of meaning in present-day society. Represented in their entirety and then by enlarged fragments, they were then obfuscated by thick painting and gauze, both aimed at moving the viewer away from the object depicted and therefore from the fears intrinsic to it.

Another artist who filtered images as a way of taking his distance from them was the American-born Peter Saul. The subjects of the works on display at the solo show held at La Tartaruga on December 21 were comics,

Coca-Cola bottles, packaging typical of the food industry over which the artist used wide, colorful brushwork. It was the artist's pictorial manipulation of commercial images that kept these works distant from the 'object-oriented' research of Roy Lichtenstein and Jim Dine, and closer to the more 'artisanal' experiments that were being carried out by the 'Scuola di Piazza del Popolo,' which De Martiis offered a great deal of support to over the course of that same year, 1963. Indeed, if we leave out the group show held on October 14 for commercial reasons (with gouaches, drawings and graphic works) and the solo show of Kline's work (November 16), organized in wake of the *post mortem* retrospective that had just been dedicated to him by the Galleria Civica d'Arte Moderna in Turin, 1963 was the year when La Tartaruga's gallerist began to emerge as a 'talent scout' for, and mentor to, the youngest generation of Roman artists.

1964: American Invasion

The 1964 calendar of events began with a solo show of the German artist Peter Brüning (January 11), followed by an exhibition of the work of the Spanish painter Antoni Tàpies (February 1), as well as by La Tartaruga's participation in *II Mostra mercato nazionale di arte contemporanea*, which opened on April 1 in the rooms of Palazzo Strozzi in Florence. Nevertheless, most of the events proposed during the year were once again dedicated to the 'Scuola di Piazza del Popolo.'

After the group show with works by Angeli, Bignardi, Festa, Fioroni, Kounellis, Lombardo, Mambor, Tacchi (March 5), and before the show dedicated to Angeli, Ceroli, Festa, Fioroni, Lombardo, and Tacchi (June), on April 15 De Martiis welcomed to the gallery an important Kounellis exhibition. Instead of the black-painted letters and symbols that had been on display four years earlier, this time the artist presented his more recent, lyrical canvases, where the schematic and anti-naturalistic figurative elements (a rainbow, a moon, the Port of Piraeus) were represented so as to express the echoes of the Greek culture they evoked.

In the fall, on November 11 the gallery opened a solo show of the sculptor Mario Ceroli, born in Abruzzo but Roman by adoption. On display were his wooden works (including *La pantera* and *Il telefono*), which related to each other and to the surrounding space, creating a sort of *ante litteram* environment. After an apprenticeship with the sculptor Leoncillo, in 1958 Ceroli had obtained his first solo exhibition at the Galleria San Sebastianello in Rome. In 1959 he abandoned the use of ceramics in his works, and began experimenting with wood, cutting out letters, numbers, and figures often borrowed from the Italian cultural repertoire. In 1963 he had met De Martiis, who had been brought to his studio by Cy Twombly,[5] and this had led to the idea of organizing an exhibition for the following year.

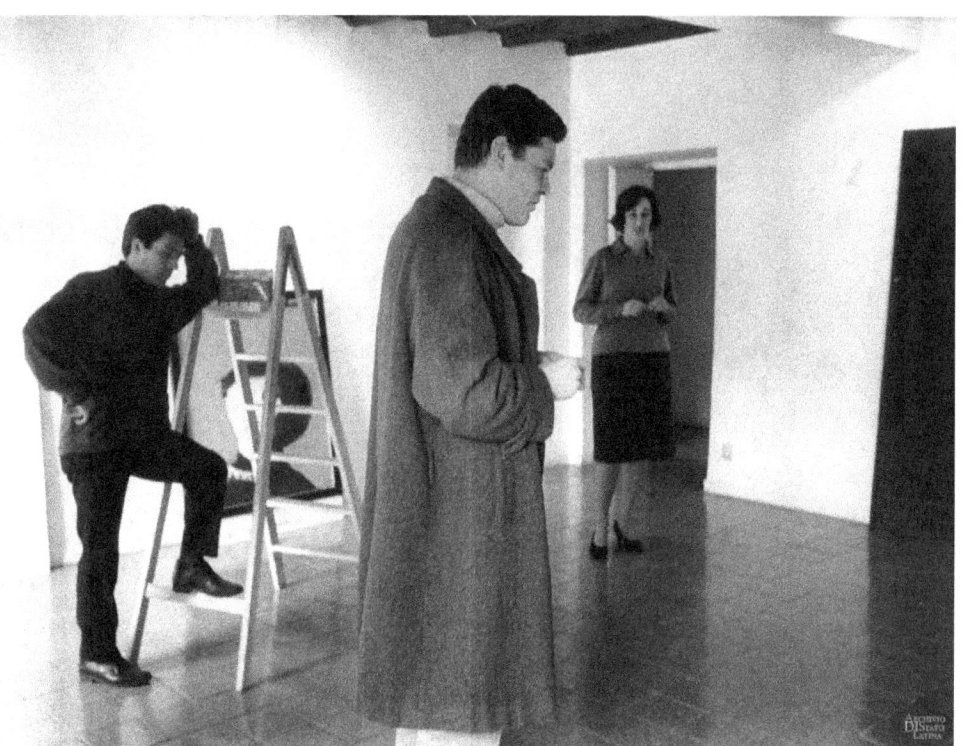

FROM THE LEFT: TANO FESTA, FRANCO ANGELI AND
GIOSETTA FIORONI ON THE OCCASION OF THE *ANGELI,
BIGNARDI, FESTA, FIORONI, KOUNELLIS, LOMBARDO,
MAMBOR, TACCHI* EXHIBITION, MARCH 5, 1964
PH.: PLINIO DE MARTIIS

Also established for the purpose of promoting the 'Scuola di Piazza del Popolo' was the *Premio "La Tartaruga,"* an exhibition that also included a competition, inaugurated on October 19, 1964, whose participants were: Angeli, Baruchello, Bignardi, Festa, Fioroni, Lombardo, Kounellis, Mambor, Mauri, Rotella, Santoro, Schifano, Tacchi, Dorazio, Perilli, Sanfilippo, Saul, and Twombly. De Martiis invited one hundred names from Italy's art and culture milieu to visit the exhibition, each one of them receiving a card on which they could express their preferences. Nonetheless, the award was not given to one of the young talents of the 'school,' but rather to the more 'traditional' painting of Perilli.

The initiative, which was inspired by the *Strega* literature prize, confirmed the gallerist's close attention to the publishing world; attention that in June of the same year was manifested with the publication of *Catalogo 1*. Founded for the purpose of solving the problem of the press's lack of interest in more recent art, *Catalogo 1*, with its magazine format, aimed at documenting the exhibitions held at La Tartaruga through critical, literary, and poetic texts, and with photographs related to the artists and their works.[6]

However, in any discussion of the programming at La Tartaruga in 1964 mention must be made of the most important Italian exhibition of the year: the 32nd Venice Biennale celebrating American Pop Art whose Grand Prize went to Robert Rauschenberg. This edition

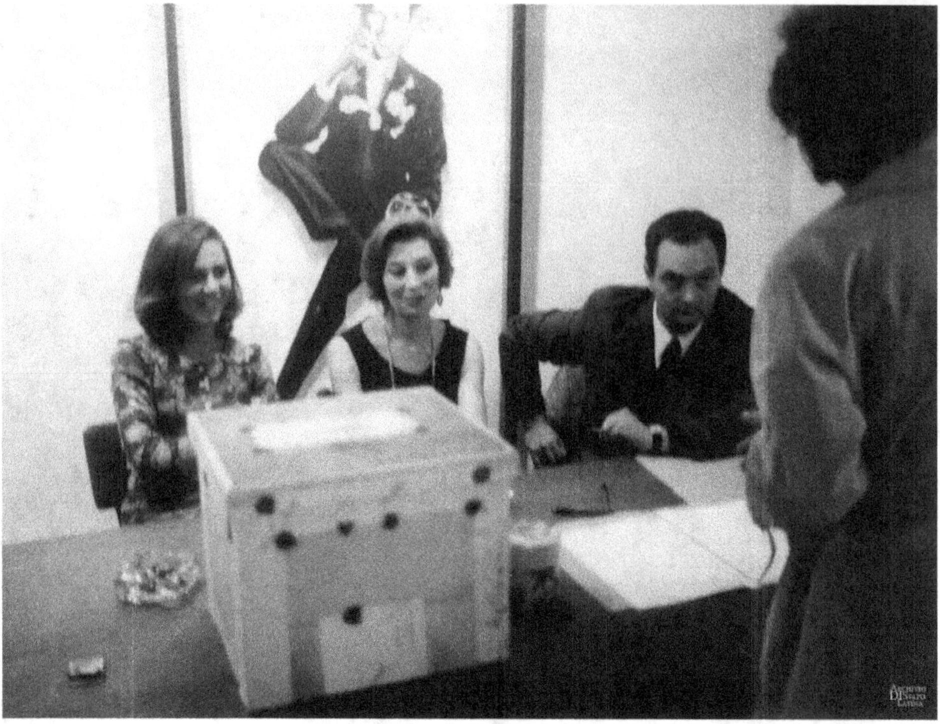

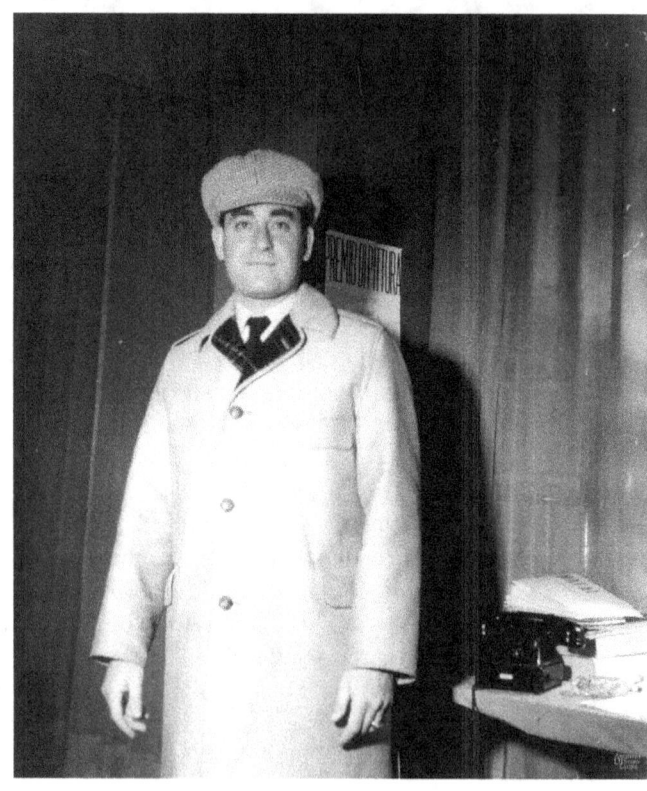

NINNÌ PIRANDELLO AND CESARE VIVALDI PRESIDE OVER THE VOTING FOR THE PREMIO "LA TARTARUGA," OCTOBER 19, 1964 PH.: PLINIO DE MARTIIS

GIORGIO FRANCHETTI ON THE OCCASION OF THE PREMIO "LA TARTARUGA," OCTOBER 19, 1964 PH.: PLINIO DE MARTIIS

of the event was aptly referred to as the 'American Biennale' because of the influence of the collectors and the American markets on the Italians. Indeed, it was Leo Castelli and Ileana Sonnabend who pushed for an exhibition to be held in the former U.S. Consulate in San Gregorio, where seven works by Dine, twenty (including *Flags*) by Jasper Johns, more than twenty (including the *Combine-Paintings*) by Rauschenberg, five by Stella and Chamberlain, and eight by Oldenburg, among others, were on display. Also keeping in mind how close Castelli was to Alan R. Solomon, the director of the Jewish Museum in New York and the commissioner of the American exhibition at the Biennale that year, it should come as no surprise that half of the American artists whose works were showcased in Venice were a part of the Galleria Castelli, and that the suspicion arose among the Italians that this might have been an attempt on the part of the American art market to 'colonize' Europe.[7]

De Martiis visited the Biennale in June 1964 together with the members of the 'school' invited to show their work at that year's edition: they were Angeli, Castellani, Festa, Fioroni, Schifano. He also brought with him the young Turin artist Giulio Paolini to whom he intended to dedicate a solo show in the fall; however, Franchetti was against it so it never came about.[8] For the artists 'of Piazza del Popolo' seeing the United States Pavilion was so game-changing that many of them and their friends (including Baruchello, Tacchi, Ceroli, Mambor) soon decided to move to the United States to get to know the 'inventors' of Pop research in person. Nevertheless, against what might seem to be the case, if we look back at La Tartaruga's activity in 1964 and in the following years, we can see how the visit to the 'American Biennale' did not in any way influence De Martiis' choices when it came to the exhibitions at the gallery, as he continued to support the young Roman artists without ever surrendering to the temptation to promote the much more popular American Pop artists. Actually, the American invasion of the Biennale stimulated De Martiis to demonstrate that Roman artistic research was original and not subordinate to what was going on across the Atlantic. Perhaps the discovery at the same time of Michelangelo, Metaphysics, and Futurism by the Italian critics[9] was dictated by the same need: to uphold the importance of Italian art history in relation to the more recent international experiments. A claim that could at the same time derive from the bitter confutation of the American 'myth' on the part the Roman artists who had moved to the Big Apple. As early as 1964 in fact, Baruchello described the Americans as follows: "You have to see these people from close up and talk to them if you are to understand the advertising trick they represent. It's almost like being in Rome, and I guarantee Tano Festa is almost more genuine than Dine."[10] Festa himself, in 1965, would describe just how hard it was to live and work in the United States, even though he was at the same time trying to convince De Martiis to collaborate with the New York gallerist Ben Birillo. Festa felt that it could be "an opportunity to establish […] a bridge with New York. Something that, up until now, contrary to what it looks like, has never occurred."[11] Two years later, Ceroli, as well, observing the same problems as the ones described by Festa, would admit: "I would give anything to go back to Rome […] here I can't seem to work at ease, I feel like I'm drowning in quicksand."[12] In 1966 Tacchi would be the one to admit, with some sadness: "All told the people here are sad, they don't have what we have, that is, the opportunity for relationships with things, instinctively, ingeniously."[13] The most disillusioned, harshest description of America was provided by Angeli when he wrote, in 1967: "Naturally, what strikes you the most is the huge importance that money has, without which it's hard to be considered as persons with a brain and feelings. One thing that strikes you when you arrive is the overabundance of objects old and new, food, candy, chocolate.

Catalogo 1

CATALOGO — S.m. Enumerazione di più oggetti in qualche ordine. Dire, Raccogliere, Scegliere. Catalogo per ordine d'alfabeto, per ordine di materie, Catalogo numerato — Compito, imperfetto — Bene o male ordinato, critico, ragionato Può il catalogo essere l'arida enumerazione, può portare schiarimenti non brevi, notizie pellegrine, anche ragionamenti profondi. — Fare, Rifare, Compilare, Compire, Stampare un catalogo — Segnatam. di libri. Il libraio dà il catalogo de' libri ch'egli tiene da vendere, lo stampatore, degli stampati da lui. Gli eredi fanno fare il catalogo della biblioteca indegnamente redatta, per spacciarla a rotta qua e là in tutte parti d'Europa, onta ai maggiori e alla patria, infamia a sé. — Catalogo d'edizioni rare. Di tutte le edizioni d'un libro medesimo Di tutte le opere d'un autore solo — Segnatam. di biblioteca pubblica. Cercate nel catalogo Libro che non si trova in catalogo Cancellarlo dal catalogo Aggiungervelo Mettere nel catalogo un libro acquistato, Levarlo dal catalogo, quando non si ha più. dice il libraio e che ha biblioteca o libreria propria. — In biblioteca ben regolata, una delle spese ordinarie è quella del catalogo — Catalogo di quadri, di altre opere d'arte in una galleria, esposte in mostra, da vendere. — Catalogo di monete. — Di piante. — Di stelle. — Il volume manoscritto o stampato Far leggere il catalogo Terzo volume del... — Il catalogo de' Santi Franch. Sacch. Op div 133 6 Nel catalogo delle Vergini. — Per estens. Girol. Nel catalogo che delle virtù del Vescovo fa l Apostolo (In questo e sim. senso meglio enumerazione o altro meno erudito) — Di cose e pers Catalogo delle navi in Omero. Macr Omero, in capo del suo catalogo colloca la Boezia, tralasciando Micene, di dove era il Re, capitano dell'armi supremo — Aus In serie di catalogo recansi le milizie, i capitani, le navi. — In questo senso familiarm. non suona lode. M'ha fatto un lungo catalogo de' suoi titoli. Segner Crist. Instr 1 19 18 Voi... mi venite attorno piangendo, e mi recitate un lungo catalogo di quei mali che vi circondano (dal Dizionario della Lingua Italiana nuovamente compilato dai Signori Nicolò Tommaseo e Cav Bernardo Bellini)

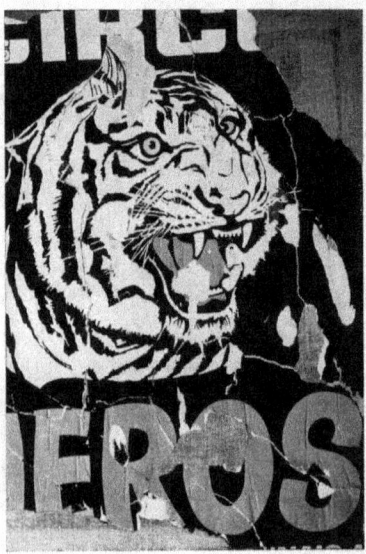

CATALOGO 1, ROME, JUNE 1964

RIGHT: JANNIS KOUNELLIS AND PINO PASCALI ON THE OCCASION OF THE FIRST PINO PASCALI SOLO SHOW AT LA TARTARUGA, JANUARY 11, 1965
PH.: PLINIO DE MARTIIS

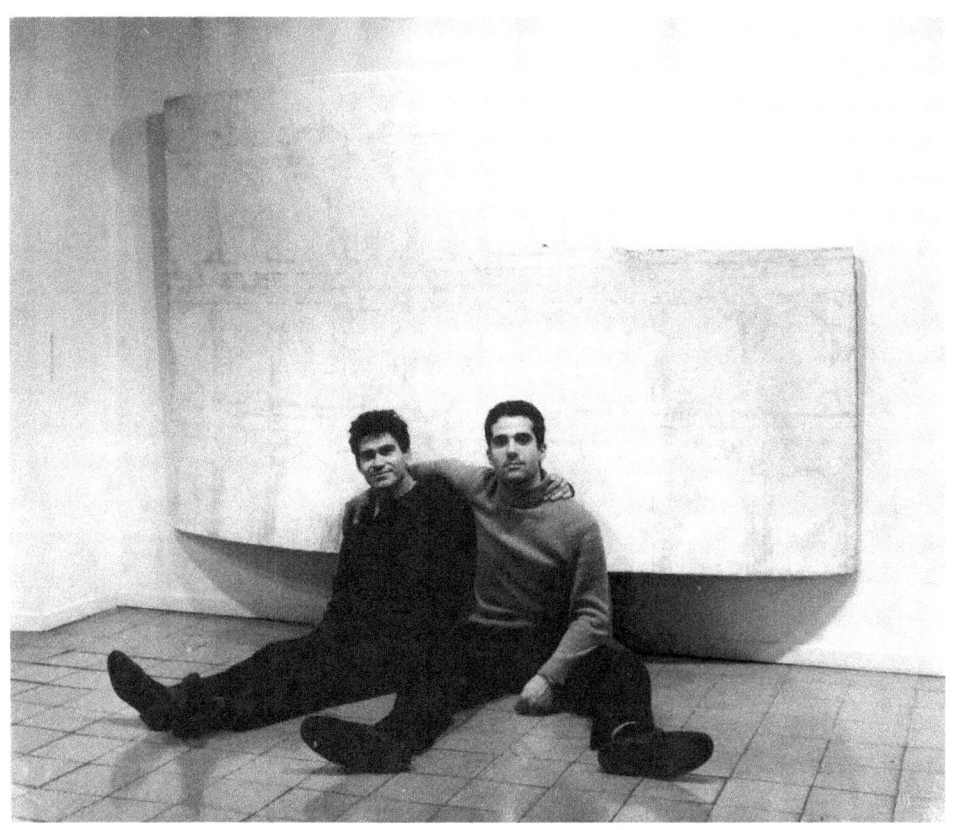

[…] And all this has a strange feeling of death. If you scratch the surface of what covers everything you will find the gravestone of one of your ancestors."[14] Between 1964 and 1967, it was likely that this deep disillusionment with American art and culture encouraged De Martiis and his artists to move away from the pro-American research and to discover a totally Italian artistic-cultural identity, declaring themselves to be its epigones.

1965: The Practice of the Environment

As foreshadowed by the Ceroli show in 1964, the practice of the environment returned to La Tartaruga the following year with the first solo show of the work of Pino Pascali (January 11). Born in Bari, he had trained at the Fine Arts Academy in Rome where his talent as a set designer was noted. After making models, drawings, and short films for several programs on RAI-TV, and after devoting himself to painting in the New Realist style, he turned his attention to New Dada and Pop Art. At La Tartaruga Ceroli conceived the exhibition of his so-called 'reliefs' not as a sum of sculptures, but as a work capable in itself of conversing with the visitors and with the host environment. He thus took part in research that, from Duchamp's urinal (1917), by way of the totem made by Schwitters in his own home (mid-1930s), to Fontana's *Ambiente nero* (1949), encouraged artists to shift their attention from the complete object per se to the relationship that it establishes with the surrounding space and with the viewer. The dissemination of the practice of the site-specific installation (works conceived in relation to their host space) and of the environment (works designed as fully-fledged ambients) is

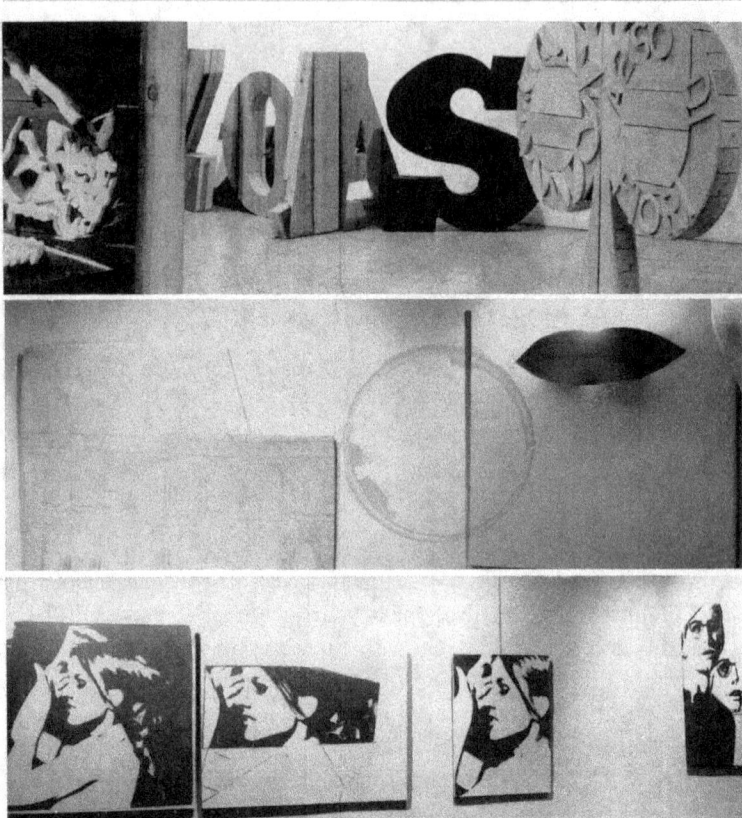

CATALOGO 2, ROME,
FEBRUARY 27, 1965

based on this. Allan Kaprow had coined the term 'environment' by calling the sound work he presented in 1958 at the Hansa Gallery in New York *Untitled Environment*. And Kaprow had also been the one to publish the book *Assemblage, Environments & Happenings* (H. N. Abrams, New York) in 1966, in which he traced the origins of these operative modalities in Rauschenberg's *Combine-Paintings*. In parallel, Yves Klein with *Le Vid* (1958), Arman with *Le Plein* (1960), Oldenburg with *The Store Two* (1962), Warhol with *Box Scultures* (1964), and Robert Morris with *Mirrors and Cubes* (1964) had established the guidelines to conceive space as an integral part of the work of art. Pascali further developed these experiments, characterizing the environment he outlined as being strongly Italian: made up of sculptures portraying the Colosseum, ruins of columns, and a tuff-covered wall, the space appeared to be an ironic homage more to the history and culture of Rome than to the typical objects of mass media culture 'sacralized' by American Pop. This was also thanks to De Martiis who suggested that the artist remove the label "Souvenir of Roma" from his *Colosseo* because the same words could be found in Lichtenstein's works. However, if De Martii's intention was to create a distance between Pascali's experiment and the work taking place across the ocean, while his suggestion was a good one at the time, he would later make a mistake. De Martiis' would refuse to show for the first time ever Pascali's new series of the works, because he believed they were too similar to the 'pro-American' Scarpitta's unusable cars.[15] Scarpitta's *Armi* consisted of sheet metal, pipes, metal mesh, wheels, bolts, plywood and wood, assembled and made uniform by military paint, and thus used to build cannons, missiles, machine guns, missile launchers, and anti-aircrafts on a scale of 1:1. These were first displayed at the Galleria Sperone in Turin in January-February 1966, thanks to Michelangelo Pistoletto's intercession.

Unlike Pascali's *Armi*, De Martiis felt that Giosetta Fioroni's *Sali d'argento* were indeed wholly 'Italian': hence, the decision to present them on the occasion of a solo show inaugurated on January 30, 1965. In these works, the typically American readymade object was replaced by an object that was reproduced in a way that was apparently the same as the original one, but was actually different in terms of its size, color, and shadows. To make them, the artist took an image from magazines or books published during the same period, she outlined their shapes, and then she reproduced them in the white space of the canvas, replicating them several times by using different densities of ink, and blurring certain parts. The viewer was thus invited to experience not the mass media world in itself, but the subjective emotion that derived from it and that was channeled through painting.

Based on the same need to confute the presumed subordination of Roman artistic research with respect to what was going on in the United States, soon afterwards De Martiis decided to exhibit a work by Giacomo Balla in the gallery. The idea was based the news that in 1963, at the National Gallery of Canada, Oldenburg had shown a bedroom: *Bedroom Ensemble*. "Aware that nothing's new under the sun, but informed that in 1912 [...] our Giacomo Balla had painted a bedroom with abstract motifs,"[16] and on February 18, 1965 De Martiis presented *Una camera da letto di Balla*. The title referred to the wooden bed that the Futurist artist, after returning to Rome from a period spent in Germany, had had built by a furniture factory between 1912 and 1913, which he then decorated with the motif of the *Iridescent Compenetrations* he had conceived in 1912. Now on display at La Tartaruga, that bedroom showed how the paternity of the 'popular' research aimed at presenting the everyday as a work of art, and the operative modality of the environment, were both wholly

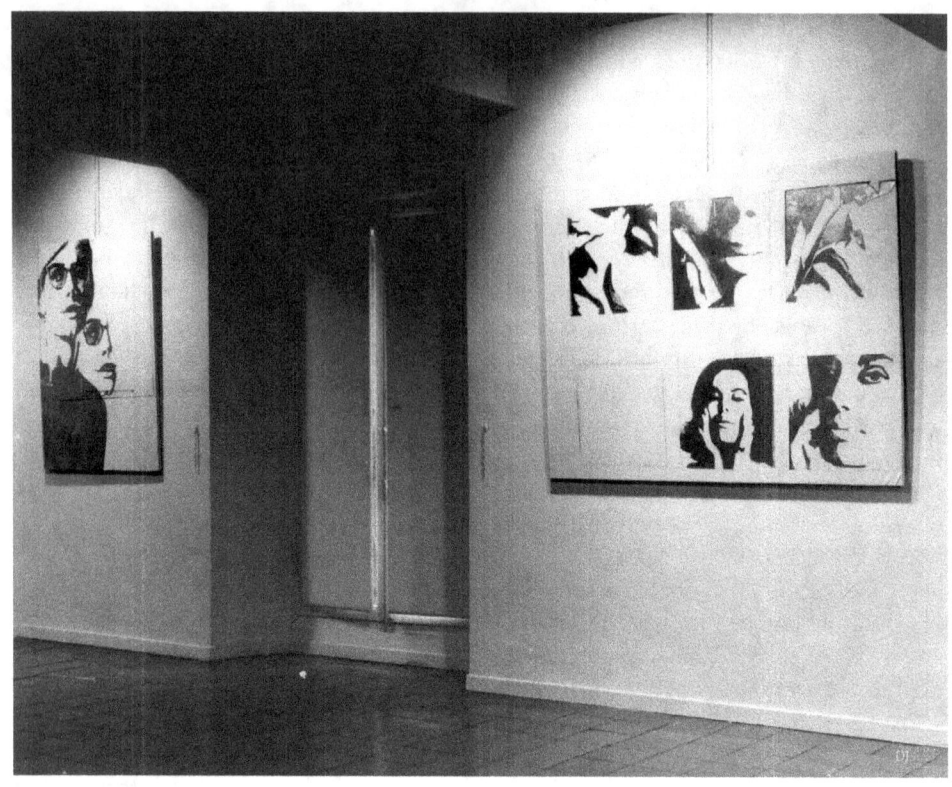

EXHIBITION VIEW OF *GIOSETTA FIORONI*, JANUARY 30, 1965
PH.: PLINIO DE MARTIIS

Italian. But not only that: the installation of the bedroom considerably influenced some of the artists of the 'Scuola di Piazza del Popolo,' first among whom Mario Schifano. From New York Schifano wrote to De Martiis as follows: "I read in an Italian newspaper that you had a show with one of Balla's rooms; I was so happy you can't imagine; I don't know whether you will believe me, but I very much love Balla and him alone. [...] Plinio, when I come back to Italy please let me do a show in your gallery; and in the catalogue or on the 'card' or the 'brochure' [...] we'll write 'A COLORI PER RAGIONI SENTIMENTALI' and the show will be a 'BOOM'!"[17] The enthusiasm for Balla's bedroom thus seems to have inspired the series of works that Schifano made in 1965, titled *Futurismo rivisitato a colori*, exhibited for the first time at La Tartaruga on the occasion of the solo show inaugurated on January 21, 1967.

After the exhibition dedicated to Balla, De Martiis continued to support the research being done by young Roman artists, welcoming the solo shows of Tacchi (March 27), Mambor (April 21), and Festa (October 22).

Born in Rome in 1940, Tacchi had debuted in 1959 at the Galleria Appia Antica with Schifano and Mambor, and later entered the entourage of the artists 'of Piazza del Popolo.' For his first solo show at La Tartaruga, he presented his so-called quilted *Tappezzerie* on which black-enamel figures are often portrayed either sitting or reclining on armchairs or sofas, perhaps inspired by the Balla environment that he had recently seen in the gallery. The scenes

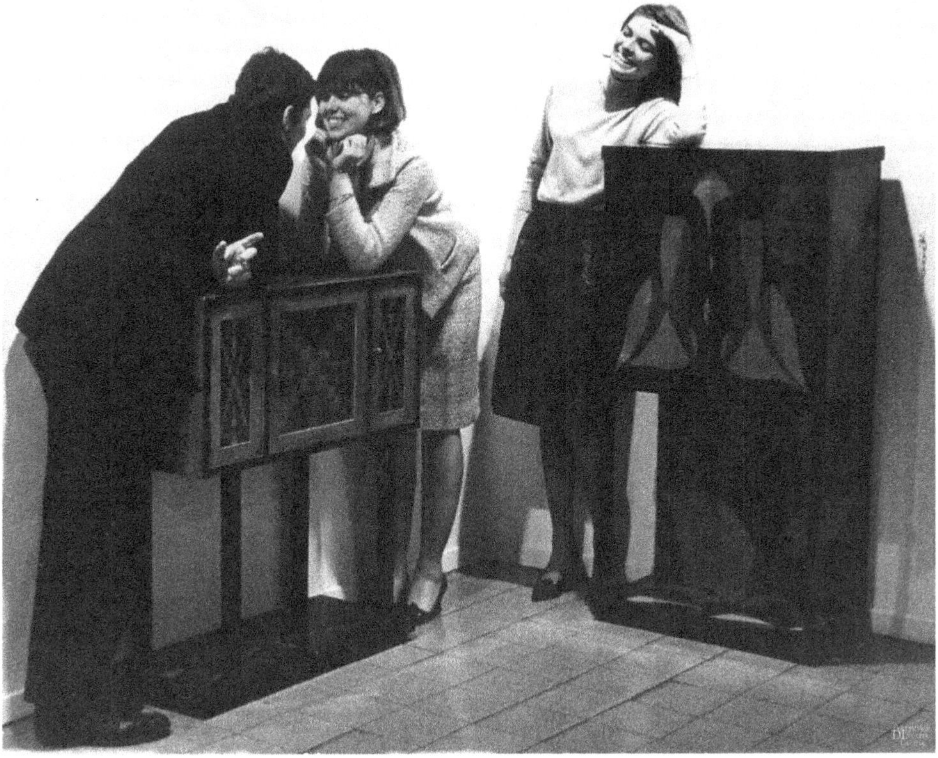

EXHIBITION VIEW OF *UNA CAMERA DA LETTO DI BALLA* AND SOME VISITORS DURING THE OPENING, FEBRUARY 18, 1965
PH.: PLINIO DE MARTIIS

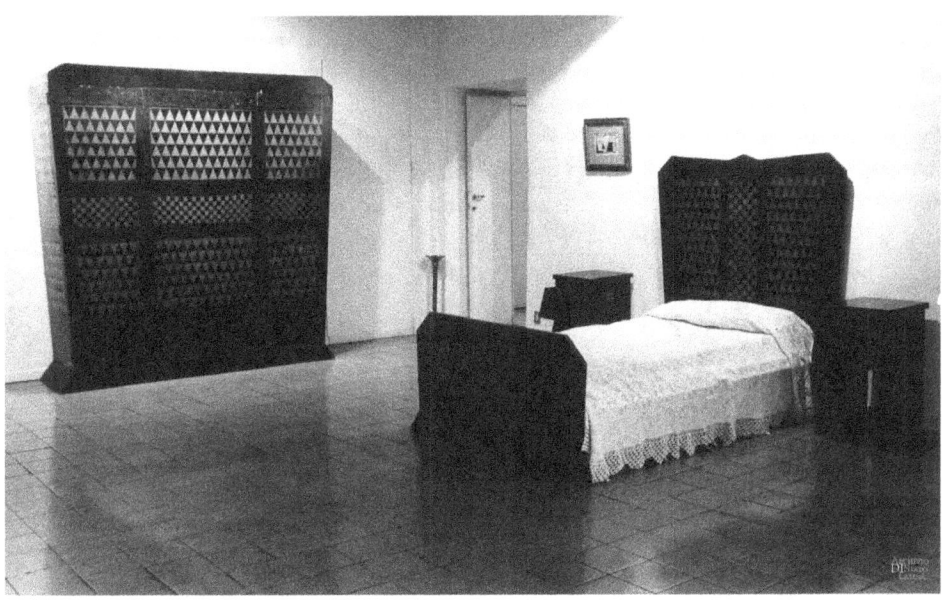

represented are rather ambiguous, however, even when the reference to famous actual figures or ones who had by that time entered the collective imaginary was evident. A case in point is the golden female body set against a black background inspired by the gold-painted female character in Goldfinger, the third film in the *James Bond* series released in 1964.

Renato Mambor, who was born in Rome in 1936, had instead met De Martiis in the early 1960s when he visited him in the gallery. After the wooden monochromes painted with industrial paint (1960), and after the *Segnali stradali* (1961) in which the geometric signs were reminiscent of the slanted stripes on the backs of trucks, the artist made his first *Uomini Statistici* (1962): paintings that initially represented the stylized man used for pedestrian signs, followed by the human shapes used in statistics, at first printed on monochrome canvas and later repeated over and over again by using a rubber stamp. The intent behind these works, exhibited at La Tartaruga, was that of involving the viewer in a learning process aimed at revealing the meaning taken on by reality once it had been deprived of its specific attribute.[18]

Lastly, after the Perilli exhibition (May 6) and a group show dedicated to the 'Scuola di Piazza del Popolo' (in June), a solo exhibition of Festa's work was held (October 22). On display were several canvases characterized by small framed images placed above the main subject of the work, which is often a sky, or a detail from a masterpiece by Michelangelo or by other old masters of Italian art. The small framed images evoke the vertical sliding of a film: hence, the reference is to cinema, not so much as a mass communication tool, but rather as a practice intrinsic to Roman culture given the presence of Cinecittà.

It should come as no surprise, then, that Festa was not the only Roman artist to include cinema in painting: in those years, numerous other artists (including Angeli and Schifano) chose the movie camera as an alternative to the paintbrush, just as numerous filmmakers presented their films as visual works inside art galleries. This was the case of the Beat filmmaker and actor Taylor Mead. Introduced to De Martiis thanks to a ticket he had been given by Rotella in Paris, on January 17, 1965 he screened three critically-acclaimed short films at La Tartaruga.[19]

In the meantime, in the spaces of Piazza del Popolo experiments continued to be conducted on the practice of the environment. On December 10, after a solo show by Castellani (November 12), Ceroli installed several sculptures that asked visitors to intervene as a character among the characters (the wooden shapes), or rather, as an actor among the elements of a pseudo-set. In *Ultima Cena*, for instance, the space left empty in between the twelve silhouettes of the apostles evokes a missing figure: that of the viewer. In *La scala*, instead, the shapes, apparently about to climb up or down steps, outline a series of opposite paths; while underlying *Piper* are the endless motions of the clients/silhouettes so packed into an elevated track that none of the real viewers looking at the work from the outside can enter. Lastly, the *Piazza d'Italia* reminiscent of de Chirico is conceived as an evocative place of connection between the pseudo-theatrical rooms/scenes intrinsic to the other sculptures displayed (*La casa di Dante, Balcone, Bocca della Verità*). The exhibition thus became a work

CESARE TACCHI ON THE OCCASION OF HIS FIRST SOLO SHOW AT LA TARTARUGA, MARCH 27, 1965
PH.: PLINIO DE MARTIIS

RENATO MAMBOR ON THE OCCASION OF HIS FIRST SOLO SHOW AT LA TARTARUGA, APRIL 21, 1965
PH.: PLINIO DE MARTIIS

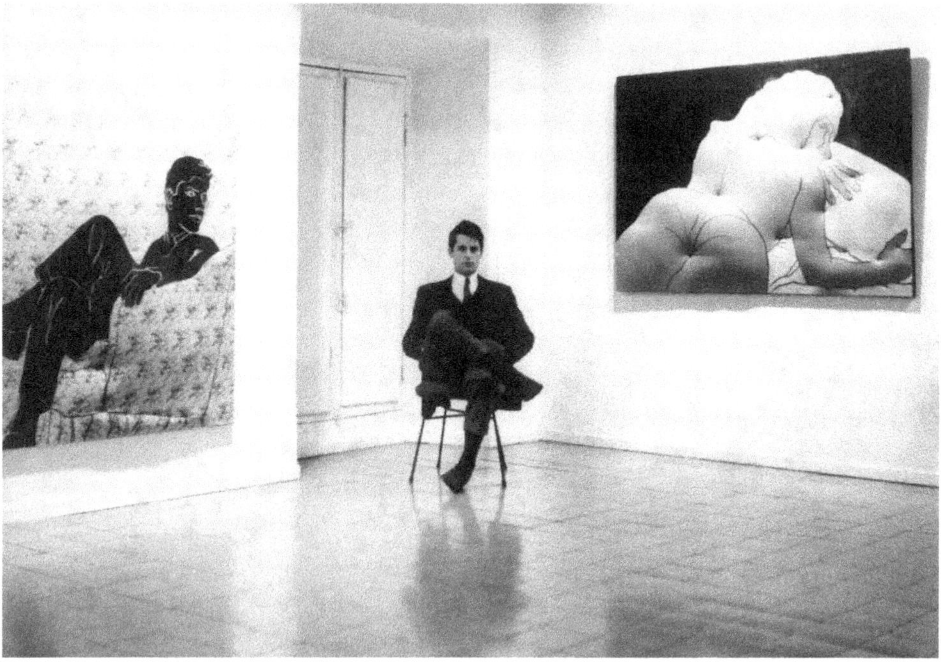

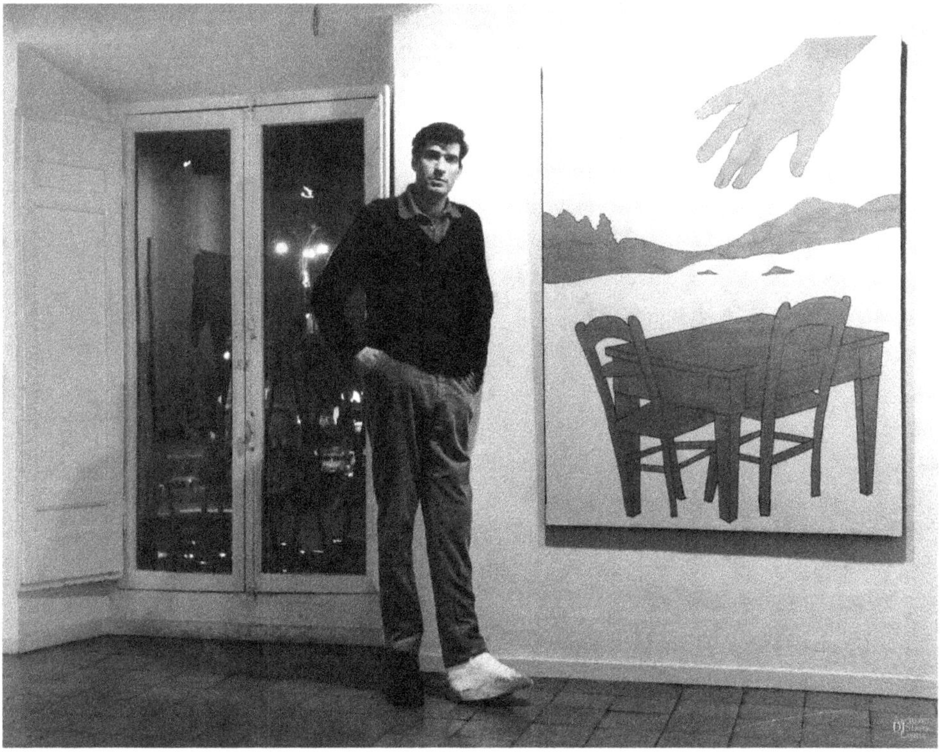

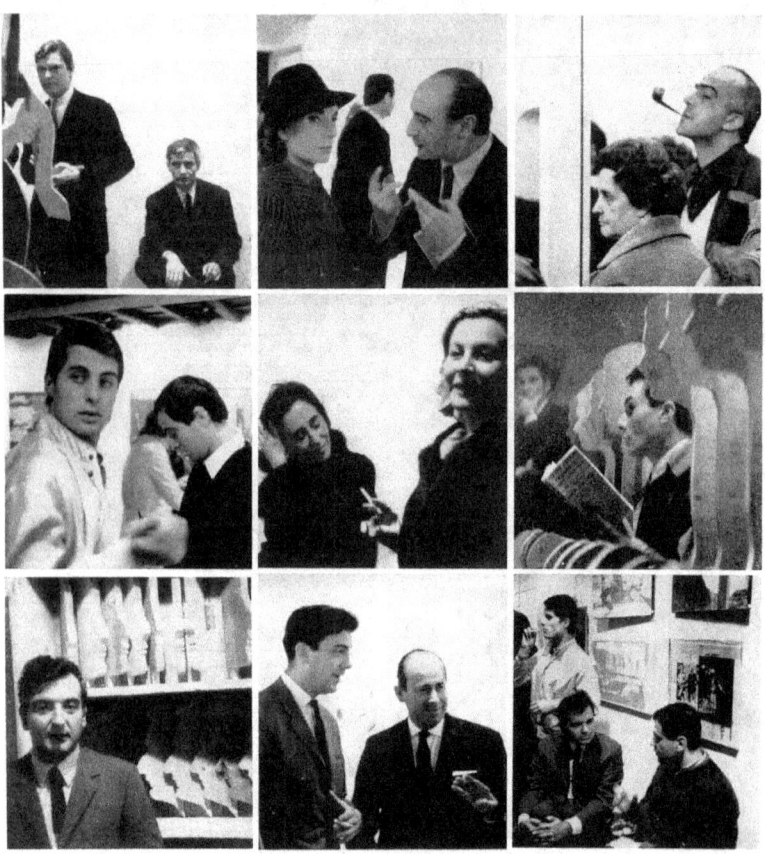

CATALOG 3, JUNE 10, 1965

ILARIA BERNARDI

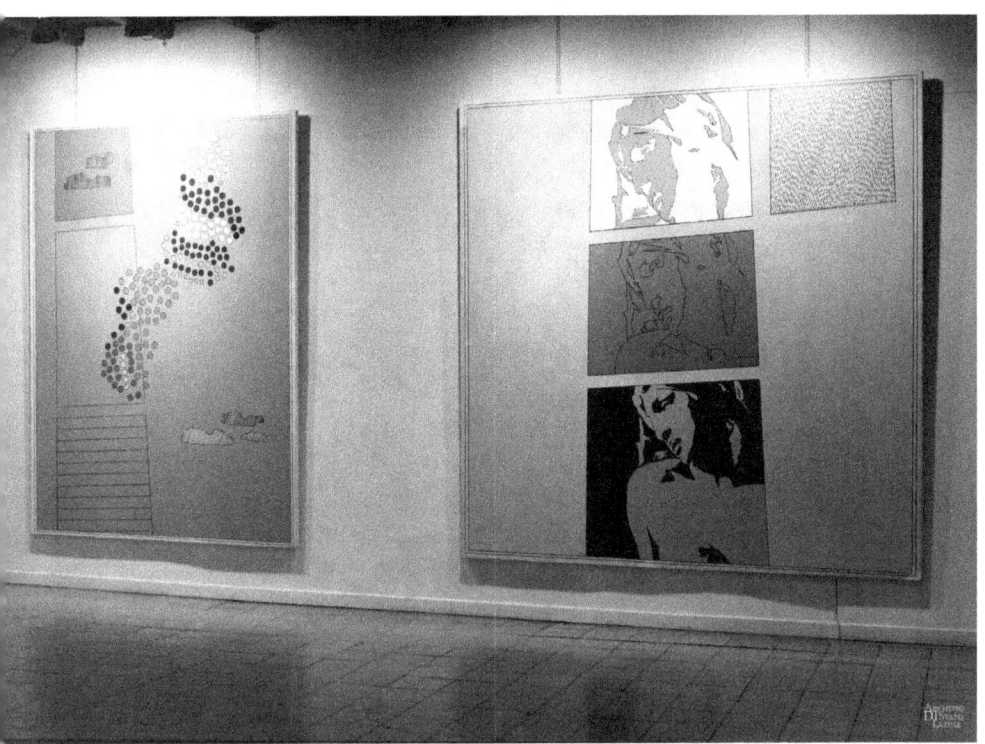

EXHIBITION VIEW OF *FESTA*, OCTOBER 22, 1965
PH.: PLINIO DE MARTIIS

in its own right meant for the active (not only contemplative) enjoyment of the viewer. It also anticipated the research between art and theater developed soon thereafter by Ceroli himself, via his collaboration with the filmmaker Luca Ronconi that began with *La Cina*. The artist had made the installation in 1966 and presented it to La Tartaruga on November 19 of the same year on the occasion of a solo show. It consists of a compact series of large wooden silhouettes, all of them the same, and depicted as they walk, alluding to the serial nature of the era of consumption, but above all to the 'serial' ideology underlying Chinese society. Nevertheless, this seriality does not mean a perceptive bombing aimed at dissuading the viewer's action and thus turning them into a viewer who is a part of the system. Rather, it assumes an environmental and performative value: the viewer, seeing that the space of the gallery is almost completely occupied by the sculpture, feels the need to move around it to be able to better see its parts, hence becoming an actor in their own right. It was based on this scenographic-theatrical value that Ronconi chose to include *La Cina* in the set design of his *Riccardo III*, performed at the Teatro Stabile in Turin in 1967.

The theatricalization of art that De Martiis would welcome to the gallery, especially between 1967 and 1968, was the direct consequence of the experiments on the environment that were developed in those years by some of the members of his 'school.'

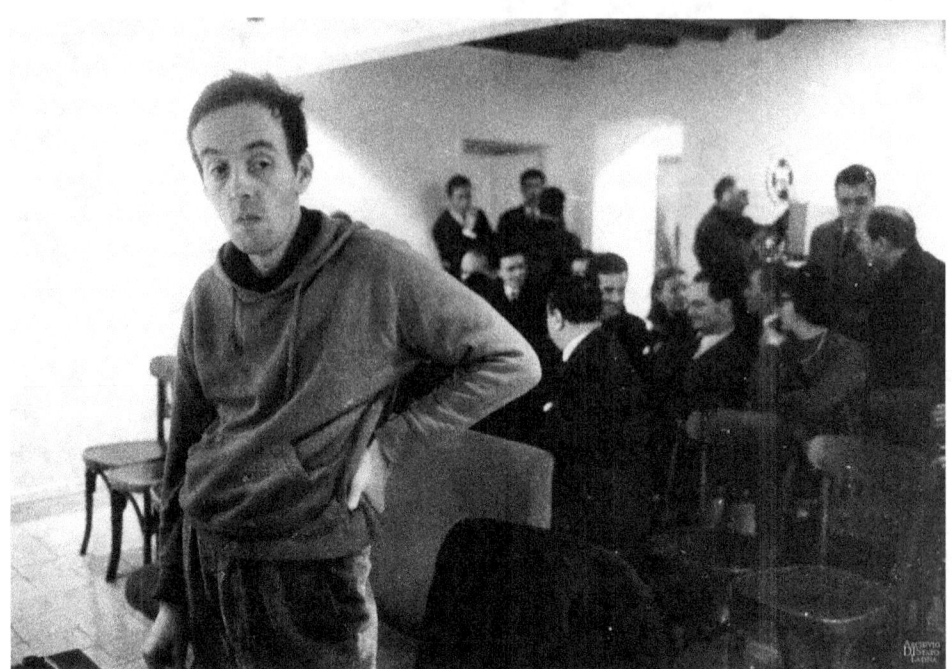

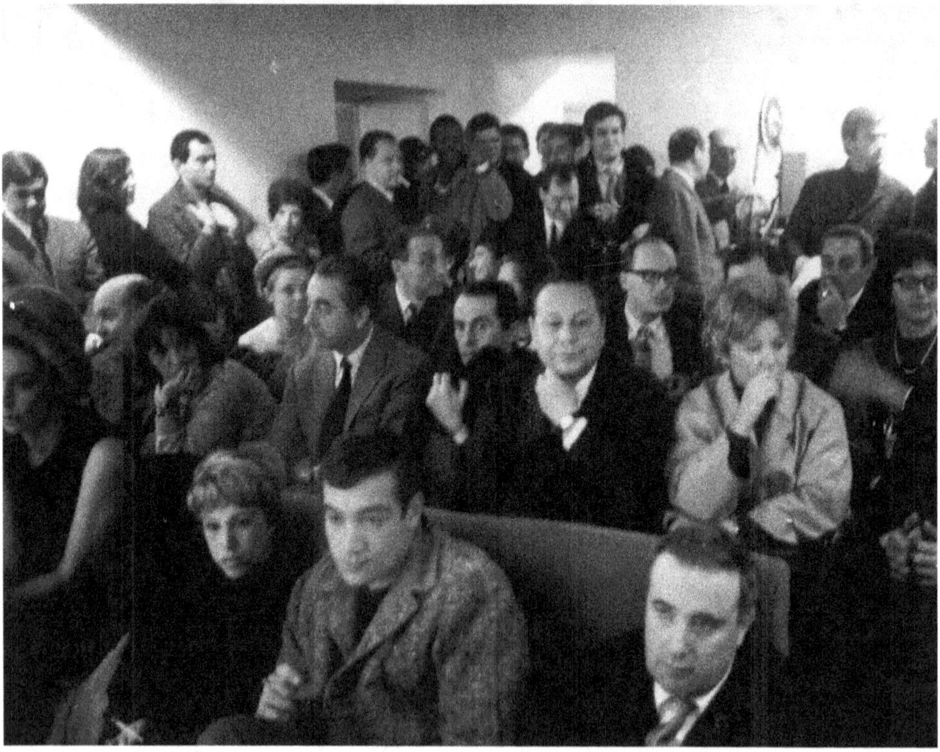

TAYLOR MEAD AND THE AUDIENCE AT THE GALLERY ON THE OCCASION OF
THE SCREENING OF THREE OF HIS SHORT FILMS, JANUARY 17, 1965
PH.: PLINIO DE MARTIIS

1966: Upholding Rome's Independence from New York

Nineteen sixty-six at La Tartaruga was a year filled with events, once again most of them dedicated to the artists of the 'Scuola di Piazza del Popolo.' They included: *Roma 1966 realtà dell'immagine* on June 10; the group show that opened on December 15 with works by Baruchello, Ceroli, Festa, Mambor, Fioroni, Kounellis, Lombardo, Mauri, Pascali, Tacchi, Twombly; Sergio Lombardo's first solo show and the presentation of his *Gesti tipici* (February 5); lastly, the aforementioned solo show of Ceroli's works that included *La Cina* (November 19). Exceptions to this were the first solo show in Italy of the German artist Gerhard Richter (January 20), the tribute to Capogrossi and Fontana (March 2) and the solo show of Müller-Brittnau (May 13). Of all these events, the most relevant was the Richter exhibition. Born in Dresden in 1932, the artist had had his first solo show at the Galleria Schmela in Düsseldorf in 1964, followed by his participation in other exhibitions held especially in Germany, Switzerland, and in the Netherlands. In early October 1965, De Martiis had gone to Richter's studio in Düsseldorf to discuss the details of the exhibition: he would have preferred to show sixteen works but not ones of landscapes or animals, leaving the selection up to the artist and his friend Manfred de La Motte.[20] The works that were presented at La Tartaruga were photo-pictures, that is, works obtained by projecting photographs taken from the news that Richter then copied over in black and white, using the traditional oil technique, but with the addition of the blurring effect typical of snapshots taken with a flash. In any case, both the critics and the Roman public showed little interest in the artist's work, and only one photo-painting (*Pyramide*) was sold.[21]

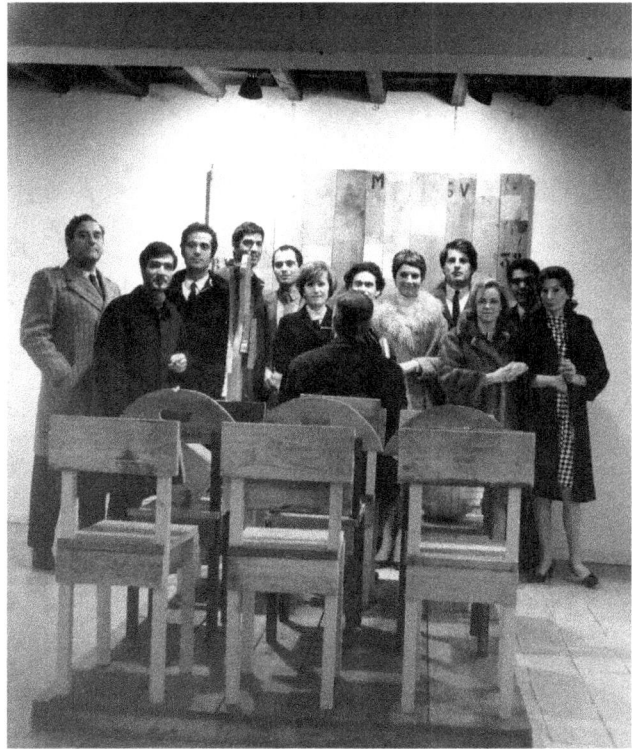

GIORGIO FRANCHETTI, SERGIO LOMBARDO, PINO PASCALI, RENATO MAMBOR, MARIO CEROLI, ROSSANA PALMA, JANNIS KOUNELLIS, PAOLA PITAGORA, CESARE TACCHI, CARLA VAPIO, VITTORIO RUBIU, NINNÌ PIRANDELLO, GIORGIO DE MARCHIS (FROM BEHIND) ON THE OCCASION OF THE *CEROLI* EXHIBITION
PH.: PLINIO DE MARTIIS

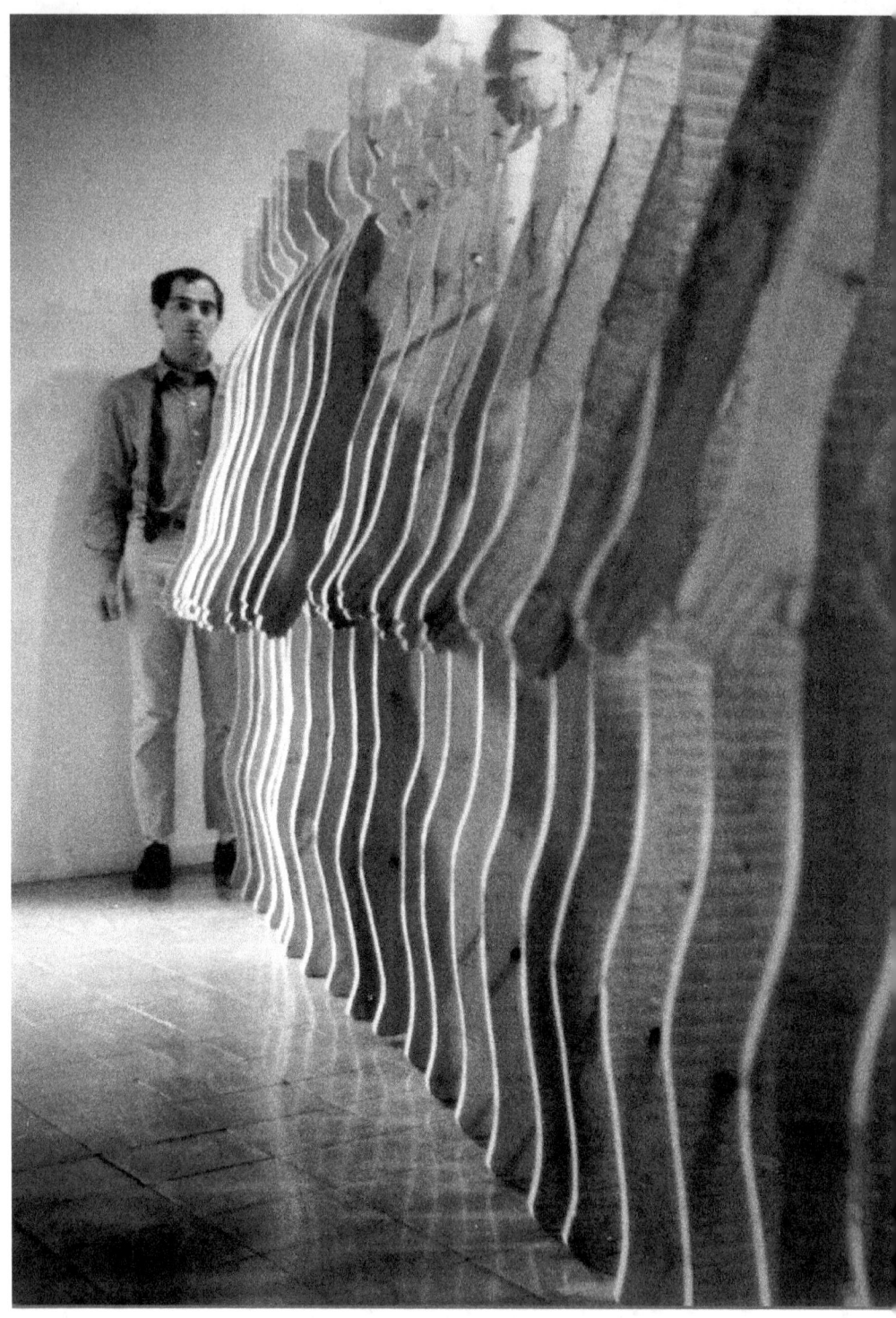

MARIO CEROLI WITH *LA CINA* (1966) EXHIBITED ON THE
OCCASION OF HIS SOLO SHOW, NOVEMBER 19, 1966
PH.: PLINIO DE MARTIIS

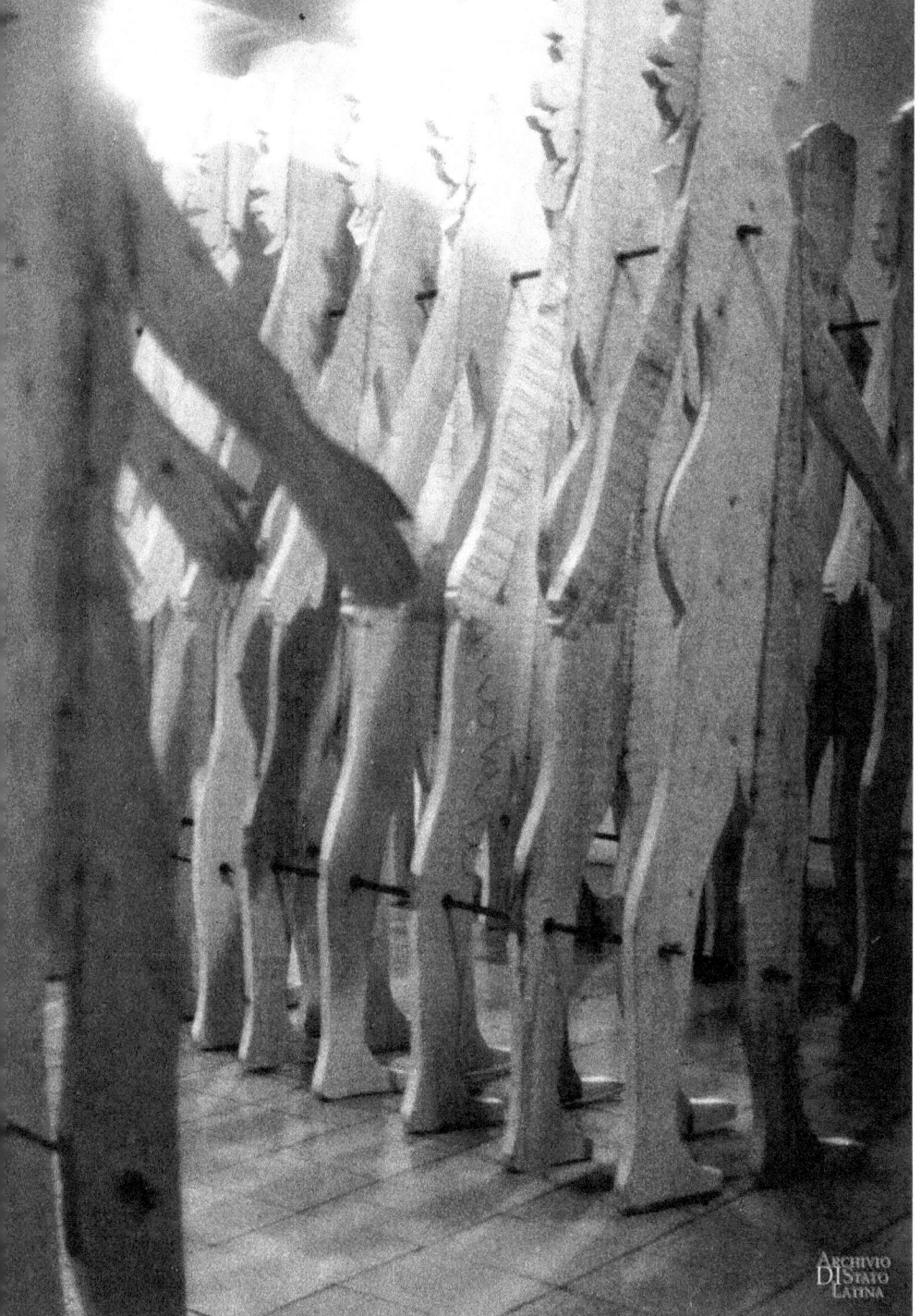

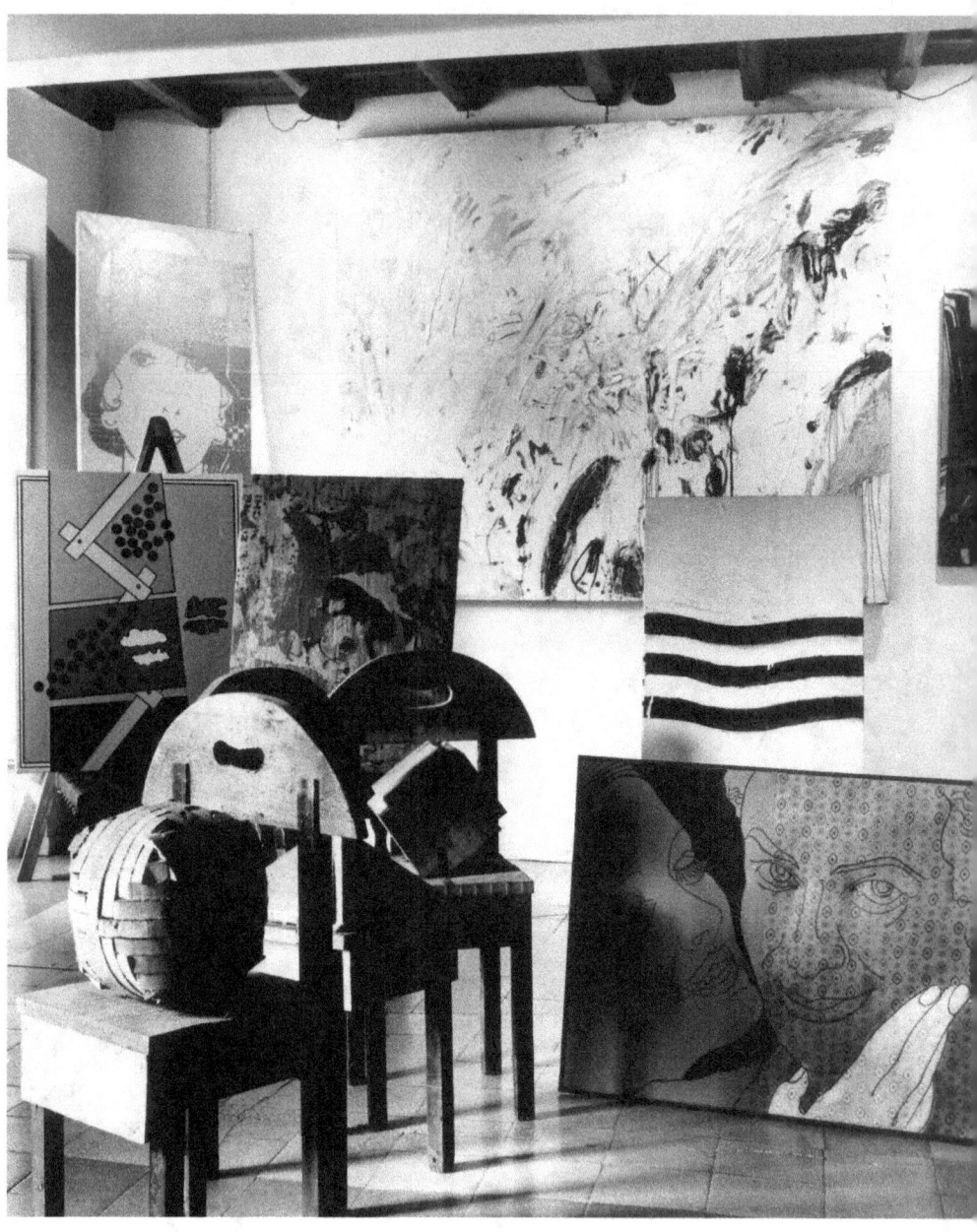

VIEW OF LA TARTARUGA WITH WORKS BY (FROM THE LEFT): MARIO CEROLI, TANO FESTA, FRANCO ANGELI, GIOSETTA FIORONI, CY TWOMBLY, JANNIS KOUNELLIS, CESARE TACCHI, AROUND 1966
PH.: PLINIO DE MARTIIS

RIGHT: SERGIO LOMBARDO IN THE STUDIO WITH SOME OF THE WORKS LATER EXHIBITED AT HIS FIRST SOLO SHOW AT LA TARTARUGA, FEBRUARY 5, 1966
PH.: PLINIO DE MARTIIS

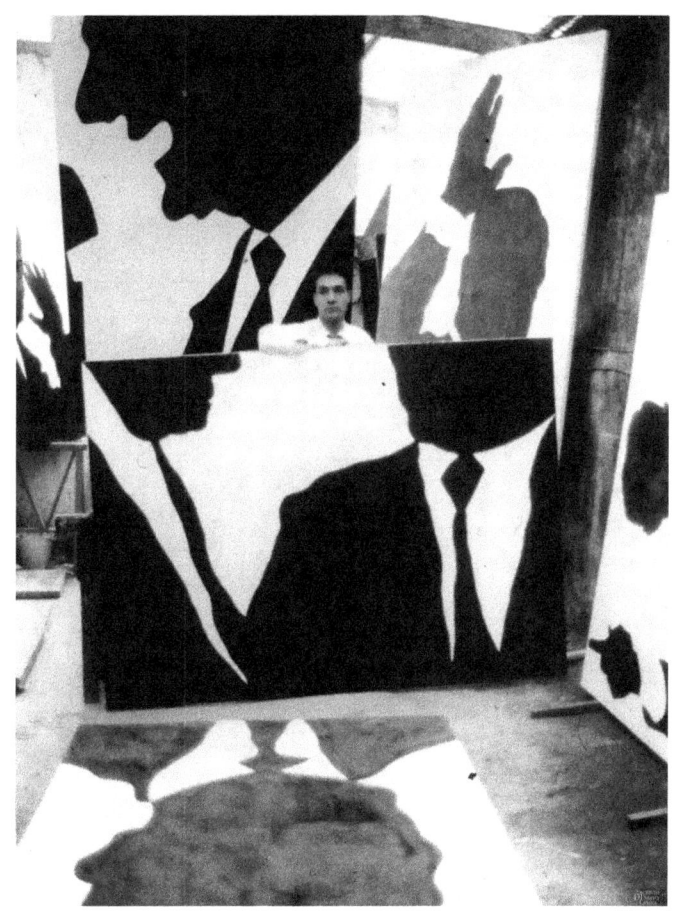

The reception of Mimmo Rotella's solo show (April 27) of the decollages he had produced between 1954 and 1966 was the complete opposite. That same year, De Martiis also included him in two group shows (in April and in September) dedicated to the members of the 'Scuola di Piazza del Popolo,' as if to underscore the wholly Italian ascendancy of their research. And for this very same reason several of Rotella's works were shown on November 3 along with those of the American Pop artists Jacquet, Lichtestein, Rauschenberg, Rosenquist, and Warhol. Rotella belonged to the previous generation of artists, and had been internationally acclaimed for some time. In 1951 he had shown his work at the Paris *Salon des Réalités Nouvelles*, and between 1951 and 1952, thanks to a scholarship he was awarded by the Fullbright Foundation, he had gone to the United States, where he had met Rauschenberg, Oldenburg, Twombly, Pollock, and Kline. After being visited by Restany in Rome in 1958, he had embraced Nouveau Réalisme, and in 1961 he had shown his work at the Paris show titled *À 40° au-dessus de Dada* curated by the same French critic. According to De Martiis, his decollages, which he began making in 1953, confirmed that Italian, not American, research was the first to understand that mass media images could be used in art. Ever since the 1950s Rotella had in fact chosen the advertising poster as an artistic expression: he had begun tearing posters off the city walls, gluing fragments of them on canvas, and then presenting

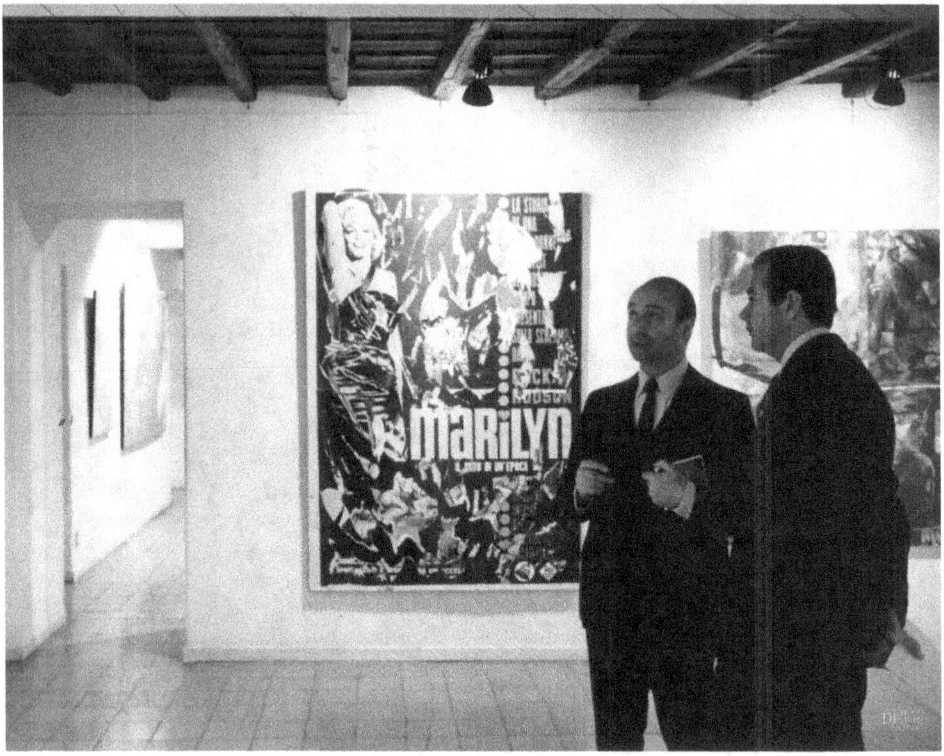

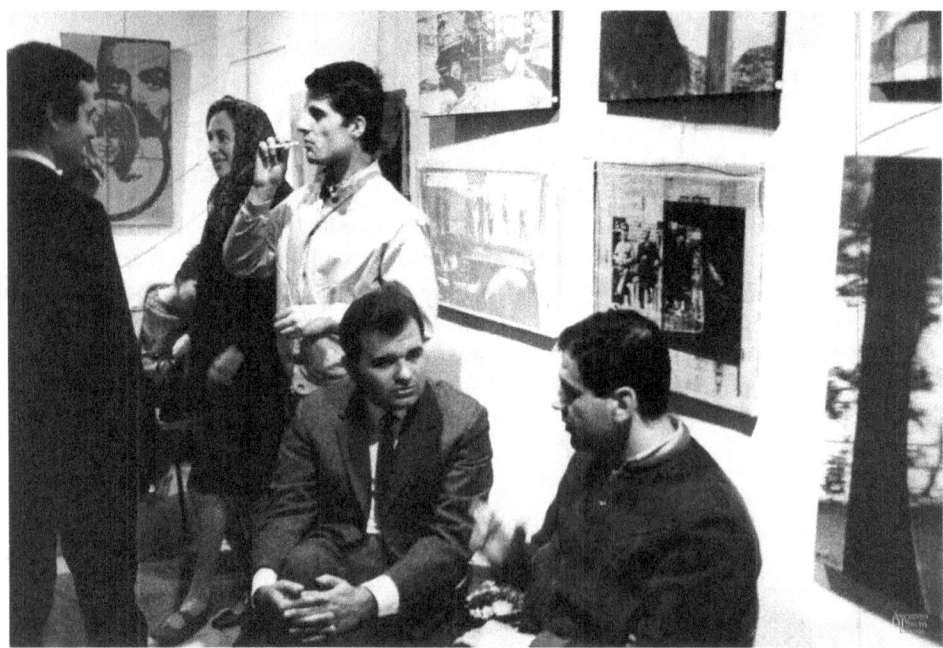

MIMMO ROTELLA ON THE OCCASION OF HIS SOLO SHOW *ROTELLA. DECOLLAGES - REPORTAGES 1954-1966*, APRIL 27, 1966

PINO PASCALI, GIOSETTA FIORONI, CESARE TACCHI, MAURIZIO FAGIOLO DELL'ARCO, TANO FESTA ON THE OCCASION OF THE *MIMMO ROTELLA* EXHIBITION PH.: PLINIO DE MARTIIS

either the whole advertisement detached from the billboard and later torn, or the relative back, in works that were almost monochrome. "We cannot group together certain names without thinking of others, for instance, the "back story of Mimmo Rotella," wrote Calvesi in 1967, convinced, like De Martiis, that the research conducted by La Tartaruga's young Roman artists "did not correspond to a translation [of American Pop, Editor's Note], but rather to a tradition, and above all to an authentically Italian condition."[22]

1967-1968: Spilling over into Action

The second half of the 1960s, both nationally and internationally, was characterized by the "dematerialization" and the "de-aestheticization" of the work of art,[23] by way of ephemeral operative modalities like the site-specific installation and performance. In Italy this experimentation was especially developed by the Arte Povera movement, thus defined in 1967 by Germano Celant, and presented by him for the first time ever in September of the same year at the group show *Arte Povera – Im-Spazio* hosted by the Galleria La Bertesca in Genoa. The works of Boetti, Fabro, Kounellis, Paolini, Pascali, and Prini were on display in the *Arte Povera* section, while those of the Roman artists Bignardi, Ceroli, Icaro, Mambor, Mattiacci, and Tacchi were instead showcased in the *Im-Spazio* section. During the later exhibitions dedicated to Arte Povera, mostly the Turinese members of the movement showed their work (above all Anselmo, Boetti, Fabro, Paolini, Penone, Pistoletto, and Zorio), hence, excluding the Romans, even though they resembled each other in the themes they dealt with and the methods they used. In those years, in fact, Turin and Rome were parallel engines of the same shift from the painting to the event, but they were also considerably different. As Carolyn Christov-Bakargiev explains, while the former city was an industrial center and the local artists reacted to serial manufacturing by using non-artistic materials, the latter was considered a city of entertainment; as the headquarters of RAI and Cinecittà, it was the favorite venue of actors, filmmakers, and international theater companies like Living Theatre and Jerzy Grotowski's Towards a Poor Theater.[24] What greatly influenced the Roman artists was the direct experience of the above-mentioned theatrical experiments that took the performance back to its origins and, conceiving it as a cathartic ritual and collective representation, abolished the traditional division between the scene and the audience. Equally important was the renewed interest in Antonin Artaud's Theatre of Cruelty and in the Futurist Theater, but above all in the theatrical experiments put forward by Carlo Quartucci, Luigi Squarzina, Mario Ricci, Giancarlo Nanni, Luca Ronconi, and Carmelo Bene. Hence, in Rome in the second half of the 1960s, the cinema and the theater constituted a collective visual identity, fueled by a constant comparison with the representatives of the various disciplines, the habitués of the same galleries and of the same places that were popular with society. And it was precisely from these relationships that the first movement of art toward the 'scenographic' installation and the 'theatrical' action was born. Suffice it to think, for instance, to the site-specific works presented on the occasion of events like *Lo spazio dell'immagine* (Foligno, 1967), but also to Ceroli's "scenoscultura,"[25] to the "theatricality[26] of Pascali's environments, and to Kounellis' "event."[27]

De Martiis was an attentive recipient of the most recent developments in artistic research, after the solo shows dedicated to Manzoni (January 9) and to Schifano (January 21) and before the Twombly solo show (April 3); and on March 6 he became the promoter of a performance to be carried out in the streets of Rome. It was Eliseo Mattiacci who

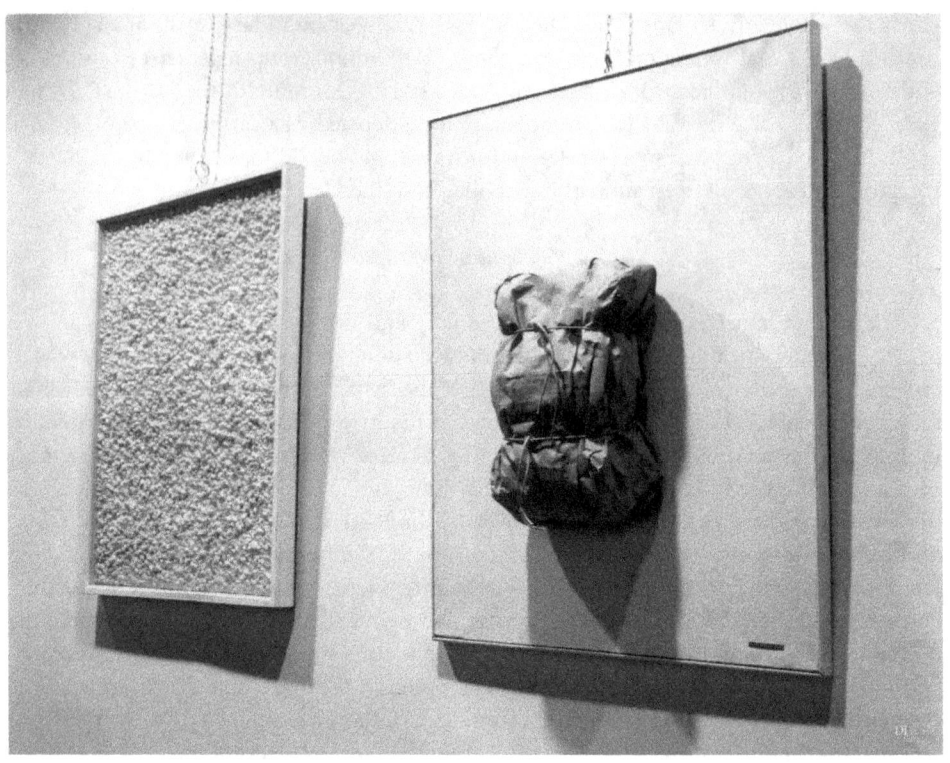

EXHIBITION VIEW OF *PIERO MANZONI*, JANUARY 9, 1967
PH.: PLINIO DE MARTIIS

conceived and organized a procession by the citizenry to carry a large, jointed, nickel-plated iron tube, 150 meters long and painted in "Agip" yellow, as far as La Tartaruga. After reaching the gallery, the artist wound the tube all around himself and occupied the whole room. Born in Cagli (Pesaro) in 1940, after moving to Rome in 1964, Mattiacci had produced some small assemblages of tubes inside transparent boxes that De Martiis had found to be interesting, although he had suggested to the artist that he make others, using a tube with the widest possible diameter available on the market.[28] This led to the action that was staged in 1967 in the streets of Rome and the resulting environment in the gallery itself.

This similar spilling over of the artwork into action, or into the potentially performative environment also characterized the two solo shows held soon afterwards at La Tartaruga by Ettore Innocente (May 2) and Paolo Icaro (June 13).

Born in Rome in 1934, Innocente was trained at the Fine Arts Academy in Rome under Toti Scialoja, and he debuted in 1965 at the Galleria La Salita. He then joined Plinio De Martiis' circle, participating in 1966 in the group show *Roma 1966 realtà dell'immagine*. The artist's solo show the following year was described by the press as "art that, having abandoned the easel painting and sculpture on a pedestal, builds objects with a great variety of materials and with a great variety of symbols, occupying space in a theatrical way, in a sort of performance where the visitor also participates."[29] On display were several variously

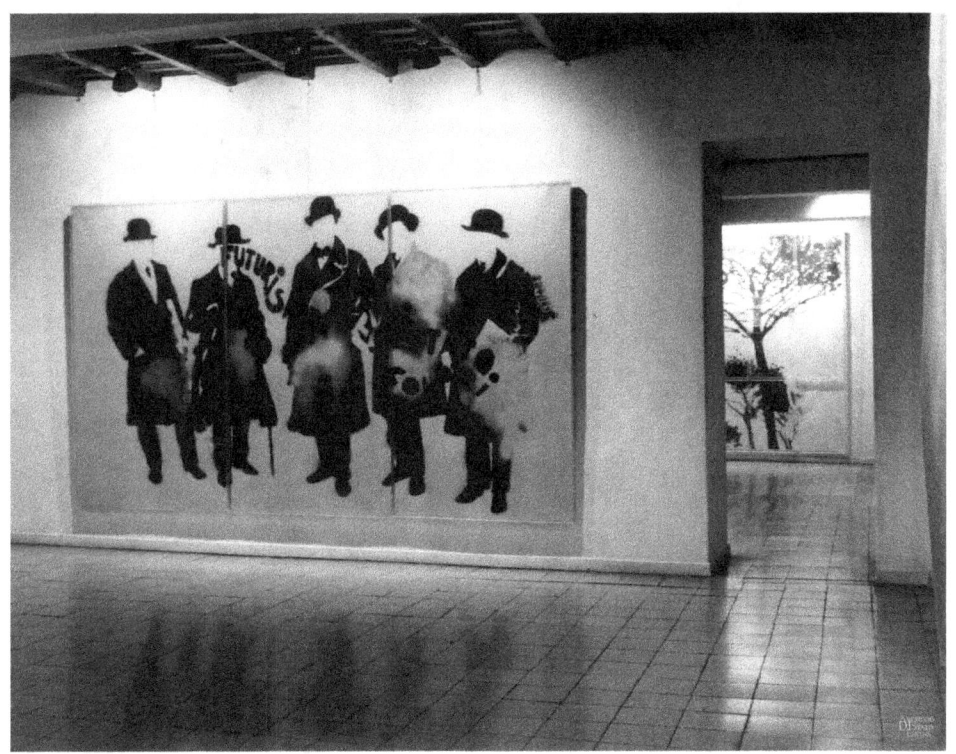

EXHIBITION VIEW OF *MARIO SCHIFANO*, JANUARY 21, 1967
PH.: PLINIO DE MARTIIS

sized plastic boxes that included the shaped forms of flowers, leaves, and everyday objects. The aim was to occupy the space of the gallery and trigger the involvement of the viewer not only from an optical point of view, but from a tactile one as well.

Involving the viewer even more was Icaro's *Gabbia Plinio-minio*. The structure took up the entire surface area of the display room, and could also be walked across inside. Born in Turin in 1936, after an apprenticeship in the studio of the sculptor Alberto Mastroianni, Icaro moved to Rome in 1960. In 1965 he went to New York where he met Ceroli on the occasion of the artist's solo show at the Galleria Bonino. The two of them started spending a great deal of time together, so much so that it was Ceroli himself who chose the word *Gabbie* to ironically define those forms of space that Icaro had built inspired by the "cast iron buildings" of New York, and to talk to De Martiis about his friend when he returned to Italy. Hence, the *Gabbia Plinio-minio*, whose title refers to the name of the gallerist and to the reddish lead-based antirust (minium) used to paint it. The distance between the bars corresponds to the size of the artist's pelvis, however the overall dimensions of the structure are what underlie its intrinsic performative dimension: occupying the entire room of the gallery, the *Gabbia* invites the visitor to enter it. At the opening Pascali showed how this was done by hanging from it ape-like.[30]

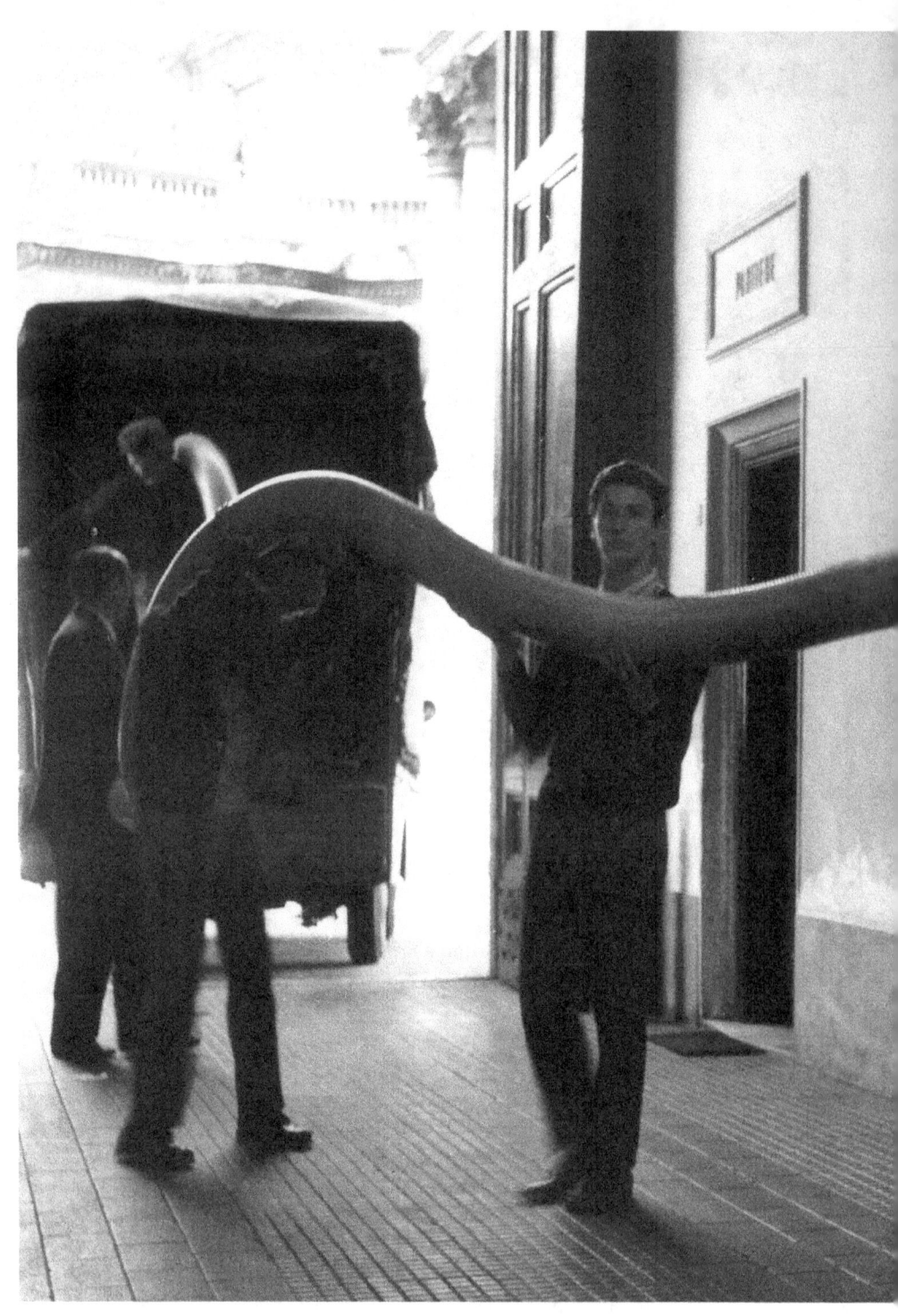

PROCESSION PRECEDING THE INSTALLATION OF *TUBO SNODABILE* BY ELISEO MATTIACCI
PH.: PLINIO DE MARTIIS

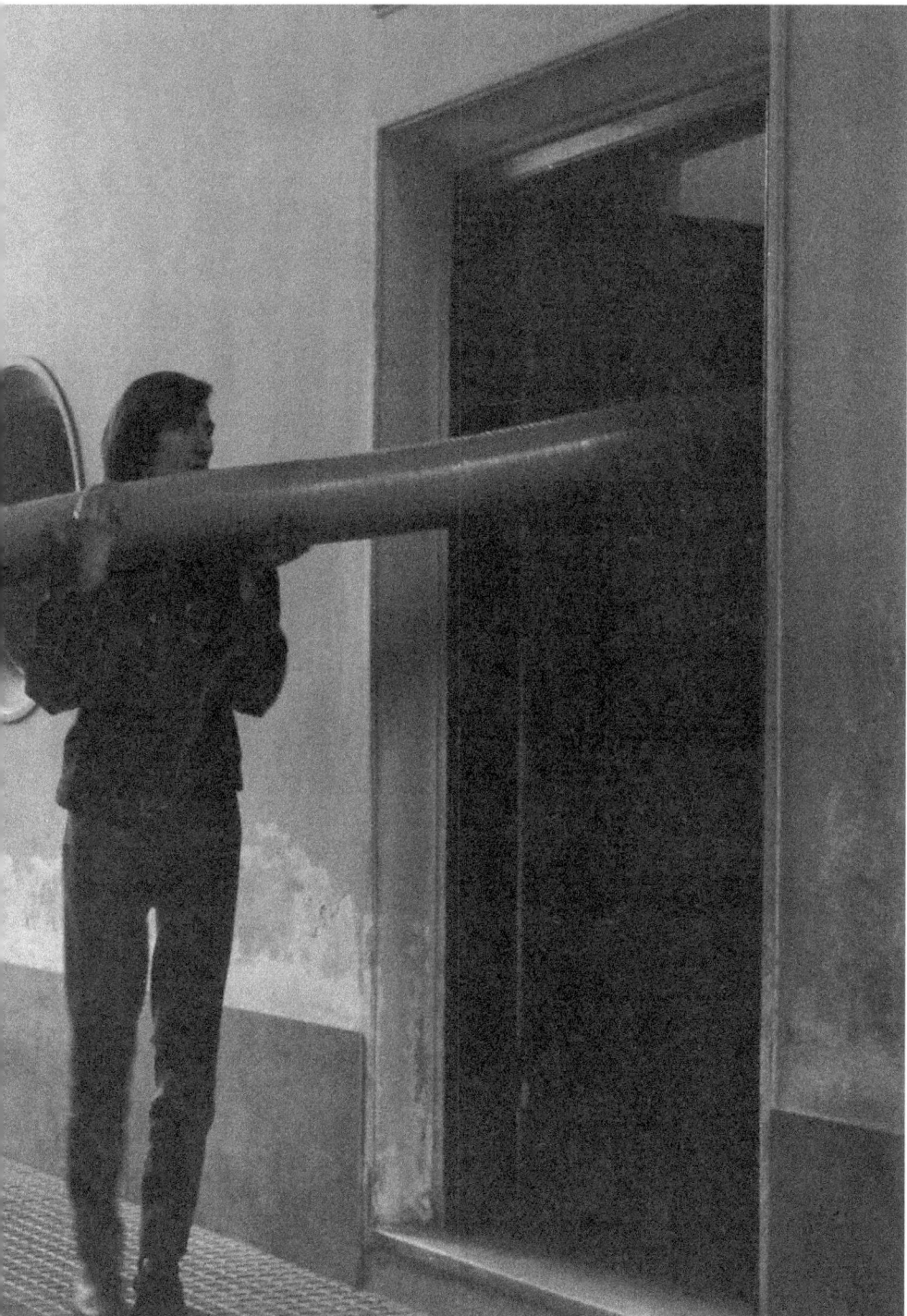

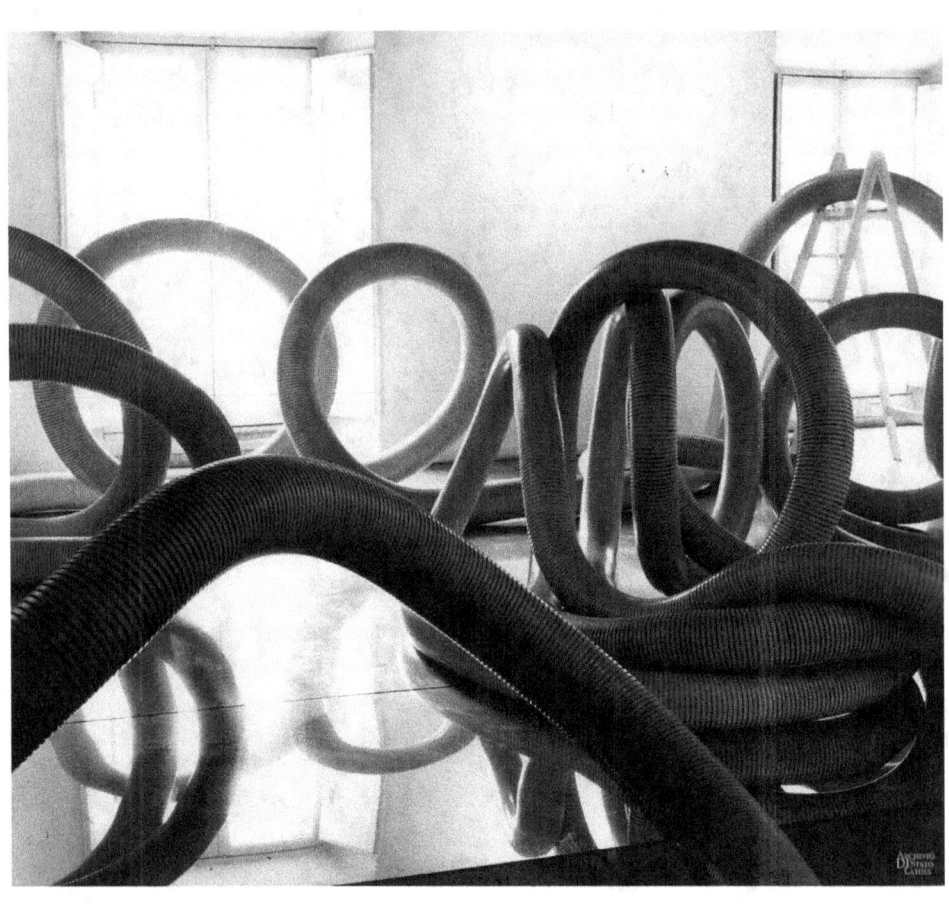

EXHIBITION VIEW OF *ELISEO MATTIACCI*,
MARCH 6, 1967
PH.: PLINIO DE MARTIIS

LEFT: OPENING OF THE FIRST PAOLO ICARO SOLO
AT LA TARTARUGA, JUNE 13, 1967
PH.: PLINIO DE MARTIIS

The theatricalization of art that occurred on the occasion of the aforementioned exhibitions, but also thanks to numerous events both in Italy and abroad,[31] marked Pop Art's definitive surpassing by process art. Consequently, the 'Scuola di Piazza del Popolo,' which had been constituted in the wake of 'popular' experimentation, ceased to exist. De Martiis was well aware of this, as he demonstrated by collaborating with the group exhibition *8 pittori romani* held at the Galleria de' Foscherari in Bologna from April 8 to 28, 1967. The aim of the event was to take stock of the 'Scuola di Piazza del Popolo' as it headed toward its end.[32] The Burri retrospective had the same goal: on December 4 it was La Tartaruga's last event in 1967, and it was conceived to mark the end of a 'school' through the work of one of its most important points of reference.

But the end is always followed by a new beginning, which for De Martiis corresponded to his support for and promotion of the theatrical dimension of art. It should come as no surprise that in 1968 the gallery's activity began with an action, performed on February 10, on the occasion of the exhibition of works allegedly by Andy Warhol, but actually 'forged' by his assistant Gerard Malanga for the purpose of investing the proceeds in funding for a film he had begun in Sicily. During the inauguration, Malanga organized a performance in which several people dressed up as cowboys and Indians were filmed dancing in front of the works on display. The twenty silk-screen prints and two paintings depicted, either in part or whole, the photograph that had been taken by an anonymous reporter of the lifeless body of Che Guevara, killed on October 9, 1967 in Bolivia: in the background an officer in uniform ascertains the death and recognizes the body, bringing a handkerchief to his nose because the body has already begun to decompose, while a man in a white coat, perhaps a doctor, points to the mortal wounds. No one, neither De Martiis, nor the critics, nor the artists, nor the reporters present realized that the works hadn't been made by Warhol, however, they still welcomed the show enthusiastically.[33]

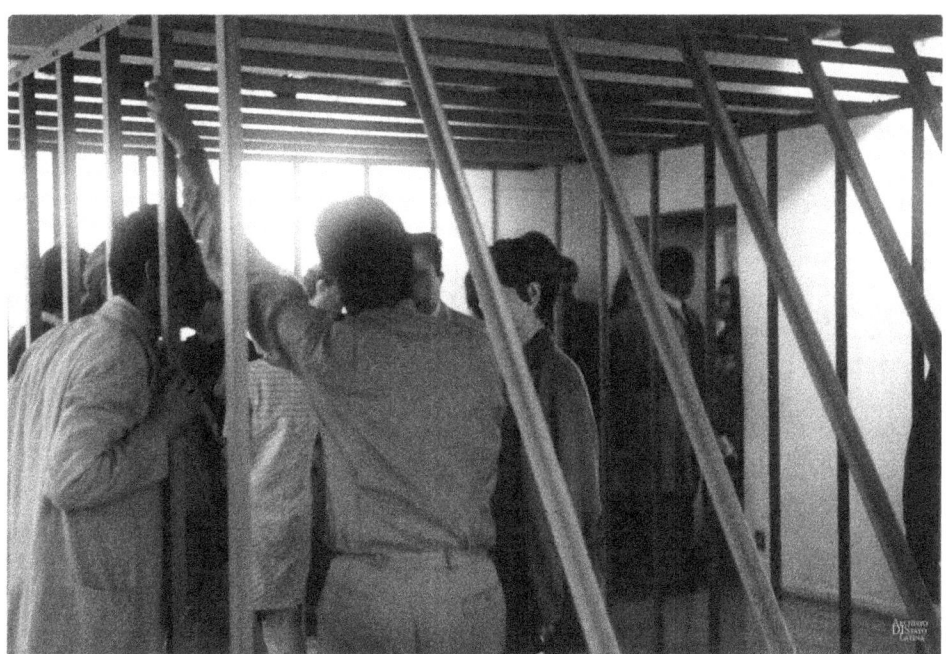

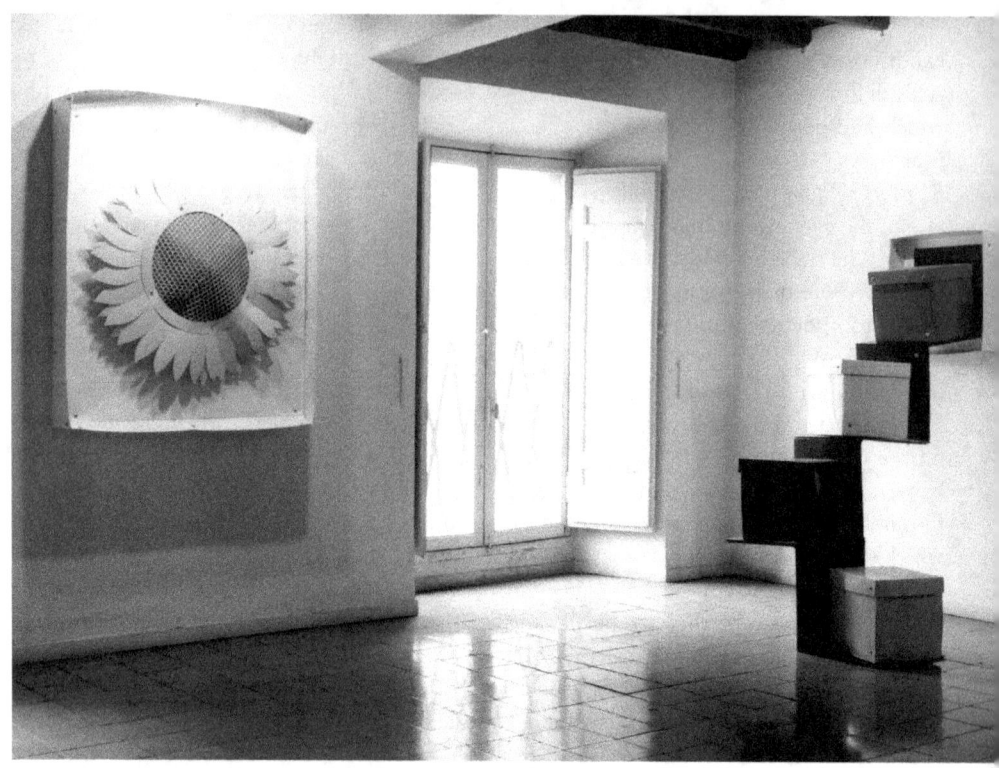

EXHIBITION VIEW OF THE FIRST ETTORE INNOCENTE SOLO SHOW AT LA TARTARUGA, MAY 2, 1967.
PH.: PLINIO DE MARTIIS

Less than two months had passed when La Tartaruga hosted another 'performative' exhibition. It was the solo show of the work of Tacchi, which opened on April 5, 1968 after the exhibition dedicated to Angeli (March 126) and the Twombly retrospective (March). Having surpassed the *Tappezzerie* in Pop style, Tacchi had now become interested in the relationship between reality, the artistic given, and the viewer, making objects that resembled furniture but were unable to be used: "The viewer will find themselves perceiving these object-paintings, sensitively so, and should feel, more than gaze, experience sensations, that is [...] The object does not abolish a space but rather replaces it and influences it intimately, relative to its potential for physical fruition."[34] It was probably the previously mentioned *Bedroom Ensemble* shown by Oldenburg in 1963 at the National Gallery of Canada that had served as a model: once again there was an unusable bedroom, where the furniture and the objects were made while keeping in mind their projection on the two-dimensional surface of the photograph (the right angles were acute and the bed was a sort of parallelogram). But while for the Oldenburg installation it was a chain that kept the viewer at a distance, for Tacchi's objects the titles themselves (*Sedia con l'acqua, Poltrona chiusa, 2 sedie bucate*) expressed the fact that they could not be used by the public. By so doing the Roman artist warned the viewer and asked that they give those objects a meaning/function that they then proved not to have. The truth is that the model closest to the one the artist seems to have looked to for their conception was not so much Oldenburg's installation as Balla's *Camera da letto* at La

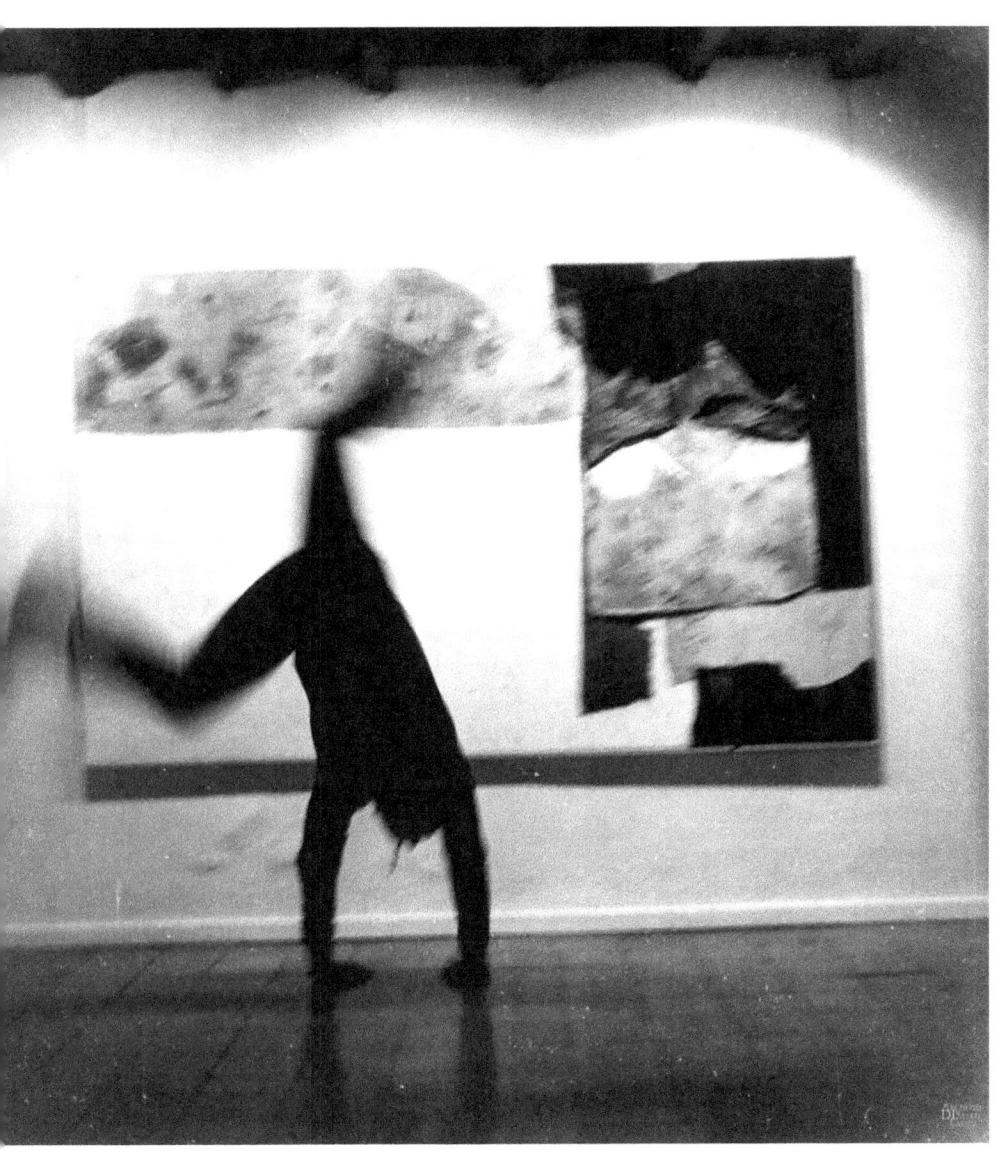

PINO PASCALI ON THE OCCASION OF THE
ALBERTO BURRI EXHIBITION, DECEMBER 4, 1967
PH.: PLINIO DE MARTIIS

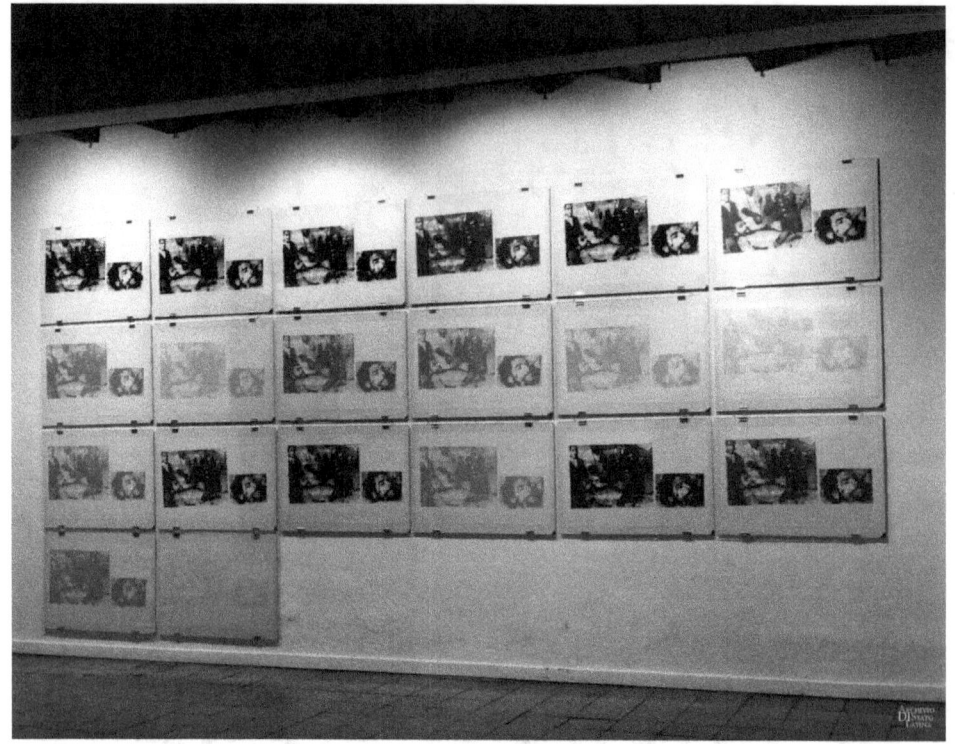

EXHIBITION VIEW OF *UN QUADRO E VENTI SERIGRAFIE DI ANDY WARHOL PER "CHE" GUEVARA*,
FEBRUARY 10, 1968
PH.: PLINIO DE MARTIIS

Tartaruga on February 18, 1965, which Oldenburg himself may have been inspired by.[35] As we are reminded by Calvesi, in 1912 Balla had made a bedroom featuring furniture with a wavy " and sightly trapezoidal surface [...]" that "tilted forwards" and therefore practically impossible to use.[36] Hence, fifty years after it was made, Oldenburg createsd a similar bedroom ensemble with furniture shapes that were skewed and therefore unable to be used; while Tacchi, on his part, made equally unusuable objects and at the same time bestowed relief on the chromatic element (for instance, in the *Poltrona rossa*) in the same way that Balla had painted his bedroom with the motif of the *Iridescent Compenetrations*.

Through the experimentations hitherto described La Tartaruga gradually went from being a place where works could be bought to one where ephemeral and therefore unsellable interventions could be staged, in line with the anti-capitalist protests that were underway at the same time. In Italy, starting from around 1965, after the period of the so-called 'economic miracle' that had witnessed considerable faith in social, political, and economic progress, a period of recession and deep dissent as concerned society began: society was seen as individualistic, anti-democratic, and interested solely in the pursuit of collective interests. The occupation of the School of Architecture at the University of Rome in February 1968 marked the turning point for the protests: debate and confrontation that had essentially been peaceful turned into revolutionary action. The protests were also influenced by a number of texts that were either published or rediscovered in that period. Whereas the

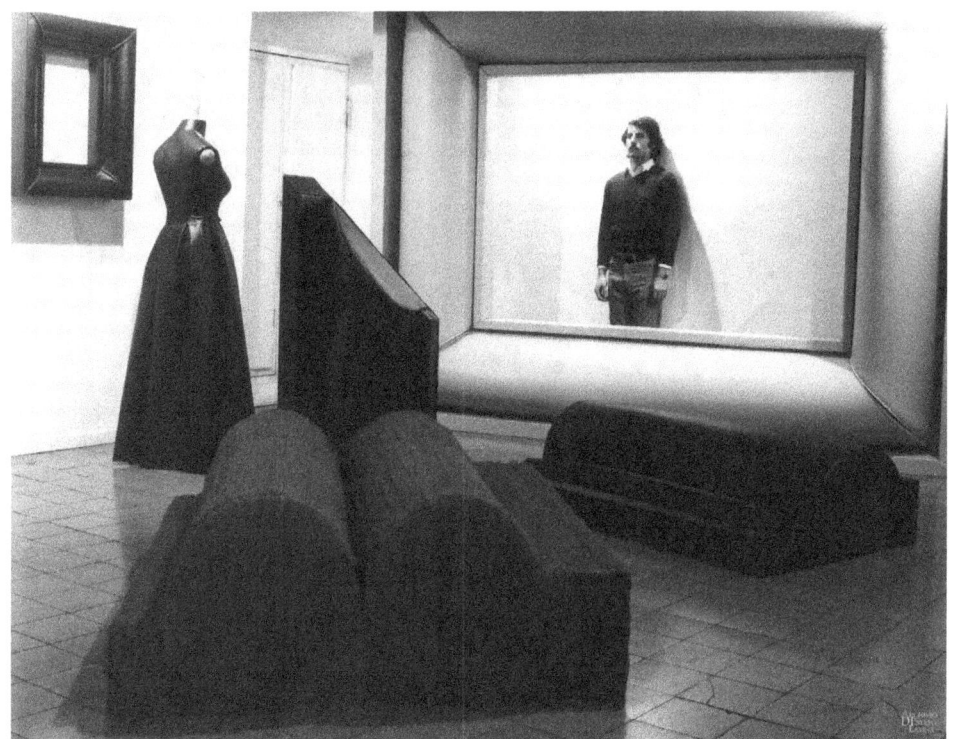

CESARE TACCHI ON THE OCCASION OF HIS SOLO SHOW,
APRIL 5, 1968
PH.: PLINIO DE MARTIIS

philosophies of Kant, Hegel, and Marx were criticized as being excessively deterministic, the critical theory developed from the 1930s by the 'Frankfurt School' (Theodor Adorno, Max Horkheimer, Herbert Marcuse, and Erich Fromm) lay the ideological foundations for the protests. In particular, Marcuse's writings became the main point of reference, exalting the power that was intrinsic to the imagination and to creativity.[37] This led to the development of artistic experimentation aimed at transcending Modernism and the vertical fruition of painting and sculpture, in favor of a disseminated aesthetic, one that was capable of giving back to humans the creative potential that had been atrophied by the alienating industrial society and of impressing change in our experience. In line with what was postulated by the American pragmatist John Dewey in *Experience and Nature* and in *Art as Experience*,[38] the sole successful experience is that of aesthetics, which does not just take place before a work of art in the traditional sense, but by living an everyday experience induced by whichever object is capable of arousing appreciation, perception, and pleasure. Therefore, each individual is a potential artist, as Duchamp himself had postulated as well.

De Martiis, who agreed with these theories, tried to immediately put them into practice, conceiving in the 'hottest' month of the protesting (May 1968) an event that was capable of "bringing art to the level of an experience that can potentially be participated in by everyone, and that encourages a sort of meta-individual solidarity in the experience itself."[39] This was the daily event titled *Teatro delle Mostre*.

una mostra ogni giorno

1	MERCOLEDI		
2	GIOVEDI		
3	VENERDI		
4	SABATO		
5	DOMENICA		
6	LUNEDI	GIOSETTA FIORONI	(LA SPIA OTTICA)
7	MARTEDI	CIRO CIRIACONO	(MEDIUM)
8	MERCOLEDI	REPLICA	
9	GIOVEDI	GIULIO PAOLINI	(AUTORITRATTO)
10	VENERDI	ETTORE INNOCENTE	(CAMERA FIORITA)
11	SABATO	EMILIO PRINI	(2 OGGETTI DI RIMBALZO)
12	DOMENICA	PAOLO ICARO	(2 POMERIGGI IN 3 O 4)
13	LUNEDI	PIER PAOLO CALZOLARI	(UN VOLUME DA RIEMPIRE PER MEZZ'ORA)
14	MARTEDI	FRANCO ANGELI	(QUATTORDICI MAGGIO)
15	MERCOLEDI	ENRICO CASTELLANI	(IL MURO DEL TEMPO)
16	GIOVEDI	PAOLO SCHEGGI	(INTERFIORE)
17	VENERDI	MARIO CEROLI	(DAL CALDO AL FREDDO)
18	SABATO	CESARE TACCHI	(CANCELLAZIONE D'ARTISTA)
19	DOMENICA		
20	LUNEDI	PAUSA	
21	MARTEDI	ALIGHIERO BOETTI	
22	MERCOLEDI	GINO MAROTTA	(UNA FORESTA DI MENTA)
23	GIOVEDI		
24	VENERDI	RENATO MAMBOR	(SPEDIZIONE DI CLAUDIO PREVITERA)
25	SABATO	FABIO MAURI	(LUNA)
26	DOMENICA		
27	LUNEDI	LAURA GRISI	(VENTO DI SUD EST)
28	MARTEDI	SYLVANO BUSSOTTI	(LA PIÚ RARA RARA)
29	MERCOLEDI	LORETO SORO	(FILARMONICI)
30	GIOVEDI	NANNI BALESTRINI	(I MURI DELLA SORBONA)
31	VENERDI	GOFFREDO PARISE	

CALENDAR COMPILED DURING THE *TEATRO DELLE MOSTRE*,
MAY 6–31, 1968

May 6-31, 1968: The Teatro delle Mostre

"The term art gallery and its role deserve to be discussed further. So that we can understand whether it is still necessary as a go-between, or is actually a hindrance."[40] In 1966 this was how De Martiis reflected on the situation of the Italian private exhibition system at the time in relation to the recent process art and site-specific art, to then state, the following year, that "private galleries are no longer of any use. To whom are you going to send these things that [...] turn the exhibition into something poised between a cultural event and a performance at theater? We should abolish private galleries and create city (communal) museums."[41] This led to the idea of organizing, at the height of the student protests in May 1968, an event that could subvert the common conception of the artwork as an object that can be sold, redefine the function of the art gallery by transforming it from a site for exhibition and sale to a place of experience that would allow the artist and the visitor to come to terms with each other on equal footing in the unfolding of the event; lastly, this could be something that would free the gallerist from the role of art dealer and instead transform him or her into an activator of a system of 'theatrical' communication/information."

Between March and April 1968, published for the first time ever was the news of the opening of the *Tartaruga show*,[42] soon to acquire the official title of *Teatro delle Mostre*. What made the event that was held from May 6 to 31 unique was the exhibition format: rather than setting up an exhibition lasting the usual month, the gallerist chose to change the exhibitions on a daily basis; twenty exhibitions, "one exhibition every day from 4 to 8 pm" – as the subtitle of the poster informed its readers,[43] – conceived each time by a different artist connected to another artist, much like a series of links in the same chain. De Martiis established neither the order among the artists nor which works they presented. All he did was suggest that they conceive actions or site-specific installations that could be arranged in the morning, when the gallery was closed, and presented in the afternoon. When one of the artists invited found the right idea, the gallery would be made available to then for an entire day.

The improvisation was actually improvisation that was controlled by the gallerist himself, who wanted the event to be a single and total work of art. To do so, De Martiis decided to restore the tradition of the so-called 'sign-posters,' asking each of the artists to make one and to hang it on the wall along with those of the other invited artists. He also set up a daily schedule that encouraged their mutual collaboration when taking one exhibition down and installing the following one. Each intervention had to be the result of a group effort, directed *ex alto* by De Martiis himself: *Teatro delle mostre*, Calvesi explained, "does not so much mean theatrical exhibitions, to my mind, as exhibitions that alternate, that succeed one another according to a script, or direction."[44] This direction was also manifested in the creation of the catalogue, which was drafted *after* the event had ended. Not only did the gallerist use his camera to take all the pictures that were published therein based on the layout designed by Magdalo Mussio, who was the editor of the magazine *Marcatrè*, but he also personally translated the event from an aesthetic standpoint by manipulating the images with cuts, color tones, blurring, particular angles, images up against the light, and the frequent use of the motion effect.[45] And in view of the publication of the catalogue De Martiis asked Calvesi to come down from his traditional *cathedra* as a critic to instead participate in the events along with the other viewers,

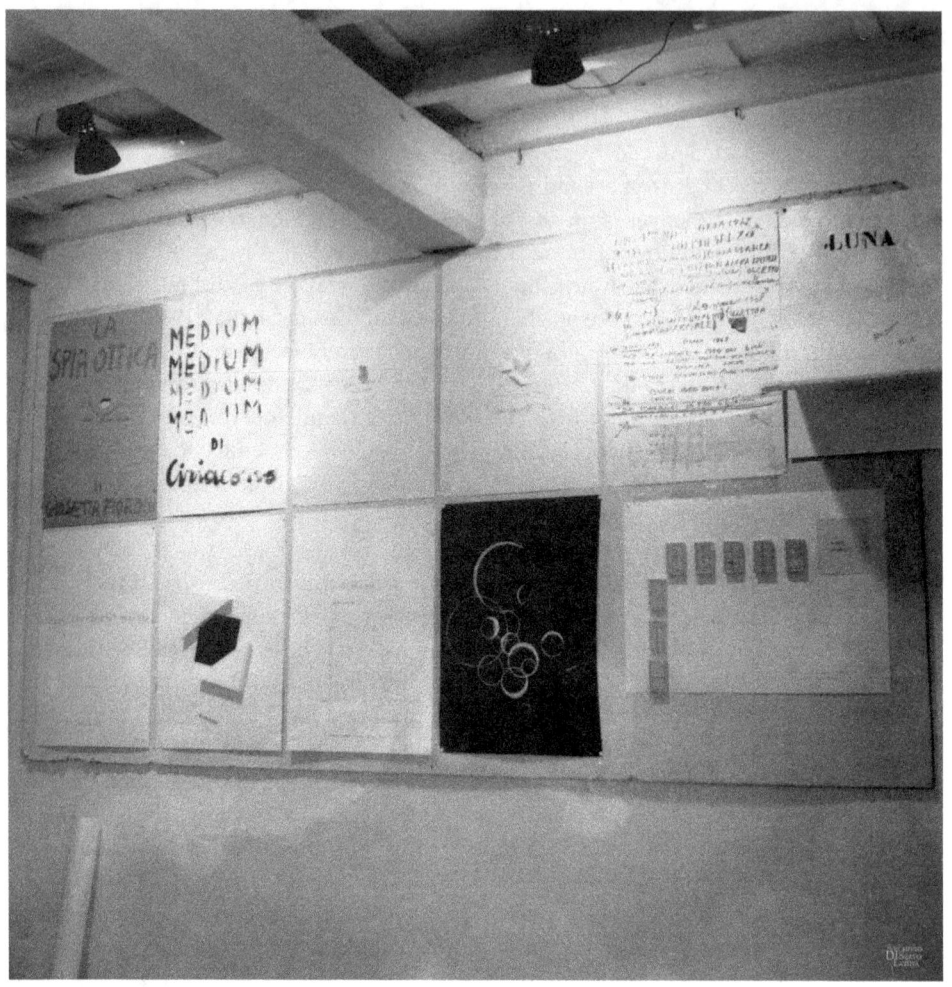

PAOLO SCHEGGI, *INTERFIORE*, THE INSTALLATION PRESENTED ON MAY 16, 1968 ON THE OCCASION OF
THE *TEATRO DELLE MOSTRE*, MAY 6-31, 1968
PH.: PLINIO DE MARTIIS

and to write a text that could provide, thanks also to Achille Bonito Oliva's captions, not an interpretation but rather the direct experience of the event. The *Teatro delle Mostre* was thus part of the discussion at the time of criticism's interpretative role before the new operative modalities aimed at the dematerialization of the artwork.

However, this particular event was especially in line with the avant-garde theater of the Living Theatre, of Quartucci, Nanni, and Carmelo Bene, as well as of specific art events that had recently been held both in Italy and abroad,[46] and especially in Rome. These included: *No Stop Teatro 12 ore*, that is, one action after another for 12 hours by artists, intellectuals, and musicians in March 1967 at Feltrinelli on Via del Babuino; Pistoletto's solo show at the Galleria L'Attico where, for the opening on February 12, 1968, the public was invited to wear stage costumes just like the artist himself; Pascali's solo show *Bachi da setola* held at L'Attico on March 25, 1968, consisting of brushes laid out in a row on the ground so that they

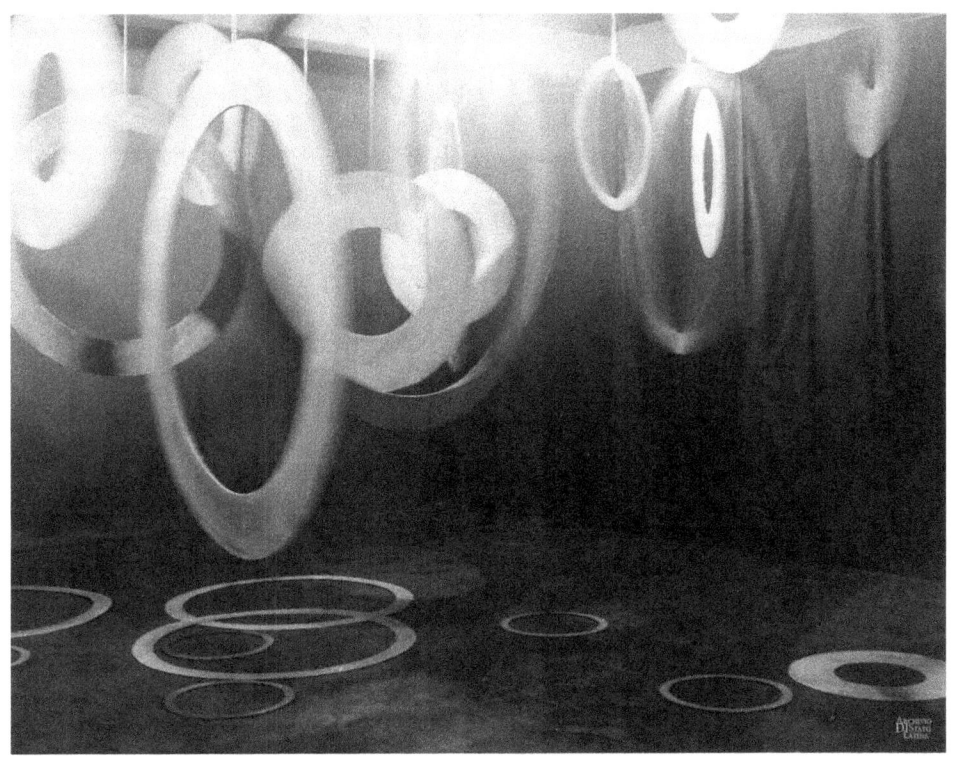

EXHIBITION VIEW OF THE SIGNS-POSTERS MADE BY EACH OF THE ARTISTS INVITED TO THE *TEATRO DELLE MOSTRE*, MAY 6-31, 1968
PH.: PLINIO DE MARTIIS

resembled long worms; lastly, the opening of *Il Percorso*, a solo show held in March at the Studio Arco d'Alibert, where the artists were invited to present not finished works, but, rather, their installation in progress.

As instead concerns the protagonists of the *Teatro delle Mostre*, on the one hand, these were the principal members of the 'Scuola di Piazza del Popolo' (Fioroni, Angeli, Ceroli, Tacchi, Mambor, Mauri) as well as the protagonists of the Roman cultural milieu who had already collaborated or who were habitués of La Tartaruga (Innocente, Icaro, Marotta, Castellani, Soro, Ciriacono, Balestrini, Parise, Grisi, and Bussotti); on the other, they were artists who lived in Northern Italy, who had never shown their work at De Martiis' gallery, but who were still rather well known in Rome (Paolini, Scheggi, Prini, Calzolari, and Boetti).[47] The presence of the poet and intellectual Balestrini, of the writer Parise, and of the musician Bussotti was instead based on the need to foster an operative osmosis between different disciplines.

COVER OF THE CATALOG
TEATRO DELLE MOSTRE,
MARCALIBRI/LERICI PUBLISHER,
JUNE 1968

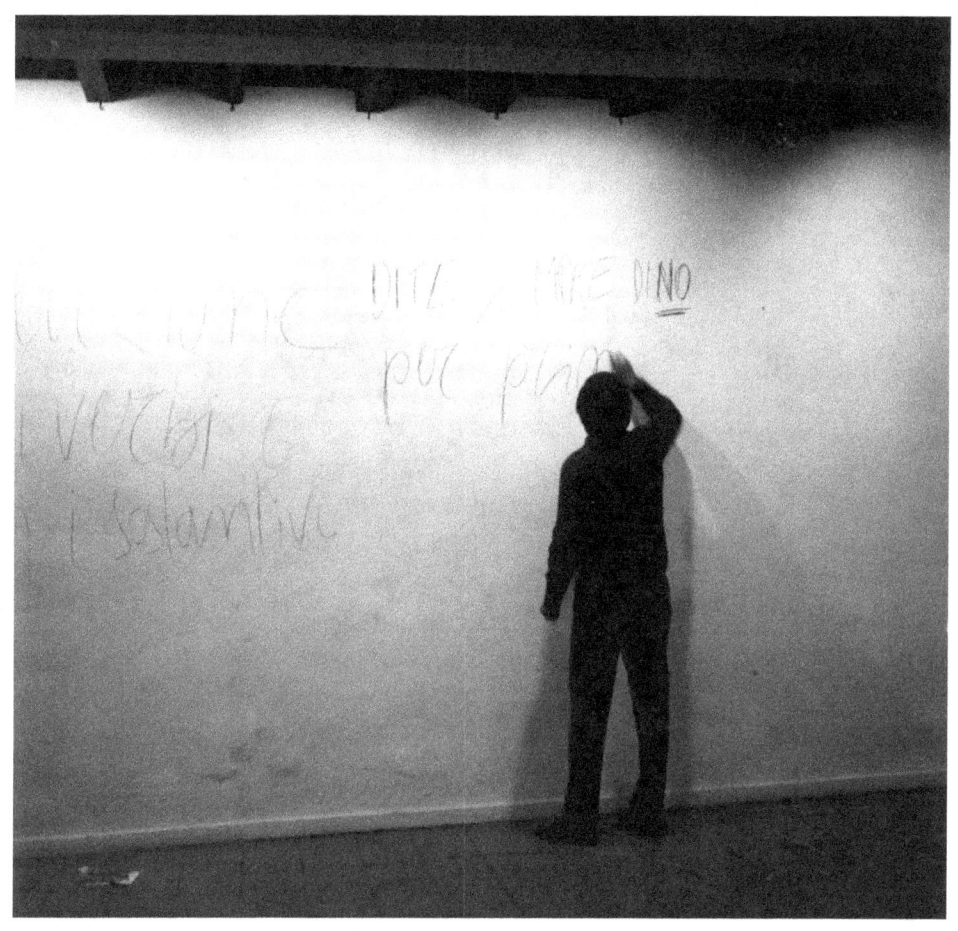

NANNI BALESTRINI, *I MURI DELLA SORBONA*, THE ACTION PRESENTED ON MAY 30, 1968, ON THE OCCASION OF *TEATRO DELLE MOSTRE*, MAY 6-31, 1968
PH.: PLINIO DE MARTIIS

What especially stood out in the actions and installations conceived by the twenty-one artists who had been invited was how in line they were with the international art scene. Fioroni, for instance, by inviting viewers to look, through a *Spia ottica* placed on the door of the display room, at the actress Giuliana Calandra carrying out everyday actions in a bedroom, evoked Duchamp's *Étant donnés*, a work that had been shown for the first time at the Philadelphia Museum of Art in 1966. A second common denominator of the actions and installations presented at the *Teatro delle Mostre* was the playful/child-like component: Marotta's *Foresta di menta*, created with green plastic strips hanging from the ceiling so that the public could make room for itself, harkened back to the "wood of *Snow White and the Seven Dwarfs*."[48] Lastly, the reference to the sociopolitical context at the time was also alluded to, especially by Balestrini's action: while telephoning from Paris he dictated the words he read on the walls of an occupied Sorbonne, so they could be transcribed on the walls of La Tartaruga by the artist friends and intellectuals present there, and so that he himself could write them down once he returned to Rome.

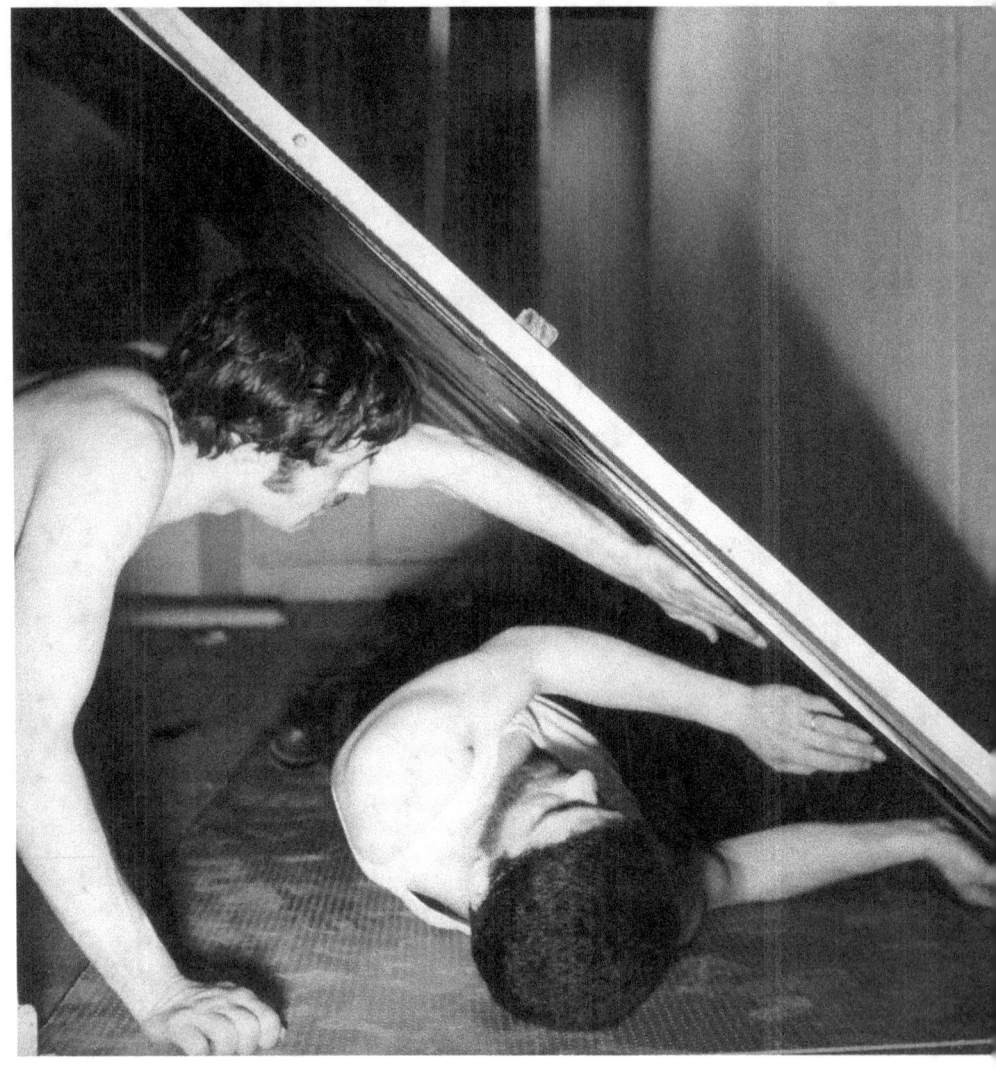

ALIGHIERO BOETTI AND LORETO SORO WHILE SETTING UP OF
THE INSTALLATION *UN CIELO* PRESENTED BY BOETTI ON MAY 21,
1968, AS PART OF *TEATRO DELLE MOSTRE*, MAY 6-31, 1968
PH.: PLINIO DE MARTIIS

The *Teatro delle Mostre* thus had the merit of capturing the current needs of Italian and international avant-garde research, and of having evoked on a daily basis the exciting climate of the protests under way. But not just that. The event's greatest merit was having codified a curatorial style, the one enacted by De Martiis, and that would be reproposed for many exhibitions over the course of the following years, eventually becoming a successful 'format' for today as well.[49]

June-October 1968: Toward the Closing of the Gallery

In an interview by Oreste Del Buono in May 1968, De Martiis revealed that the *Teatro delle Mostre* was a sort of experiment aimed at verifying whether or not there were the premises to bring to completion his plan to "transform the gallery into a fully-fledged theater with people having to pay a ticket to get in."[50] That idea as well as the intention of bringing the Festival to Milan, Turin, and Genoa[51] remained on paper, but once it had ended the question arose as to whether it was still possible to conduct the usual exhibition activity in the gallery, or which even more innovative events deserved to be put forward.

As he waited to discover new paths to take, De Martiis decided to ideally extend the Festival, presenting three exhibitions in the months of June, each of them again lasting a day. The Roman artist and architect Gianfranco Fini set up *Il grande schermo* the evening before Robert Kennedy was assassinated (this occurred right after midnight on June 5, 1968). The installation consisted of twenty-four television sets that broadcast, with the audio off and in a loop, just three images: the route Kennedy took from the hotel lobby to the site where he was killed, the shooting, and the lifeless body of the presidential candidate lying on the floor his face covered in blood.[52] A few days later, on June 11, at the center of the exhibition room, arranged on a table was a cash register on which a chart announced the title of the situation activated by Gianfranco Baruchello: *Finanziaria Artiflex*. Behind the table, sitting on a chair, was Pascali's partner, Michèle, who was selling to visitors boxes inside plastic containers arranged to the sides of the register, each of which contained either a 5 lire coin on sale for 10, or a 10 lire coin on sale for 5. The aim was to verify the ability of the potential customers to give up making a profit and instead abandon themselves to the poetic game of a loss of value. When the action came to an end, the only boxes that remained were the ones containing a 5 lire coin sold for 10. The following day Baruchello enacted another intervention: a sign hanging from the ceiling and bearing the title of the action (*Sala d'attesa Artiflex*) made available to visitors several benches so they could sit down and converse, as if they were in a company waiting room. The artist, thanks to the fake company title "Artiflex" conceived in late 1967, chose to simulate industry to analyze the subtle merchanding processes it implemented.[53] Although Lorenza Trucchi named both Fini and Baruchello as being among the protagonists of the Festival,[54] *Il grande schermo*, *Finanziaria* e *Sala d'attesa Artiflex* can be considered further but separate examples of the avant-garde research of which De Martiis the previous May had wanted to be the mentor.

"Galleries have finally exhausted their function," he declared in December 1968. "Nowadays, only someone who believes in a stable, peaceful society can hang a painting in their home […]. So why should there be exhibitions? They're just the umpteenth ceremony for very few people."[55] On the basis of this belief the curtain was lowered on the gallery stage, and in October 1968 La Tartaruga's historical headquarters in Piazza del Popolo closed. It was also a sign that an era had come to an end. An era that, according to the critic Giorgio De Marchi, symbolically ended on September 11, 1968, with the sudden death of Pino Pascali, that is, of one of the principal members of the 'Scuola di Piazza del Popolo,' from that moment on destined to be disperesed.[56]

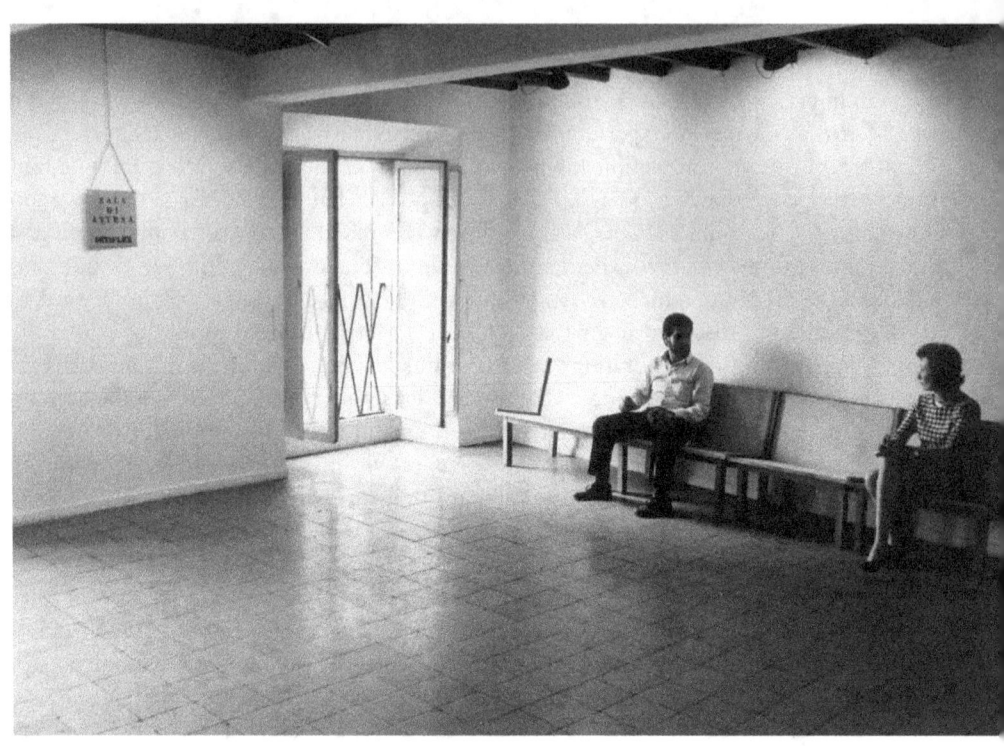

LORETO SORO AND NINNÌ PIRANDELLO ON THE OCCASION OF THE EXHIBITION
GIANFRANCO BARUCHELLO: SALA D'ATTESA ARTIFLEX, JUNE 12, 1968
PH.: PLINIO DE MARTIIS

1. Pirani Federica, "Intervista a Plinio De Martiis," in Calvesi M. – Siligato R. (eds.), *Roma anni '60. Al di là della pittura*, exhibition catalogue (Rome, Palazzo delle Esposizioni, December 20, 1990 – February 15, 1991), Edizioni Carte Segrete, Rome 1990, p. 341.

2. *Oltre l'Informale* was the title of the *IV Biennale Internazionale d'Arte* held from July 7 to October 7, 1963, in San Marino marking the transcending of Informal art by the Italian artistic research at the time.

3. Festa Tano, letter written to Plinio De Martiis, London, December 7, 1963 (Archivio di Stato di Latina, Fondo La Tartaruga, busta 24).

4. Festa Tano, letter written to Plinio De Martiis, London, January 24, 1963 (Archivio di Stato di Latina, Fondo La Tartaruga, busta 24).

5. Mario Ceroli in conversation with Ilaria Bernardi, Rome, December 1, 2009, in Bernardi Ilaria, *Teatro delle Mostre, Roma, maggio 1968*, Scalpendi editore, Milan 2014, p. 187.

6. This would be followed by *Catalogo 2* and *Catalogo 3* published on February 27, 1965 and June 10, 1966, respectively, *Catalogo 4* was drafted in 1969, but it never went to print.

7. For further information on that edition of the Biennale, see: Solomon Alan R. (ed.), *USA. XXXII Esposizione Biennale Internazionale d'Arte Venezia 1964 / International Biennal Exhibition of Art Venice 1964*, The Jewish Museum New York, New York 1964.

8. Cf. unpublished statement made by Maddalena Disch (Director of the Fondazione Giulio e Anna Paolini, Turin) in conversation with Ilaria Bernardi, February 19, 2010.

9. Referenced are the exhibitions and publications released in those years mentioned in Crescentini C. – D'Orazio C. – Pirani F., *Roma pop city 60-67*, exhibition catalogue (Rome, MACRO - Museo d'Arte Contemporanea Roma, July 13 – November 22, 2016), Manfredi Edizioni, Rome 2016. Furthermore, as early as 1962, Calvesi wrote to De Martiis that he was a staunch supporter of the existence of "an avant-garde Roman 'tradition,' of an abstract sense with Dadaist-like points, that started with Balla, passed through Prampolini, and fertilized during this postwar period; […] of the importance of Burri's 'Origine' group, as an environment; […] of the relationship between the Divisionism of Balla and Dorazio" (Archivio di Stato di Latina, Fondo La Tartaruga, busta 31).

10. Baruchello Gianfranco, letter written to Plinio De Martiis, New York, April 16, 1964 (Archivio di Stato di Latina, Fondo La Tartaruga, busta 21).

11. Festa Tano, letter written to Plinio De Martiis, New York, May 8, 1965 (Archivio di Stato di Latina, Fondo La Tartaruga, busta 24).

12. Ceroli Mario, letter written to Plinio De Martiis, New York, 1967 (Archivio di Stato di Latina, Fondo La Tartaruga, busta 23).

13. Tacchi Cesare, letter written to Plinio De Martiis, New York, October 25, 1966 (Archivio di Stato di Latina, Fondo La Tartaruga, busta 29).

14. Angeli Franco, letter written to Plinio De Martiis, New York, January 1967 (Archivio di Stato di Latina, Fondo La Tartaruga, busta 21).

15. On the relationship between Pascali and De Martiis, see: Pirani Federica, "Intervista a Plinio De Martiis," *op. cit.*, p. 340.

16. Berenice, "Camera da letto in competizione pop," in *Paese Sera*, Rome, March 11, 1965.

17. Schifano Mario, letter written to Plinio De Martiis, New York, 1965 (Archivio di Stato di Latina, Fondo La Tartaruga, busta 28).

18. Cf. Renato Mambor in conversation with Ilaria Bernardi, Rome, December 3, 2009, in Bernardi Ilaria, *Teatro delle Mostre, op. cit.*, p. 191.

19. Cf. Locatelli Luigi, "I cinematografari 'pop' hanno ripreso fiato," in *Il Giorno*, January 28, 1965.

20. Cf. Richter Gerhard, letter written to Plinio De Martiis, October 10 and December 21, 1965 (Archivio di Stato di Latina, Fondo La Tartaruga, busta 26).

21. Richter Gerhard, letter written to Plinio De Martiis, February 21, 1966 (Archivio di Stato di Latina, Fondo La Tartaruga, busta 26).

22. Calvesi Maurizio, "8 pittori romani," in *Angeli - Ceroli - Festa - Fioroni - Kounellis - Pascali - Schifano*

- *Tacchi*, exhibition catalogue (Bologna, Galleria de' Foscherari, April 8-28, 1967), Bologna 1967, n. pag.

23. Referenced are the texts: Lippard Lucy, *Six Years: The Dematerialization of the Art Object from 1966 to 1972*, University of California Press, Berkeley 1972, and Rosenberg Harold, "De-aestheticization," in Id., *The De-definition of Art*, Secker & Warburg, London 1972.

24. Carolyn Christov-Bakargiev, in Gilman Claire, "L'arte povera a Roma," in Guercio G. – Mattirolo A. (eds.), *Il confine evanescente. Arte italiana: 1960-2010*, Electa, Milan 2010, p. 49.

25. Celant Germano, "La scenoscultura di Ceroli," in *Casabella* 326, July 1968, pp. 60-62.

26. Hahn Otto, "Pascali: una nuova concezione dell'arte," in *Cartabianca* 2, May 1968, pp. 6-7.

27. Boatto Alberto, *A Rose is…*, in *Jannis Kounellis. Il giardino, i giuochi*, exhibition catalogue (Rome, Galleria L'Attico, March-April 1967), Rome 1967, n. pag. For an accurate reconstruction of the most important group and solo shows concerning the theatricalization of art in those years, see Celant Germano (ed.), *Identité italienne: l'art en Italie depuis 1959*, exhibition catalogue (Paris, Centre Georges Pompidou, June 25 – September 7, 1981), Centro Di, Florence 1981.

28. Cf. Giosetta Fioroni in conversation with Ilaria Bernardi, Rome, December 6, 2009, in Bernardi Ilaria, *Teatro delle Mostre*, op. cit., p. 175.

29. [No author], "Ettore Innocente", in *L'Espresso Sera*, May 14, 1967.

30. Cf. Paolo Icaro in conversation with Ilaria Bernardi, Tavullia (Pesaro-Urbino) April 7, 2010, in Bernardi Ilaria, *Teatro delle Mostre*, op. cit., p. 182.

31. For more on this, see: *ivi*, pp. 11-15.

32. Cf. Calvesi Maurizio, "8 pittori romani," op. cit., n. pag.

33. Among the many articles that were published for the occasion, see: Trucchi Lorenza, "Arte per tutti. Warhol alla 'Tartaruga,'" in *Momento Sera*, February 24, 1968.

34. Tacchi Cesare, letter written to Plinio De Martiis, June 20, 1966 (Archivio di Stato di Latina, Fondo La Tartaruga, busta 29).

35. The news of the existence of Balla's *Camera da letto* had appeared for the first time in 1952 when Ettore Colla published several studies about it in the magazine *Arti Visive*.

36. Calvesi Maurizio, [no title] in *Una camera da letto di Balla*, exhibition catalogue (Rome, Galleria La Tartaruga, February 18, 1965), Rome 1965, n. pag.

37. Marcuse Herbert, *Eros and Civilisation. A Philosophical Inquiry into Freud*, 1955 and Id., *One-Dimensional Man. Studies in the Ideology of Advanced Industrial Society*, 1964.

38. Dewey John, *Experience and Nature*, 1925 and Id., *Art as Experience*, 1934.

39. Calvesi Maurizio, "Arte e tempo," in *Teatro delle Mostre*, exhibition catalogue (Rome, Galleria La Tartaruga, May 6-31, 1968) Marcalibri/Lerici editore, Rome 1968, n. pag.

40. Plinio De Martiis, in *Qui Arte Contemporanea* 1, July 1966, p. 6.

41. Plinio De Martiis, in *Espresso Sera* 8, May 28, 1967, p. 45.

42. [No author], "Tartaruga show," in *Flash Art* 7, March-April 1968, p. 2.

43. The formula for the event, "one exhibition per day," might have been suggested by Paolini himself: cf. Bernardi Ilaria, *Teatro delle Mostre*, op. cit., p. 15.

44. Calvesi Maurizio, "Arte e tempo," op. cit., n. pag.

45. Cf. Sergio Giuliano, "Cancellazione d'artista di Cesare Tacchi: esposizione, catalogo e documento fotografico tra la fine degli anni '60 e l'inizio degli anni '70,'" in *RolSA, Rivista on line di Storia dell'Arte. Dipartimento di Storia dell'Arte. Università di Roma* 2, 2004, n. pag.

46. As concerns Italy let us recall in particular: *Con temp l'azione* in 1967 in Turin and *Spazio dell'immagine* in Foligno the same year. Outside of Italy: *9 Evenings: Theatre & Engineering*, a cycle of performances organized by Robert Rauschenberg and

by the engineer Billy Klüver, between October 13 and 23, 1966 at the 69th Regiment Armory of New York (promptly described by Ceroli in a letter he wrote to De Martiis from New York in 1966 (Archivio di Stato di Latina, Fondo La Tartaruga, busta 23); *19:45-21:55 Dies alles Herzchen wird einmal Dir gehören*, am event held on September 9, 1967 at the Galerie Dorothea Loehr in Frankfurt on the occasion of which the curator, Paul Maenz, had asked the artists invited to create ephemeral interventions during the period of time mentioned in the title of the exhibition; *Intermedia '68*, a festival that took place in New York and that included alternating videos, performances, music, poetry, and performances of different kinds, staged by eleven artists, including Allan Kaprow and Dick Higgins.

47. The truth of the matter is that other artists were supposed to have taken part in the event (Schifano, Pistoletto, Festa, Fabro, Pascali, Kounellis), but did not do so for various reasons (for example Kounellis and Pascali had signed an exclusive contract with the gallerist Sargentini; Schifano was in America). Cf. Calvesi Maurizio, "Cronache e coordinate di un'avventura," in Calvesi M. – Siligato R. (eds.), *Roma anni '60, op. cit.*, p. 31.

48. Parise Goffredo, *Conversazione su nastro*, audiocassette recorded and transmitted the last day of the *Teatro delle Mostre* (Archivio di Stato di Latina, Fondo La Tartaruga, Audio and video materials).

49. Referenced in particular are: *Amore Mio, Vitalità del Negativo* (1970), *Informazioni sulla presenza italiana* (1971), *24 ore su 24* (1974), and the more recent *Ogni sera con Elisabetta Catalano* (Rome, Galleria Pio Monti, 2009) and *Il teatro delle esposizioni* (Rome, Villa Medici, 2010). This section is in part from Bernardi Ilaria, *Teatro delle Mostre, op. cit.*, which may be referred to for further information.

50. Del Buono Oreste, "Arte: il teatro delle mostre," in *Panorama* 110, May 23, 1968. A few days later, the gallerist announced the second project (nor was this one ever realized) that intended to transfer the entire event to Milan, Turin, and Genoa (Cf. "Non c'è niente di indiscreto," in *Il Tempo*, June 4, 1968).

51. Cf. ibid.

52. Trucchi Lorenza, "Il festival della disobbedienza," in *L'Europa*, June 22, 1968, p. 58.

53. Cf. Trini Tommaso, *Introduzione a Baruchello. Tradizione orale e cultura popolare in una pittura d'avanguardia*, Milan 1975.

54. Trucchi Lorenza, "Il festival della disobbedienza," *op. cit.*, p. 58.

55. Plinio De Martiis, in *Made in-bollettino della Modern Art Agency*, Naples, December 1968, n. pag.

56. Pirani Federica, "Intervista a Giorgio De Marchis," in Calvesi M. – Siligato R. (eds.), *Roma anni '60, op. cit.*, p. 336. This paragraph is in part taken from: Bernardi Ilaria, *Teatro delle Mostre, op. cit.* See for further information.

CONCLUSION
THE
MAIN EVENTS
FROM 1969 TO 2004

The years from 1969 to 2004 correspond to a period of predictable 'agony' for La Tartaruga: although it remained a venue for artists and intellectuals, it quickly lost its role as a gallery of reference for Italian avant-garde experimentation. A posteriori, Fabio Sargentini would thus describe the *Teatro delle Mostre* as "a dying gesture," for soon afterwards Plinio De Martiis was forced to shut down his activity because it was incapable of keeping up with the more recent trends in international artistic research.[1] The truth of the matter is that it was not at all a question of being incapable, but of respect for one's story: La Tartaruga had been born from an idea by the gallerist's artists friends in the 'Scuola romana' in the 1950s, and in the following decade it had been a veritable forge for the city's youngest talents, making way for a new 'school.' After the *Teatro delle Mostre*, to be able to continue to promote the most recent avant-garde research, De Martiis would have had to begin supporting the Italian and international exponents of Arte Povera, process art, and Conceptual art, whose dissemination and success in the second half of the 1960s had, however, sanctioned the decline of the 'Scuola di Piazza del Popolo.' Backing research such as this would have meant, for De Martiis, betraying his own identity and that of his artists. Hence, the inevitable decision to close the gallery and continue to support his artist friends behind the scenes.

It should come as no surprise that the new headquarters of the gallery (now called Studio La Tartaruga), opened by De Martii's wife Ninì in 1969 in Rome on Via Principessa Clotilde 1/A, offered as its first show *Archivio 1954-1969* (February 19): a selection of photographs taken by De Martiis with a Rolleicord 6x6, representing the greatest names in the first fifteen years of his exhibition activity. Nor is it surprising that, after the Giulio Paolini solo exhibition in 1969, between 1970 and 1971 the Studio La Tartaruga hosted exhibitions mostly dedicated to the artists of the 'Scuola di Piazza del Popolo,'[2] or to those who had shown their work there in the 1960s.[3] There were only three new entries: the Romans Gianfranco Notargiacomo (on March 5, 1971 the first of two other solo shows was dedicated to his work, held on June 11, 1974 and February 6, 1976) and Enea Ferrari (May 18, 1971), as well as the Milanese Vincenzo Agnetti (March 26, 1971).

Soon after midnight of New Year's Eve, on January 1, 1971, Ninì passed away unexpectedly. De Martiis, after completing the exhibition calendar for 1971 by himself, decided to close La Tartaruga from 1972 to 1973. In the following ten years he reopened it several times, always in Rome: on April 9, 1974 on Via Ripetta no. 22; on December 19, 1974 on Via Pompeo Magno 6/b, and after closing for two years, on March 3, 1980 in Piazza Mignanelli no. 25, where it stayed open until 1984. Between 1974 and 1984, the focus was mostly on theater, cinema, music, and visual poetry,[4] organizing, for instance, a cycle of four days of poetry readings titled *Corpus Scripsit*, curated by Nanni Cagnone (June 3-6, 1975). In parallel, De Martiis continued to promote some of the artists of the 'Scuola di Piazza del Popolo,'[5] he rediscovered the previous 'Scuola romana,'[6] and he supported some of the youngest Italian artists that in the future would not achieve the success that the gallerist had hoped for, however.[7] The only exhibitions that were dedicated to artists who had never shown their work at La Tartaruga, but who were well-known, were those of the works of Ettore Spalletti (February 26, 1975), Davide Mosconi (March 25, 1975), and Claudio Parmiggiani (January 15, 1976).

The multiple and diverse directions undertaken by De Martiis in his exhibition activity in the 1970s would not allow him to assign a specific identity to the gallery. The turnaround did not take place until May 3, 1978 with the first solo show of Franco Piruca, an artist, born in Catania in 1937, who, by returning to the painting of a classicist matrix, wanted to fill the gap that had been left by the ephemeral performances in public and private exhibition venues. After Piruca's solo show, De Martiis became even more convinced of the need on the part of Italian artistic research to rediscover its classical and pictorial origins. After the *Laboratorio di poesia* curated by Elio Pagliarani (June 22, 1978), he closed La Tartaruga and began to converse about painting with a group of artists, eventually constituting the so-called 'Sei pittori' group: Alberto Abate, Stefano Di Stasio, Salvatore Marrone, Nino Panarello, Franco Piruca, and Piero Pizzi Cannella. At the same time that the pictorial research of the Transavanguardia promoted by Achille Bonito Oliva was developing, De Martiis dedicated to 'Sei pittori' and to other kindred artists numerous exhibitions[8] starting from 1980, the year that La Tartaruga opened in Piazza Miglianelli no. 25.

Nevertheless, the return to painting that was meant to restore a specific identity to the exhibition space was short-lived. Paradoxically, at the very moment when this research was acknowledged – in 1984 Calvesi coined the word Anacronismo[9] when it was introduced at the Venice Biennale –, De Martiis decided to once again close the gallery, perhaps because he realized that the original group of 'Sei pittori' had become something different, something that he could not share. He thus decided to turn to art publishing. After publishing *La Tartaruga. Quaderno 1* in 1984 with texts about his activity, in La Tartaruga's new Roman venue on Via Ripetta no. 19 (from 1986 to 1987), which would later move to Via Sant'Anna no. 18 (from 1989 to 1993), he initiated the publication of *La Tartaruga. Quaderni di arte e letteratura*. These were brochures inspired by the journal *L'Italiano* by Leo Longanesi in terms of the contents that hovered between art and poetry as well as the format, and printed, from 1986 to 1993, once or twice a year by the publisher De Luca. In addition to his publishing activity, De Martiis also curated exhibitions in various venues, collaborating with different galleries,[10] including: the Galleria Contini in Venezia (from 1980 to 1982), the Galleria Marino in Rome (from 1983 to 1984), and above all the Galleria Netta Vespignani in Rome (from 1989 to 1997)

APPENDIX

1954-2004
CHRONOLOGY

Listed in chronological order on these pages are all the activities linked to the Galleria La Tartaruga and carried out by Plinio De Martiis from the beginning of his activity as a gallerist in 1954, to his passing in July 2004. They include solo and group shows, publishing experiences, film screenings, poetry or literary readings held at La Tartaruga, along with the gallery's participation in national and international fairs, as well as collaborations with exhibitions organized by public or private institutions, both Italian and foreign.

Within each year and for each event mentioned, the following are indicated: the date the event opened and/or closed ("n.e.d." – no exact date – is used when this information is unknown), the title, as well as any details included in the inventory of the gallery archive, or deduced from other sources and deemed of interest. The proven existence of invitations, foldouts, brochures, cards containing information, bulletins, catalogues produced on the occasion of the individual exhibitions is in brackets.

As for the above-mentioned publications, the following are indicated when available: title (only when it is different from the title of the event it is related to), publication date, publisher (only when it is not La Tartaruga), whether or not there are texts and, if known, the names of the respective authors. The same bibliographical data are provided with regard to magazines, periodicals, and books produced during the same years by the gallery independently of the specific exhibitions, when these are deemed to be important.

For some of the events that took place during the event-filled and most important years from 1954 to 1968, also provided because it is considered to be of interest, is a short quotation in the original language from the reviews written during the same period, or from one of the above- cited publications or informative materials produced by the gallery itself.

Reproduced at the bottom of the page and in an abbreviated form is the relevant bibliographical information indicated in its entirety corresponding to the activity to which the quotation refers.

Furthermore, the closings and the relocations of La Tartaruga are listed under the year and month (if known) when they took place.

The chronology from 1954 to 2000 includes only the activities and information that could be proven based on the sources, that is, based on the inventory and documents in the gallery archive, currently held in the Archivio di Stato di Latina, but also based on articles published in the newspapers and magazines at the time of the survey held at the Biblioteca Nazionale Centrale di Roma.

1954

February 25: the gallery opens on Via del Babuino no. 196, Rome, with an exhibition titled *"Cosacchi da ridere." Litografie di Daumier Cham & Vernier*. On display are forty lithographs from the volume *Les Cosaques pour rire*, published by Le Chiavari, Paris 1954. [Invitation].

> "Now I propose to turn to one of the most important men, not only in caricature but also in modern art, to a man who every morning gives the Parisian population a laugh, who, every day, supplies the need of public gaiety, and gives it something to feed on [...] Until now only artists have appreciated the serious vein that lies hidden there, and the fact that it deserves serious study. The reader will have guessed that Daumier is he man I am referring to."
> (Baudelaire Charles, No Title, in the invitation to the exhibition, Rome 1954)

March 10: *Giovanni Omiccioli*.

March 20: *Eva Fischer*. On display is a series of paintings from the cycle known as 'delle Biciclette.'

> "Alla 'Tartaruga' Eva Fischer presenta [...] il ciclo delle 'biciclette.' Dobbiamo constatare che potenziando le qualità inventive a lei proprie la Fischer sforza di far diventare 'personaggio' l'umile mezzo di trasporto. Ora a prescindere dal contenuto e passando a considerare la consistenza più o meno estetica del nuovo dipingere, dobbiamo sottolineare la sua spiccata tendenza al grafismo [...]. Ma codesta tendenza si svolge in senso pittorico o in senso decorativo? Ecco il problema. Un problema al quale la Fischer ci auguriamo sappia rispondere più chiaramente nelle prossime opere."
> (Sciortino Giuseppe, "Le pittrici," in *La fiera letteraria*, March 20, 1954)

April 1: *Pierluigi Sonetti*.

April 13: *Piero Sadun*.

April 26: *Antonio Vangelli*. On display is a series of paintings from the cycle known as 'del Circo.'

> "Antonio Vangelli espone un suo 'Ciclo del Circo' alla galleria 'Tartaruga.' Diciamo subito che è la più bella delle mostre sinora fatte dalla nuova galleria di via del Babuino. [...] I piccoli quadri, che in questi giorni espone alla 'Tartaruga,' sono espressioni proprie alla personalità dell'artista romano e non solo lo qualificano e definiscono meglio, ma chiariscono e accrescono le sue ben note e stimate qualità. Il circo è, per l'artista, un appiglio realistico per dar corpo alle immagini poetiche che urgono alla sua fantasia; e sono immagini di una grazia, di una finezza, di una delicatezza che commuovono."
> (Sciortino Giuseppe, "Mostre Romane," in *La fiera letteraria*, April 26, 1954)

May 8: *Litografie di Forain*. On display in the room are engravings by: Francisco Goya, Théodore Gericault, Honoré Daumier, Eugène Delacroix, Èdouard Manet, Pierre-Auguste Renoir, Alfred Sisley, Berthe Morisot, Paul Cézanne, Pablo Picasso. [Invitation].

May 19: *Henry Inlander*.

May 29: *Sante Monachesi*.

June 10: *Eva Llorens*.

June 24: *Detomi*.

November 10: *Mino Maccari*. On display are engravings and drawings. ["Bollettino della galleria," November 1954, published by Istituto Grafico Tiberino (Rome), with a text by Nicola Ciarletta, an interview with the artist, and a newsletter].

"Maccari è l'esempio più spontaneo e coerente della confusione odierna tra pittura e letteratura. [...] Tracciare una figura sulla carta è come tracciare delle lettere. Infatti nelle figure di Maccari si intuiscono varie grafie: ora corsive, ora diritte, qua piegano a sinistra come la scrittura di certe donnine esagitate, là si gonfiano come certi caratteri ampollosi; talvolta precipitano dal rigo come la grafia dei depressi, talaltra se ne levano giubilanti come dittatori. Nello stesso tempo la scrittura di una lettera è come il disegno di una figura. [...] Malgrado il suo impersonale decoro, un vocabolario può mutarsi in un teatro amenissimo."
(Ciarletta Nicola, "Dove le parole diventano segni, e i segni parole," in *Bollettino della galleria*, November 1954, n. pag.)

November 24: *Armando Buratti*. ["Bollettino della galleria," November 1954, published by Istituto Grafico Tiberino (Rome), with texts by Maurizio Calvesi and Elio Filippo Accrocca, and a newsletter].

"La leggerezza, il distacco dei bianchi di Buratti, può essere il simbolo della sua pittura. È nei bianchi che meglio si avverte lo sciogliersi dell'umanità dolcemente riservata di Buratti nell'acuto sommesso della sua poesia. [...] Gli oggetti vi si stendono e vi si aprono, serbando una struttura puramente esterna, di piani piegati alla luce; i tetti verdi, le staccionate bianche, i carretti azzurri acquistano una candida evidenza di realtà in questo ordinato telaio spaziale. [...] Una delle cose più belle è il quadro con tre barche: la vivezza dei verdi, dei rossi, degli azzurri affiora pur nel tono di luce così trattenuto toccando un effetto intimo e squisito; mentre il modo di tagliare e disporre le tre barche, di organizzarne con genialità le strutture, testimonia una completa capacità di impaginazione, e lascia intravedere in Buratti ancora molte, nuove possibilità, anche in altre direzioni."
(Calvesi Maurizio, "Armando Buratti," in *Bollettino della galleria*, November 1954, n. pag.)

December 11: *Birolli - Consagra - Corpora - Fazzini - Franchina - Gentilini - Guttuso - Leoncillo - Mafai - Pirandello - Raphael - Turcato*. [*Bollettino della galleria*, December 1954, published by Istituto Grafico Tiberino (Rome), with an anonymous introduction, an extract from a text by Charles Baudelaire, and a newsletter].

"Il dibattito sugli orientamenti artistici si è intensificato e complicato negli ultimi anni, sì che il pubblico, e qualche volta persino la critica stessa, rimangono perplessi. Ci è sembrato utile riunire un limitato numero di artisti, di diverso orientamento e di opposte correnti, i quali nella loro opera hanno sempre mantenuto una coerenza interna ed una personalità, legate sempre ai principi ed ai valori fondamentali della pittura. [...] Questa nostra mostra vuole essere soltanto una prima indicazione e, limitata a pochi, non intende escludere nessuno dei tanti altri artisti che fanno parte del clima più vitale di oggi."
(No Author, "Birolli - Consagra - Corpora - Fazzini - Franchina - Gentilini - Guttuso - Leoncillo - Mafai - Pirandello - Raphael – Turcato," in *Bollettino della galleria*, December 1954, n. pag.)

December 30: *Luigi De Angelis*. [*Bollettino della galleria*, December 1954, published by Istituto Grafico Tiberino (Roma), with texts by Carlo Bernari, Vasco Pratolini, Alfredo Mezio, and a newsletter].

"Marine, porti, carrozzelle, velieri all'ancora, trofei di frutta, paesaggi marittimi dove la biacca è un ricordo popolaresco del mare canuto di omerica memoria […]. Questi quadretti dove la poesia è inseparabile da un minimo di artigianato sono forse la sola contropartita all'intellettualismo dell'artista torturato ed enciclopedico, in un'epoca che fa un uso esagerato dei termini di esperienza e di angoscia."
(Mezio Alfredo, "Luigi De Angelis," in *Bollettino della galleria*, December 1954, n. pag.)

1955

January 18: *John Bratby*. [*Bollettino della galleria*, January 1955, published by Istituto Grafico Tiberino (Rome), with a text in Italian and in English by Derek Hill, and extracts from reviews dated to September 1954 on the artist's work].

"I quadri di John Bratby ci rivelano agevolmente l'uomo che li ha dipinti. […] Ora ha imparato a conoscere il mare e sta imparando a conoscere i paesi sui colli intorno a Roma. […] La sua sincerità potrà destare impressione, la stessa, sgradevole, impressione che si prova scoprendo una spiacevole verità su noi stessi. Uno dei suoi occhi spalancati potrà penetrare troppo profondamente, perché possa riuscire piacevole, ma tant'è: la realtà che egli ci presenta non la possiamo cambiare. Bisogna ascoltare la verità, quale che sia l'emozione che ne risulti. Nulla è taciuto e nessuna spiegazione ci viene offerta."
(Hill Derek, "John Bratby," in *Bollettino della galleria*, January 1955, n. pag.)

February 3: *Francesco Trombadori*. On display is a series of landscapes on canvas. [*Bollettino della galleria*, February 1955, published by Istituto Grafico Tiberino (Rome), with texts by Libero de Libero and Velso Mucci, and a bibliographical note on the artist].

"Francesco Trombadori espone una serie di paesaggi alla Galleria della Tartaruga, paesaggi campestri e paesaggi cittadini, soprattutto di Roma. […] Certi ammassi di verde della campagna siracusana intorno a case e muri su cui la luce si diffonde largamente come per esempio nel quadro intitolato: 'La salina' […]; quel paesaggio intitolato: 'Paesaggio 1955', tutto case, alberi e ombre; l'atro intitolato: 'La casa bianca,' fatto d'un grande folto di verde che avvolge la casa; il 'Passaggio a livello' in cui la strada tra siepi, si perde in una impressionante lontananza; 'Vista del Mare' dal piano invaso da una vasta ombra; 'Ponte Cavour' in cui la massa del ponte sorge bianca come un'apparizione da un'acqua dai profondi riflessi son tutte opere che colpiscono in questa mostra per intensità e concretezza raggiunte."
(Pensabene Giuseppe, "Obelischi e paesaggi nelle mostre romane," in *Il Secolo d'Italia*, February 6, 1955)

February 21: *Mario Mafai*. On display are recent works. [*Bollettino della galleria*, February 1955, published by Istituto Grafico Tiberino (Rome), with an anonymous introduction and notes by the artist].

"Si aveva tutti l'aria di deporre ogni nostro capriccio o antagonismo in fatto di pittura ai piedi del grande autoritratto che ci accoglieva all'ingresso della galleria, uno degli autoritratti meno

convenzionali e narcisisti dipinti in questi ultimi anni, e nel quale sembra che Mafai abbia voluto raccontarsi [...]. Come questi peperoncini, quest'uva, queste viole e questi fiori che chiamare natura morta è convenzione che li falsa e sminuisce."
(D'Arrigo Fortunato, "Mostre. Mario Mafai alla Tartaruga," in *Vie Nuove*, March 13, 1955)

March 11: *Giulio Turcato*. [*Bollettino della galleria*, March 1955, published by Istituto Grafico Tiberino (Rome), with texts by Vlaminck and Alfredo Mezio, artist's statements, and a newsletter].

"Un quadro di Turcato esposto nella nostra Galleria: 'Bambino ribelle che viene ripreso dalla madre'. Abbiamo cercato di farci spiegare dal pittore il significato di questo titolo. 'Mi sembra che questo sia stato un problema delle nostre generazioni. Ognuno di noi ha cercato di scappare dalla propria educazione, dalle condizioni del proprio ambiente, dalle abitudini inveterate'".
(No Author, "Una visita a Turcato," in *Bollettino della galleria*, January 1955, n. pag.)

March 23: *Antonio Scordia*. [*Bollettino della galleria*, March 1955, published by Istituto Grafico Tiberino (Roma), with an anonymous introduction, a biographical note about the artist, a list of the works exhibited delle opere esposte, and a newsletter].
"La Tartaruga ha il piacere di presentare un gruppo di opere recenti del pittore Antonio Scordia, un esponente tra i più validi di quella giovane pittura italiana rivelatasi nel dopoguerra in un clima di approfondimento e di ricerca di nuove direzioni, sulla quale si appuntano le migliori speranze per l'arte italiana."
(Anonymous introduction, in *Bollettino della galleria*, March 1955, n. pag.)

April 4: *Ben Shahn*. On display are the drawings. [*Bollettino della galleria*, April 1955, published by Istituto Grafico Tiberino (Rome), with extracts from the artist's writings and talks, and a biographical note about the artist].

"Si afferma che l'arte astratta è l'espressione perfetta di una simile era, e questo forse è vero. Perché l'arte astratta dichiara validi solo la sua tecnica, i materiali per dipingere e la maniera di organizzarli. Rifiuta invece l'uomo, la sua vita, le sue visioni, le sue filosofie, il suo futuro. Afferma che la macchina può assorbire le nostre emozioni e contenere la nostra anima. Eppure, sono convinto che l'interesse crescente per le cose d'arte e l'aumentare delle attività artistiche, non sono altro in fondo che una ribellione contro l'assolutismo della scienza e della tecnica, un anelito verso un tocco umano, un'affermazione personale."
(Shahn Ben, No Title, in *Bollettino della galleria*, April 1955, n. pag.)

April 16: *Titina Maselli*. On display are the drawings. [*Bollettino della galleria*, April 1955, published by Istituto Grafico Tiberino (Rome), with a letter to the artist from Renzo Vespignani, a biographical note about the artist, a list of the works exhibited, and a newsletter].

"Nelle opere presenti in questa mostra è maturata una coscienza del mondo più solida ed organica, libera da ogni enfasi troppo letteraria e soggettiva. [...] Aspetti della nostra vita quotidiana che hai saputo cogliere con lucidità. Qui gli oggetti, pur conservando tutta la loro magia non sono 'inventati', non sono piegati a 'servire un effetto', ma hanno la forza e la necessità del documento."
(Renzo Vespignani, "Lettera a Titina Maselli," in *Bollettino della galleria*, April 1955, n. pag.)

April 30: *Salvatore Scarpitta*. [*Bollettino della galleria*, April 1955, published by Istituto Grafico Tiberino (Rome), with texts by Mario Mafai, Cesare Zavattini, Jack Massard, a biographical note about the artist, and a list of the works exhibited].

"Scarpitta passò attraverso l'espressionismo e l'astrattismo. Oggi, man mano, si lascia indietro i residui formalisti e non è di quelli che ancora si compiacciono fra i gingillamenti edonistici e le loro vane allusioni poetiche. Così, come i migliori, Scarpitta è alla conquista di un contenuto e, quindi, della figura a cui vuol dare una chiara funzione morale. Ed è, secondo me, una delle strade giuste, se non l'unica."
(Mafai Mario, "Salvatore Scarpitta," *Bollettino della galleria*, April 1955, n. pag.)

May 12: *A. Raphael Mafai*. On display are works dated from 1928 to 1955. [*Bollettino della galleria*, May 1955, published by Istituto Grafico Tiberino (Rome), with a text by Alfredo Mezio, a bibliography, and a biographical note about the artist].

"Raphael Mafai nella galleria 'La Tartaruga' espone, con opere più recenti, le ormai celebri pitture tra il 1928 e il 1930 già ammirate pochi anni fa allo 'Zodiaco.' E bisogna riconoscere che mai ella fu artista felice come in quella breve e fortunata stagione che vi vide la nascita della cosiddetta 'scuola romana,' permeata di un romanticismo autentico, di un lirismo acceso di bagliori crepuscolari e di sensualità greve e angosciata."
(Bellonzi Fortunato, "Le esposizioni collettive degli artisti di Roma e Provincia e del V Maggio della pittura romana," in *Domenica*, May 29, 1955)

May 28: *Antonio Cardile*. [*Bollettino della galleria*, May 1955, published by Istituto Grafico Tiberino (Rome), with texts by Corrado Cagli and Giovanni Omiccioli, and a biogaphical note about the artist].

"Malgrado nell'intero corso dell'attività grafica di Cardile non siano avvertibili accenni autobiografici agli anni di guerra, di prigionia, di sanatorio, di esilio, il timbro di tutta la sua opera è certo determinato dalle conseguenze della guerra, chiaramente leggibili nei volti, nei gesti, la disperata solitudine di questa umanità reclusa nelle 'case di cura.' da tutto esclusa, chiusa nell'ossessionante perimetro di malinconici giardini."
(Cagli Corrado, "Antonio Cardile," in *Bollettino della galleria*, May 1955, n. pag.)

November 12: *Sadun*. [Invitation].

December 20: *Giuseppe Macrì*. On display are bronze and silver sculptures. [*Bollettino della galleria*, December 1955, published by Istituto Grafico Tiberino (Rome), with a text by Leonardo Sinisgalli, an autobiography by the artist, and a newsletter].

"Pensavo ieri, – vedendo i cavallini di Macrì in bronzo e i gatti-mosca di argento […] – di veder nel gentile scultore calabrese un lontano parente dei fabbricanti di Presepi, non per cercare appiglio alle ricorrenze, ma per la nuova necessità di mortificare la nostra superbia e quella di tutti i nostri simili, di fronte a un teatrino in formato ridotto, a un mondo pieno di omuncoli poco più grandi di una pipa."
(Sinisgalli Leonardo, "Giuseppe Macrì," in *Bollettino della galleria*, December 1955, n. pag.)

December 30: *Le spalle alla natura. Quadri di: Balla - De Pisis - Mafai - Muccini - Omiccioli - Pirandello*

- *Sironi - Vespignani.* [*Bollettino della galleria*, December 1955, published by Istituto Grafico Tiberino (Rome), with extracts from texts by Max J. Friedlander, Renzo Vespignani, Fausto Pirandello, and Armand Dayot].

"Gli artisti forzarono le barriere dell'arte puramente visiva e poterono impunemente abbandonarsi al mito, alla poesia, alla satira, all'aneddoto, fin quando tradussero soltanto in forma colore i valori dell'intelletto e del sentimento. [...] La cosiddetta arte astratta trasse una ultima conseguenza: parve che dalla natura ancora troppi elementi intellettuali e psicologici confluiscono nel quadro; anelando alla pura arte visiva, si volsero le spalle alla natura."
(Friedlander Max J., *Le spalle alla natura*, from Id., *Il conoscitore dell'arte*, Einaudi, Turin 1955 and republished in *Bollettino della galleria*, December 1955, n. pag.)

1956

January 10: *Maria Petrucci*. [*Bollettino della galleria*, January 1956, Istituto Grafico Tiberino (Rome), with texts by Alfonso Gatto and Alfredo Mezio, and with a biographical note about the artist].

"Diciamo subito che questi quadri di soggetto nuovayorkese, opere di pittura e non scenografie letterarie, hanno, ben al di là d'ogni fumismo che qua e là traspare, un rapporto ineguale di delicatezza e di forza, il risveglio di un'immagine finale e liberatrice dalla chiave delle sue strutture che ne stringono il nesso. [...] Il suo linguaggio disponibile vale più della sua invenzione. Si guardi a 'La strada' o a 'Strada a Harlem': c'è persino una rozza e dura affermazione di pietà, un tentativo di fermezza epigrammatica. La luce da esterna si fa interiore, entra nella materia del colore. E l'uomo solo con pochi altri fa più foresta di una moltitudine."
(Mezio Alfredo, "Un biglietto per Maria Petrucci," in *Bollettino della galleria*, January 1956, n. pag.)

January 24: *Riccardo Francalancia*. [*Bollettino della galleria*, January 1956, published by Istituto Grafico Tiberino (Rome), with a text by Giuseppe Ungaretti, and extracts from the artist's notebook].
"L'opera di Francalancia, io la conosco da quando ebbe a manifestarsi la prima volta tanti anni fa, ed essa è rimasta, nei lunghi anni del suo progredire, sempre fedele a se stessa. La poesia che è nella parola della sua pittura, è fatta di raccoglimento affettivo, della dolcezza che è nelle forme – piante, monumenti, case, tondeggiamenti del terreno – a lungo dagli occhi amorevoli accarezzati. È poesia di forme che lodano la mano che le ha fermate in una umana luce."
(Ungaretti Giuseppe, "Francalancia," in *Bollettino della galleria*, January 1956, n. pag.)

March 20: *Sette pittori romani. Attardi - Brunori - Dorazio - Muccini - Perilli - Scarpitta - Vespignani*. [*Bollettino della galleria*, March 1956, published by Tipografia Artigiana (Rome), with an anonymous introduction and texts by the artists].

"Abbiamo raccolto nella nostra galleria un gruppo di opere di alcuni pittori romani dell'ultima generazione. Di quella generazione che in questi anni si è maturata attraverso esperienze diverse e spesso contrastanti e polemiche."
(Anonymous introduction, in *Bollettino della galleria*, March 1956, n. pag.)

April 11: *Corrado Cagli*. On display is a series of paintings from the cycle referred to as 'degli Arlecchini.' [*Bollettino della galleria*, April 1956, published by Tipografia Artigiana (Rome), with texts by Palma Bucarelli and Paolo Toschi].

"Si veda questa storia di Arlecchini: queste immagini di Arlecchino ricavate tagliando netto, con una tecnica sorprendente e prodigiosamente abile come sempre, nel tessuto colorato, astratto apparentemente, ma già contenente in sé, nello stesso ordinamento dei tasselli variopinti, la predisposizione della forma già tutta nella mente dell'artista; con sovrapposizioni di zone e velatura egli ricava da questa sua materia la forma come farebbe uno scultore dalla pietra. In quell'ordito multicolore e luminoso fino alla fosforescenza, già in sé simbolico di Arlecchino, il personaggio si forma e vive prima ancora di essere rivelato."
(Bucarelli Palma, "Corrado Cagli," in *Bollettino della galleria*, April 1956, n. pag.)

April 28: *De Gregorio - Marignoli - Raspi - Toscano*. [*Bollettino della galleria*, April 1956, published by Tipografia Artigiana (Rome), with a text by Leoncillo, and short biographical notes about the artists].

"Questi pittori [...], in un contatto diretto con la realtà, in un emozionato colloquio con essa si propongono la posizione morale e quindi estetica diversa dalle due polarizzazioni in cui si è divisa l'arte italiana in questi ultimi anni. Che tentano un superamento di quei concettualismi aprioristici dell'opera che stanno veramente diventando le uniche vere 'vecchie' posizioni dell'arte di oggi."
(Leoncillo, "De Gregorio - Marignoli - Raspi – Toscano," in *Bollettino della galleria*, April 1956, n. pag.)

May 14: *Ugo Attardi*. [*Bollettino della galleria*, May 1956, published by Tipografia Artigiana (Rome), with a text by the artist, a note signed "La Tartaruga" about the art criticism in the newspapers of the day, and a newsletter].

"Un pittore può essere moderno solo se è sincero nell'esprimere i suoi sentimenti. [...] e qui si torna al problema di sistemare insieme la cultura, la sapienza tecnica, con la spontaneità. [...] Voglio muovermi rapidamente e liberamente. Nel mio lavoro vi sono ancora tracce di qualcosa di vecchio, ma non intendo star fermo; voglio muovermi in rapporto al precisarsi in me di una coscienza più viva della vita moderna. Ritengo assurdo e dannoso restare abbarbicati al proprio passato, più che mai se questo è modesto come il mio."
(Attardi Ugo, "Ugo Attardi," in *Bollettino della galleria*, May 1956, n. pag.)

October 20: *Quadri di: Afro, Birolli, Corpora, Mafai, Moreni, Pirandello, Santomaso, Turcato, Vedova*. [Card].

November 8: *Fausto Pirandello*. [Brochure, with a letter from Lionello Venturi to the artist, and a list of the works exhibited].

"Caro Pirandello, ho veduto con molto piacere le sue ultime pitture che stanno per essere esposte alla Tartaruga. V'è un distacco, più netto di prima, dall'oggetto rappresentato nell'intento di raggiungere una più completa coerenza di forma e colore. I paesaggi sono bellissimi. [...] Dal 1951 Lei non aveva più a Roma una mostra personale, oggi si presenta rinnovato, con l'esperienza del lungo studio e dell'entusiasmo della giovinezza."

(Venturi Lionello, *Lettera a Pirandello*, in the exhibition brochure, Rome 1956, n. pag.)

December: *Adam, Braque, Chagall, Hartung, Leger, Mirò, Picasso, Singier, Soulanges*. On display are lithographs. [Card, with a list of the works exhibited].

1957

January 9: *Mario Lattes*. On display are landscapes and still lifes. [Catalogue, with a text by Libero de Libero, and a list of the works exhibited].

"Lattes si rafforzava in quella superiore unità che è propria di chi non considera la pratica dell'arte se non come una esercitazione morale. Che tale esigenza sia pungente e scrupolosa fino alla rinuncia d'ogni vanità, può vedersi ancora nelle opere che Lattes ha dipinto lo scorso anno, ora esposte alla *Tartaruga*. Il tema dei paesaggi e delle nature morte non è mutato né è mutato lo spirito da cui le visioni insorgono con quell'accento acutissimo di nostalgia per una realtà andata in pezzi e polvere, che stenta disperatamente di riamalgamare la propria sostanza. [...] Stavolta è nuovo lo spirito dell'elegia che alita sulle colline bianche della neve lunare, tra i massi lucenti della necropoli, a fiore di città remote, a volte fa un'aurora nel cielo e sui deserti pietrificati ripullula la vegetazione come una strombettata di fede."
(de Libero Libero, No Title, in the exhibition catalogue, Rome 1957, n. pag.)

January 24: *Piero Dorazio*. [Catalogue, with a text by Nello Ponente].

"La rinuncia di Dorazio alla figuratività è stato fatto spontaneo [...]. Ma non ha significato la rinuncia all'immagine, beninteso a un'immagine pittorica e non naturalistica. Tuttavia a differenza di molti suoi coetanei, l'oggetto pittorico presente in Dorazio non è stato astratto da un oggetto naturale, è una creazione puramente fantastica, più di ordine psicologico che emozionale."
(Ponente Nello, No Title, in the exhibition catalogue, Rome 1957, n. pag.)

February 7: *Antonio Scordia*. On display are lithographs and drawings. [Foldout, with a list of works exhibited and of the artist's exhibitions].

"Siamo a un passo dall'astrattismo ma senza la sua costruttività spaziale. Nella 'Marina di Fregene,' nella 'Donna sulla veranda,' nel 'Cavallo.' e soprattutto in 'Colazione sull'erba' si sente sempre il buon mestiere, ma anche una pausa di incertezza sulla strada da imboccare per tenersi alla *page*."
(Etna Giacomo, "Antonio Scordia," in *Il Giornale del Mezzogiorno*, February 28, 1957)

February 19: *Afro, Burri, Scialoja*. [Foldout].

March 4: *Leoncillo*. [Foldout, with a text by the artist, a list of the works exhibited, and a biographical note about the artist].
"La materia oggi è per me molto importante perché bene o male un volume cromatico l'avevo trovato per la mia cultura ed ora questa identità la voglio anche per la materia. [...] non una realtà descritta e ricondotta a stile, ma forma colore materia a dare direttamente l'emozione, il sentimento della natura, a 'volerla imitare' per essere un'altra natura come essa [...]. Per

questo ora ho fatto foglie, cespugli e fiori, perché così mi è parso più facile 'vedere' di nuovo le cose. Dopo ne farò altre meno naturali, quelle che mi premono di più: perché noi non siamo naturali."
(Leoncillo, No Title, in the foldout of the exhibition, Rome 1957, n. pag.)

March 18: *Antonio Corpora*. [Foldout, with a text in French by Christian Zervos and a list of the artist's exhibitions].

"Se Corpora non avesse questa natura evocatrice (a volte proprio romantica) la sua realtà non avrebbe interesse per noi, che poco amore portiamo all'edonismo decorativo ed al purismo più o meno nazionale. La sua realtà non avrebbe l'accento grave che ha, quel tono patetico e perfino drammatico. E ci sembra che in questa mostra il pittore abbia raccolto proprio il meglio di sé. I suoi quadri sono allo stesso tempo emotivi e architettati; così come la materia è, in essi, sottile, trasparente, e insieme plastica, densa."
(Guzzi Virgilio, "Mostre romane. Corpora alla 'Tartaruga,'" in *Il Tempo*, March 26, 1957)

April 3: *Mario Mafai*. [Foldout, with a text by Lionello Venturi].

"Mafai ha risolto per sé, in modo pieno ed esemplare, il problema dell'astratto-concreto. E non si dica che si tratta di stile bozzettistico. Niente di più ordinato e realizzato, niente di più rappresentativo dell'effetto pittorico, del suo amore per i colori romani, del suo attaccamento a Roma. I *Tetti* e il *Mercatino* sono ottimi esempi di questa nuova arte."
(Venturi Lionello, No Title, in the foldout of the exhibition, Rome 1957, n. pag.)

April 24: *Turcato*. [Foldout].

"Voluttà dell'arte pura, gusto dell'arabesco. Ancora. Questa 'avanguardia' è un verme solitario che per un pezzo terrà segreta la testa. […] Bisognerà gli stessi pittori […] sentano il bisogno di tornare all'occidente, il quale è sempre stato *figura*. Del resto, il quadro di Turcato dal titolo *Traliccio* sembra voler spezzare quel compiaciuto edonismo a due dimensioni. La forma trova già nello stadio della tecnica un palpito umano e si articola in uno spazio più libero".
(No Author, "Incontro con l'artista," in *Il Tempo*, May 21, 1957)

May 11: *Achille Perilli*. [Foldout, with a text by Nello Ponente and a list of the artist's exhibitions].

"Perilli è oggi maturo perché ha saputo liberare le sue premesse da quell'eccesso di intellettualismo che le caratterizzava e perché ha saputo riscoprire nella grafia semplificata e assoluta un valore fantastico. Forse oggi è più facile penetrare l'emozione di un suo dipinto perché essa è più spontanea, perché ha forse perduto in rigore teorico ma guadagnato in libertà di espressione."
(Ponente Nello, No Title, in the foldout of the exhibition, Rome 1957, n. pag.)

May 27: *Salvatore Scarpitta*. [Foldout, with a text by Cesare Vivaldi, and with a biographical note about the artist].

"Le opere raccolte nell'odierna Mostra rivelano chiaramente l'arco che Scarpitta ha tracciato dall'espressionismo astratto ad una 'nuova figurazione' del reale. La sua ultima pittura stabilisce col mondo un rapporto sempre più intensamente, sicuramente lirico […]. Lirismo

puro, sempre al color bianco, ma da cui ormai sempre più netta si libera l'immagine."
(Vivaldi Cesare, No Title, in the foldout of the exhibition, Rome 1957, n. pag.)

June 14: *Karel Appel*. First solo show in Rome. [Foldout, with a text by Willem Jacob Henri Berend Sandberg].
"Il confronto tra i quadri e gli schizzi d'un vero artista è spesso molto utile. [...] Lo schizzo, soprattutto l'abbozzo, è l'emozione intensa che pervade l'uomo nel momento della creazione [...]. I dipinti di questo pittore sono altrettante testimonianze di una una vitalità e di una forza rare unite a una lucidità impressionante."
(Sandberg Willem Jacob Henri Berend, No Title, in the foldout of the exhibition, Rome 1957, n. pag.)

October 7: *Dorazio, Nuvolo, Perilli, Scarpitta, Sterpini*. [Foldout].

October 19: *Marca-Relli. Collages pitture*. [Foldout, with a biographical note about the artist].

November 18: *Ettore Colla ferri legni*. First solo show in Rome. [Foldout].

December 5: *4 pittori contemporanei. Afro, Burri, Capogrossi, Matta*. [Foldout].

December 18: *Micro Salon*. Exhibition in collaboration with Galerie Iris Clert, Paris. Works by: Abidine, Alcopley, Alechinsky, Appel, Arbas, Arman, Arp, Baj, Beaufort, Delaney, Bellegarde, Benrath, Bertini, Bertrand, Boille, Brauner, Bro, Brüning, Bryen, Chan, Marcelle, Ch Achoune, Cesar, Chereau, Childa, Coteau, Corneille, Cousins, Crippa, Dangelo, De Silva Viera, Decaro, Anita, Dimitri, Dobaschi, Don Fink, Dorazio, Doucet, Dubuffet, Duvillier, Ernst, Engel Pank, Falchi, Fautrier, Fontana, Gaitis, Gaul, Gauthier, Gillet, Graziani, Hartung, Hba, Helman, Hennessy, Hiquily, Hossiasson, Hundertwasser, Ionesco, Jacobsen, Jamis, Jaouen, Jorn, Kallos, Kamzin Choon, Katsura, Kermadec, Kimber Smith, Kito, Klee, Klein, Kolos Vary Koskas, Kricke, Kurt-Lewy, Lago, Lam Wilfredo, Laubies, Lemborelle, Liberaki, Liles, Lucatti, Melina, Manessier, Matta, Maussion, Messagier, Michaux, Mortensen, Mubin, Nejad, Newcombe, Novelli, Omiros, Oppenheim, Pantaloni, Penalba, Perilli, Picasso, Ping-Ming, Pink Lutka, Quenti Marie, Raymond, Rioppelle, Roditi, Rotella, Sam, Scarpitta, Schneider, Selim, Signori, Sterpini, Stubbing, Sugai, Szenes, Takis, Trygyadottyr, Tsingor, Van Haardt, Vasarely, Villon, Viola, Wendt, Weber Hudo, Yves Le Monocrhome, Zack, Zangs, Zeu. [Foldout].

1958

January 7: *Miguel Ocampo*. [Foldout, with a text by Nello Ponente].

"Miguel Ocampo è architetto oltre che pittore e questo può giustificare il desiderio d'ordine che si avverte immediatamente davanti ai suoi quadri. Ma è un ordine che si adegua spontaneamente alla dimensione pittorica e il risultato è sempre distante dalla pura costruzione architettonica delle immagini. [...] Le forme si sottraggono al controllo della geometria per rivestirsi di significazione psicologica. Al di là dell'apparenza regolata si intuisce la libertà della fantasia."
(Ponente Nello, No Title, in the foldout of the exhibition, Rome 1958, n. pag.)

January 25: *Corpora, Scialoja, Turcato*. [Card].

February 8: *Bertini*. [Foldout, with a text in French by Eduard Jaguer].

"Que la peinture de Bertin soit une étonnante source de déléctation pour quiconque apprécie les recherches contemporaines, cela, je pense, est manifeste. En enet, même en ses annés où plus que jamais l'habilité technique se donne libre cours, l'on rencontre relativement peu de peintres qui sachent nous prodiguer tant de miroitantes trasparences dans la coloration, tant de souple témérité dans exploration d'un graphisme qui dégage du tumulte ses veines essentielles; mais aussi, qui sachent nous déconcerter, d'aventure, par l'angecement de la composition, la 'mise en page.'"
(Jaguer Eduard, *Vers une peinture metaphysique*, in the foldout of the exhibition, Rome 1958, n. pag.)

February 27: *Kline*. First solo show in Europe. [Foldout].

March 15: *Jorn*. First solo show in Rome. [Foldout, with a text by Cesare Vivaldi and a poem by Jacques Prévert].

"Jorn peint son univers. / Et c'est pour lui, comme pour tant de bonnes gens, son univers à soi. / Son univers Adam. / Son univers Véronèse. / Son univers de vase. / Son univers d'eau. / Son univers âtre. / Son univers luisant et solitaire où, de nuit, les passants de la route comme les poissons de la mer sont jetés contre les arbres, le roches, aveugòes par les feux tournants du progrès. / Son univers de gris-souris, de Venice ou de Bohème. / Son univers sel et aussi son univers poivre. / Son univers bouteille à la mer et mon, ton, son, nôtre, vôtre, l'autre univers de terre."
(Prévert Jacques, No Title, in the foldout of the exhibition, Rome 1958, n. pag.)

March 27: *Nuvolo*. [Foldout, with a text by Emilio Villa].

"Dopo tante esclamazioni contratte, improvvisa allusioni surreali a miti atmosferici e parvenze teurgiche, la sua pittura oggi tende a spiegare, in schemi sereni e ammirevoli, una sua intimissima vocazione alla Energia Bianca (e ancora fonti orfiche: care forse a Timeo da Locri o al Melville delle pagine sul bianco."
(Villa Emilio, No Title, in the foldout of the exhibition, Rome 1958, n. pag.)

April 13: *Gruppo 11*. On display are works by: Attila Birò, G. C. Kirchberger, Georg-Karl Pfahler, Friedrich Sieber. [Brochure, with a text by Heinz Spielmann].

"Ancora una parola su alcuni richiami ad apparizioni della Natura che qualche volta si possono ritrovare nei quadri del Gruppo 11: anche in questo caso si tratta solamente di somiglianze nell'essenza, nella struttura, e non qualche forma di ispirazione naturalistica. Questo avvicinarsi non alla Natura ma al suo Negat, appartiene alla dialettica del nostro tempo. Le vecchie frontiere fra Natura e Arte, fra sensazione e intelletto, divengono fluide."
(Spielmann Heinz, *gruppe 11*, in the brochure of the exhibition, Rome 1958, n. pag.)

April 26: *Scarpitta*. [Foldout, with texts by the artist and by Leonardo Sinisgalli].

"Parlare e spiegarsi, così come la materia che è solamente la tela stessa, rivela la sua trama e la sua forza, le debolezze e le lacerazioni. Lo stesso colore vivo farsi spento e il simbolo decadere.

Tutto questo mi ha fatto dimentico di alveari in cui inserire il mondo. [...] ho trovato appena adesso la frontalità del quadro spoglio e la sua proiezione [...]. Ho tolto l'indumento che ricopriva le mie tele. [...] Ma una cosa mi ha dato energia, ed era la scissione stessa del colore dalla problematica della materia. Separando questi ho visto, tra l'altro, il colore emergere come il tutto-quadro e non più ispessito."
(Scarpitta Salvatore, No Title, in the foldout of the exhibition, Rome 1958, n. pag.)

May 15: the single issue of *Artecronaca* is published, edited by Plinio De Martiis.

"Questo numero unico esce come primo tentativo di una cronaca che registri l'interessante e folta attività di due mesi di vita artistica delle gallerie romane. Abbiamo voluto soltanto ed esclusivamente informare seguendo un criterio prospettico non privato, ma internazionale. Abbiamo cercato di usare un linguaggio chiaro e semplice. Ci siamo riusciti solo in parte poiché, comprensibilmente, è difficile muoversi ed uscire dalla ragnatela di una critica misteriosa e parolibera (unica eccezione Lionello Venturi) alla quale siamo stati abituati. Possiamo considerare questo numero unico un numero di saggi di un giornale di cronaca artistica che abbiamo in programma di far uscire, mensilmente e puntualmente, a partire dal mese prossimo."
(No Author, "Cronaca d'arte," in *Artecronaca*, Rome, May 15, 1958, p. 1)

May 17: *Cy Twombly*. First solo show in Europe. [Foldout, with a text by Palma Bucarelli, and a short biographical note about the artist].

"Chi non ha lasciato un segno sul muro, inarrestabile impulso di tracciare un segno, di fare un gesto, puro gesto sul puro muro bianco? Solo una superficie dapprima, poi i segni si sovrappongono, creano un tempo e uno spazio, il muro ha ora una profondità. La vita è ovunque intorno, le cose aspettano solo d'essere viste. Qualcuno ha tracciato quei segni, unica irripetibile presenza di vita, struggente argomento dell'inconoscibile, filo di speranza di comunicare con l'invisibile."
(Bucarelli Palma, No Title, in the foldout of the exhibition, Rome 1958, n. pag.)

May 31: *Consagra. Disegni su pannelli*. [Foldout, with an anonymous introduction and a short biographical note about the artist].

"La Galleria ha il piacere di presentare una mostra di pannelli di Pietro Consagra. Questi disegni, su pannelli di faesite, fanno parte del lavoro preparatorio che l'artista conduce prima di accingersi alla realizzazione scultorea di ogni singola opera; così, attraverso il loro esame, è possibile rendersi conto di quali siano le attuali linee direttrici del lavoro di Consagra, ed anche avere un'idea di quale sarà la fisionomia delle sue prossime sculture."
(Anonymous introduction, in the foldout of the exhibition, Rome 1958, n. pag.)

July: *Afro, Capogrossi, Consagra, De Kooning, Kline, Marca-Relli, Matta*. First of two exhibitions. [Card].

October 4: *Brooks, Donati, Okada*. Second exhibition of two. [Card].

November 22: *Wols. Quadri e gouaches*. First solo show in Rome. [Invitation].

1959

January 13: *11 pittori italiani d'oggi*. Exhibition held to present the volume *Pittori italiani d'oggi* by Lionello Venturi, with works on display by: Afro, Renato Birolli, Bruno Cassinari, Corpora, Mario Mafai, Fausto Pirandello, Giuseppe Santomaso, Toti Scialoja, Antonio Scordia, Giulio Turcato, Emilio Vedova. [Foldout, with an anonymous introduction].

> "In occasione della pubblicazione dell'opera di Lionello Venturi 'PITTORI ITALIANI D'OGGI' edito recentemente da Luigi De Luca, siamo lieti di allestire una mostra con opere degli 11 pittori presentati nel libro. Sono i pittori che Venturi ha difeso con la sua attività di critico militante e con la ponderatezza del suo giudizio di storico dell'arte partecipando egli stesso alla loro battaglia per il rinnovamento del gusto pittorico italiano."
> (Anonymous introduction, in the foldout of the exhibition, Rome 1959, n. pag.)

January 31: *Consagra. Sculture recenti*. The exhibition was held jointly with the artist's solo show at the Galerie de France in Paris planned for March 10, 1959. [Card].

February 10: *Scarpitta, Perilli, Novelli, Accardi, Sanfilippo, Bignardi, Rotella, Marotta, Nuvolo, Buggiani*. Also on display are works by: Afro, Karel Appel, Van Wyck Brooks, Pietro Consagra, Enrico Donati, Franz Kline, Mario Mafai, Conrad Marca-Relli, Koyo Okada, Mark Rothko, Toti Scialoja, Giulio Turcato, Cy Twombly. [Foldout, with a text by Cesare Vivaldi].

> "Roma è città infingarda: si è accorta di avere quasi tutti i migliori pittori italiani [...] soltanto 'di rimbalzo' quando Parigi o New York ne hanno stabilito la fama o quando un critico acuto e coraggioso come Venturi li ha imposti [...]. Ma finalmente se ne è accorta, e non è più disposta a lasciarsi ingannare. Il lavoro di questi artisti ha messo radici ben salde, ha fruttificato culturalmente, ha preparato un fertile terreno."
> (Vivaldi Cesare, *Giovane pittura di Roma*, in the foldout of the exhibition, Rome 1959, n. pag.)

April 9: *Kline, Rothko, Scarpitta, Twombly*. [Foldout].

May 13: *Burri*. The exhibition was held in collaboration with the Galleria Blu, Milan. [Poster].

May 30: *Rauschenberg*. First presentation in Italy of the *Combine-Drawings*. [Foldout, with a short biographical note about the artist].

June 16: *Scialoja*. [Poster; published in a limited edition at the same time as the exhibition is the monograph, curated by the Galleria La Tartaruga, *Scialoja*, by Gillo Dorfles, *Quaderni di arte attuale* series, De Luca Editore, Rome 1959, with a text in both Italian and English].

July 2: *Novelli, Perilli, Scarpitta, Twombly, Vandercam*. [Poster].

November 14-28: *Novelli, Perilli, Twombly*. Exhibition held at the Galerie Aujourd'hui at the Palais Des Beaux Arts, Brussels, and organized in collaboration with La Tartaruga. [Poster; Foldout].

December 3: *Mafai*. On display are ten abstract paintings. [Foldout, with a text by Attilio Bertolucci and a list of the works exhibited].

> "Sto solo davanti alle tele [...]. Dei dieci quadri astratti [...] un gruppo è come una serie di radiografie intime, persino intimiste. I titoli: 'La luce ritorna luce' (con i gialli tramati, forse estivi, alla lontana naturalistici); 'Graffiare è come vivere' (graffiati, graffiti in azzurro su un fondo magma terroso); 'Cancellare la memoria' (i reticoli multicolori, come una memoria non cancellata, una larva del figurativo). Ma le tele più belle sono forse quelle di un altro gruppo, in cui micce si accendono e si spengono, braci si consumano, petali di rosa si sfanno. [...] alla fine quel che conta è quel che si vede, quel che diventa pittura, cioè gioia degli occhi, per sempre."
> (Bertolucci Attilio, No Title, in the foldout of the exhibition, Rome 1959, n. pag.)

No Exact Date: publication in a limited edition of the monograph *Salvatore Scarpitta*, written by Cesare Vivaldi, edited by Galleria La Tartaruga, *Quaderni di Arte Attuale* series, De Luca Editore, Rome 1959.

1960

January 12: *Novelli*. [Foldout].

January 30: *Perilli*. [Foldout, with a list of the artist's exhibitions].

February 23: *Afro. 40 disegni e gouaches 1950-1960*. [Foldout].

March 23: *Peter Brüning*. First solo show in Rome. [Foldout, with a short biographical note about the artist].

April 4: *Caniaris*. [Foldout, with a short biographical note about the artist].

April 26: *Cy Twombly*. [Foldout].

> "Per qualche anno Twombly [...] non s'è servito altro che d'un'appuntita matita nera [...]. I quadri che Twombly espone ora sono assai più complessi (anche perché vi albeggia qua è là il colore), ma non per questo meno lievi. Ve n'è uno, molto grande, in cui abbiamo letto 'Sunset' ('Crepuscolo') e poniamo che sia il titolo, per quanto le parole che l'artista americano scarabocchia sulla tela abbiano un valore grafico, non semantico. [...] In un'altra opera leggiamo 'To Leonardo': è una dedica, più che un titolo. Il teorico delle macchie d'umidità non poteva non ricevere un omaggio da questo gentile macchiatore di lenzuola, o tovaglie, da questo ariele dell'inesprimibile che pure riesce a farsi intendere."
> (Bertolucci Attilio, "Mostre. Twombly alla Tartaruga," in *Telesera*, April 1960)

May 14: *Dino Basaldella*. [Foldout].

June 4: *Kounellis*. First solo show. [Foldout].

> "Kounellis consegue [...] precisione di rapporti risalendo ad una originaria esperienza anonima collettiva di ideografia geometrica monumentale ad una impressione tipografica del ritmo e del tempo interno su una superficie fisica irrilevante, ma trasposta a spazialità di pura funzione: il foglio su cui un ragazzo fa i compiti di scuola, e l'ingegnere i suoi progetti."

(Diacono Mario, "L'alfabeto di Kounellis," in *Quaderni* della Tartaruga, February 1961, n. pag.)

October 8: *Wood*. [Foldout, with a short biographical note about the artist].

November 3: *Burri, Consagra, De Kooning, Matta, Rothko*. [Foldout].

December 3: *Opere di piccolo formato*. Afro, Balla, Burri, Brauner, Brüning, Capogrossi, Bignardi, Caniaris, Consagra, Cascella, Corpora, Dorazio, Fioroni, Fontana, Franchina, Leoncillo, Kline, Kounellis, Mafai, Marca-Relli, Marotta, Mauri, Matta, Novelli, Perilli, Rotella, Pomodoro, Scarpitta, Scialoja, Scordia, Scanavino, Turcato, Twombly, Wood. [Foldout].

No Exact Date: publication of the monograph *Album: raccolta dei cataloghi 1957-1960*, edited by Galleria La Tartaruga, Rome 1960: the volume also includes a selection of the photographic documentation related to the solo shows held at the gallery from 1957 to 1960.

1961

February: publication of *Quaderni della Tartaruga*, edited by Plinio De Martiis, with texts in Italian, English, and French by Cesare Vivaldi, Mario Diacono, James Joyce, and reproductions of works by Giosetta Fioroni, Mimmo Rotella, Mario Schifano, Jannis Kounellis, Salvatore Scarpitta, Cy Twombly.

> "I quaderni della Tartaruga non sono in vendita; vengono inviati gratuitamente, in Italia e all'estero, a critici, pittori, gallerie, musei, collezionisti, ecc. Questa pubblicazione non ha carattere di periodicità".
> (No Author, colophon, in "Quaderni della Tartaruga", Rome, February 1961, n. pag.)

March 11: *Bignardi, Fioroni*. [Foldout].
March 23: *Mario Schifano*. [Foldout, with a short biographical note about the artist].

April 22: *Castellani e Manzoni*. On display are several extroflexions by Castellani, while Manzoni stages his *Sculture viventi*. [Foldout].

June 30: *Un punto di vista. Garrubba. Fotografie*. [Foldout].

November: *Kounellis, Schifano, Twombly*. [Foldout].

December: *Rauschenberg, Twombly, Kounellis, Tinguely, Schifano*. [Foldout].

s.d.e.: publication of the monograph with a limited edition *Cy Twombly. E una parafrasi per Cy Twombly*, written by Cesare Vivaldi, Edizioni La Tartaruga, Rome 1961.

1962

January: *Quadri di: Appel, Brooks, Marca-Relli, Matta.* [Foldout].

March 8: *Turcato.* [Foldout, with a text by Emilio Villa].

"La visione di Omero al quinto libro odisseico, viene spontanea in mente quando il pittore Turcato narra per noi qualche simbolico episodio del suo incessante periplo, in punta di piedi sopra la pelle tesa nell'Europa. Questa volta l'episodio accadde tra un treno e un altro, una notte, nella stazione fuligginosa di Charleroi, dove si potrebbe sceneggiare una discensio ad inferos. Gli oblò baluginanti dei treni lasciarono trapelare lussuose rosacee epidermidi di ninfe internazionali che scivolavano all'interno dello sleeping, povere anime. [...] e allora che cosa è questa pelle butterata sulle tavole di Turcato [...] se non il simbolo del compianto, del brivido, del terrore moderno? [...] la nostra pelle è in gioco. [...] che non siamo forse noi i sambartolomei della fantasia contemporanea?"
(Villa Emilio, No Title, in the foldout of the exhibition, Rome 1962, n. pag.)

April 3: *Shiraga.* [Foldout, with a text by Michel Tapié, and a biographical note about the artist].

"Ho assistito a delle riunioni di lavoro del gruppo Gutai. [...] In questo clima si è sviluppata l'esperienza artistica di Kazuo Shiraga, che probabilmente è una delle due o tre più forti personalità della giovane pittura in oriente."
(Tapié Michel, No Title, in the foldout of the exhibition, Rome 1962, n. pag.)

May: *La materia a Roma.* On display are works by: Franco Angeli, Alberto Burri, Tano Festa, Gino Marotta, Mimmo Rotella, Salvatore Scarpitta, Mario Schifano.

June 11: *Cy Twombly.* Exhibition held at the Galleria del Leone, Venice, and organized in collaboration with La Tartaruga. [Brochure].

December: *Fontana, Twombly, Francis.* At the end of the exhibition the gallery closes its location on Via del Babuino n. 196.

1963

February 9: the gallery relocates to Piazza del Popolo n. 3, Rome, and inaugurates its new location with *13 Pittori a Roma.* On display are works by: Franco Angeli, Umberto Bignardi, Tano Festa, Giosetta Fioroni, Jannis Kounellis, Renato Mambor, Fabio Mauri, Gastone Novelli, Achille Perilli, Mimmo Rotella, Peter Saul, Cesare Tacchi, Cy Twombly. [Invitation; Catalogue, with texts by Gillo Dorfles, Umberto Eco, Edoardo Sanguineti, Nanni Balestrini, Antonio Porta, Alfredo Giuliani, Elio Pagliarani, Cesare Vivaldi].

"Sta nascendo una nuova pittura, in Europa come in America, con connotati simili eppure diversi... Sta forse sorgendo una sorta di 'realismo di massa', un'arte che si serve degli stessi mezzi della civiltà di massa per tracciarne una satira spietata?"
(Vivaldi Cesare, *Verso un realismo di "massa,"* in the exhibition catalogue, Rome 1963, n. pag.)

March 6: *Twombly*. [Catalogue, with extracts from texts by Frank O' Hara, Palma Bucarelli, Emilio Villa, Franco Marino, Cesare Vivaldi, Manfredi De La Molte, Gillo Dolfles, Pierre Restany, and a list of the artist's exhibitions].

"Le scritture di Cy sono la creazione d'una strutturazione di spazi; sopra superfici divenute sempre più ampie, che oggi raggiungono persino le dimensioni di intere pareti, l'artista riesce a costruire persino un suo 'cosmo segnico,' fatto di frammenti, di esitazioni, di appunti, di parole [...]. Codesti elementi dispersi e aleggianti nel grande spazio bianco o lievemente colorato vengono a costituire quasi delle strane costellazioni: galassie, dove 'sistemi' in rapida espansione fluttuano entro una via lattea sena confini."
(Dorfles Gillo, No Title, in the exhibition catalogue, Rome 1963, n. pag.)

April 8: *Una mostra di tre giovani pittori romani. Lombardo, Mambor, Tacchi*. [Foldout; Catalogue, with a text in Italian and in English by Sergio Lombardo].

"La nostra pittura non è protesta, ma narrazione di fatti concreti e giudizio filtrato attraverso l'Erlebnis del nostro essere nel mondo tutti i giorni; è il recupero della coscienza in una civiltà dove ogni tipo di reazione emotiva normale o abnorme è scontata nell'uniformità automatica dei comportamenti tipici."
(Lombardo Sergio, No Title, in the exhibition catalogue, Rome 1963, n. pag.)

April 24: *Bignardi*. [Foldout, with a text in Italian and in English by Forrest Williams].

"Si legge nei quadri di Bignardi un processo di meditazione propedeutica che cerca di esplorare le varie potenzialità dal mondo dei mass-media e dall'iconografia della scienza. Il problema creativo è allora quello di stabilire una relazione tra queste potenzialità che si riferiscono in modi diversi al nostro mondo e quelle del linguaggio pittorico usuale. La soluzione è un particolare dialogo attivo tra i due ordini, mosso da un'emozione sostenuta e intensamente lirica."
(Williams Forrest, No Title, in the foldout of the exhibition, Rome 1963, n. pag.)

May 6: *Festa*. [Catalogue, with a text by Giorgio De Marchis].

"Questo riproporre l'oggetto come cosa e come immagine, come apparenza e come realtà, ne fa qualche cosa di ambiguo; alla certezza del conoscerlo si unisce il sentimento che sia annuncio d'altro, cosicché più giusto pare un riferimento alla pittura metafisica esplicito in certi titoli come 'Nostalgia dell'infinito,' e il tema stesso degli oggetti di mobilio è di gusto metafisico, ma soprattutto l'aria vagamente onirica di questi oggetti così solidi e spessi cui la copertura di colore, come il bianco porcellanoso dell'obelisco, dà un valore irreale proprio nella loro veste visibile. Lo stesso tema iconografico pone l'oggetto non solo come realtà percepita, ma come soglia, o come limite, di visione, di rivelazione: la porta, la finestra, lo specchio [...]. Il recupero dell'oggetto diviene recupero del mistero. Costruire si risolve ad evocare il senso nascosto dietro il reale."
(De Marchis Giorgio, No Title, in the exhibition catalogue, Rome 1963, n. pag.)

May 20: *Baruchello*. [Catalogue, with texts by Maurizio Bonicatti and Alain Jouffroy (in French)].

"Baruchello est ces rares artistes qui, aujourd'hui, tentent de nous introduire dans un espace libre de toute référence connue. Ses objects, et tout particulièrment ses tableaux, ouvrent une

porte nouvelle dans le monde des communications intersubjectives. Ils nous donnent autant à penser qu'à voir et à imaginer."
(Jouffroy Alain, No Title, in the exhibition catalogue, Rome 1963, n. pag.)
June 6: *Angeli*. [Catalogue, with texts by Nello Ponente and Mario Diacono].

"Angeli [...] resta in contatto dialettico con i simboli e le immagini, li sottrae all'abitudine e al conformismo. Una falce e martello, la mezza luna e la stella della libera Algeria, il lutto delle croci uncinate, la banale e ridicola inutilità dello N. PAG.Q.R., non vogliono più essere manifesti, forme di condizionamento, emblemi da guardare con la coda dell'occhio. Sono restituiti ai loro significati originari o, a dir meglio, ai loro valori, che sono soprattutto morali. La sovrapposizione di una tela trasparente, variamente colorata a seconda dei quadri, non è un alleggerimento della presenza di questi simboli, ma un mezzo per accostarsi ad essi con più attenzione, una pausa che induce una riflessione."
(Ponente Nello, No Title, in the exhibition catalogue, Rome 1963, n. pag.)

October 14: *Gouaches, disegni e grafica*. Braque - Ernst - Kandinskji - Le Corbusier - Matta - Moholy-Nagy - Rauschenberg - Schwitters - Severini - Twombly - De Kooning - Fontana - Kline - Rothko.

November 16: *Franz Kline*. On display are six oils on canvas and five oils on paper made between 1951 and 1956. [Catalogue, with an anonymous introduction, an extract from an interview with the artist, and a list of the works exhibited].

"La Tartaruga presentò Franz Kline per la prima volta in Europa nel febbraio 1958, due anni prima che la personale nel padiglione degli Stati Uniti alla Biennale di Venezia lo rivelasse al grande pubblico europeo. Oggi, un anno e mezzo dopo la morte dell'artista, ormai riconosciuto come uno dei massimi protagonisti della pittura contemporanea, la nostra galleria è lieta di presentare un gruppo di suoi dipinti, di cui quattro assolutamente inediti, in coincidenza con la grande retrospettiva ordinata presso la Galleria Civica d'Arte Moderna di Torino in collaborazione con il Museum of Modern Art di New York."
(Anonymous introduction, in the exhibition catalogue, Rome 1963, n. pag.)

December 21: *Peter Saul*. First solo show in Italy. [Catalogue, with a text by Cesare Vivaldi].

"Peter Saul è il più fluente e smagliante narratore di fiabe che conti oggi la nuova pittura. Nel suo volontario esilio europeo questo giovane americano si racconta – e racconta – instancabilmente le favole, le allegorie, i miti della civiltà di massa degli *States* raccogliendoli all'unico livello al quale possono iscriversi nella memoria poetica, quello infantile [...]. Questo spiega come egli possa usare alcuni ingredienti tipici della *pop art* (i personaggi dei fumetti, le confezioni dell'industria alimentare, le bottiglie di Coca cola, gli arnesi di uso quotidiano) per costruirsi un'arte che è l'opposto dell'oggettivismo 'brutale' dei Lichtenstein e dei Dine."
(Vivaldi Cesare, No Title, in the exhibition catalogue, Rome 1963, n. pag.)

1964

January 11: *Peter Brüning*. [Invitation; Catalogue, with texts by Manfred De La Motte and Pierre Restany].

"Per quanto l'opera di Brüning determini con precisione il suo stile e lo definisca costantemente nei suoi particolari di una emotività continua e aderente ai caratteri del colore che egli ama, cioè il rosso e le sue gamme e sfumature di segno, non si può dire che la sua pittura sia il frutto di riflessioni intellettuali o di calcolo tecnico. […] La funzione del colore conserva la natura di una sua intima vibrazione di ritmo che toglie ogni staticità alla composizione."
(No Author, "Mostre d'arte. Peter Brüning," in *Il Messaggero*, January 17, 1964)

February 1: *Tàpies*. On display are fourteen paintings, four drawings, four lithographs. [Poster; Catalogue, with a text by the artist, a biographical note, a list of exhibitions, and a bibliography about the artist].

"Viviamo in un mondo sommerso dalla tecnica, soffocato dai comforts. Viviamo continuamente *distratti* dimenticando le nostre più elementari radici e perfino i nostri istinti. […] Nella mia opera io cerco di aiutare l'uomo a superare questo stato di alienazione incorporando nella vita quotidiana oggetti che lo mettano in contatto, in modo tangibile, con i problemi ultimi e più profondi della nostra esistenza."
(Tàpies Antoni, No Title, in the exhibition catalogue, Rome 1964, n. pag.)

March 5: *Angeli, Bignardi, Festa, Fioroni, Kounellis, Lombardo, Mambor, Tacchi*. [Card].

April: participation in the *II Mostra mercato di arte contemporanea*, Florence, Palazzo Strozzi, with works by Franz Kline, Jannis Kounellis, Cy Twombly, Antoni Tàpies.

"La Tartaruga con Kline, Twombly, Kounellis, Tàpies. […] questa galleria ha il merito di aver suggerito per prima e da molti anni opere ed artisti che poi si sono affermati".
(Bovi Arturo, "Criteri più rigorosi per la mostra mercato", in *Il Messaggero*, March 22, 1964)

April 15: *J. Kounellis*. [Catalogue, with a text by Cesare Vivaldi].

"Il nuovo filone d'ancoraggio è rappresentato non più dalle rigide lettere e cifre, ma da elementi figurativi molto schematici, del tutto antinaturalistici. All'inizio forse anche più elementari dei vecchi motivi tipografici […], poco a poco il dato figurale è divenuto più ricco: un arcobaleno, la luna nelle sue diverse fasi, il porto del Pireo, il mare. Poco a poco Kounellis ha insomma acquisito fiducia in se stesso, nelle proprie possibilità e nella sicurezza del proprio cammino di pittore e si è sempre meglio liberato da ogni eccessiva preoccupazione di controllo formale. In quel settore della gioventù italiana che personalmente mi sta cuore e che considero il più interessante […]. Kounellis ha un posto tutto suo e di notevolissimo rilievo."
(Cesare Vivaldi, No Title, in the exhibition catalogue, Rome 1964, n. pag.)

June: *Angeli, Ceroli, Festa, Fioroni, Lombardo, Tacchi*.

June: *Catalogo 1* is published, with a collection of texts and images related to La Tartaruga's activity.

"CATALOGO – S.m. Enumerazione di più oggetti in qualche ordine. Dire. Raccogliere. Scegliere. Catalogo per ordine alfabetico, per ordine di materie. Catalogo numerato – Compito, imperfetto – Bene o male ordinato, critico, ragionato. Può il catalogo essere l'arida enumerazione, può portare schiarimenti non brevi, notizie pellegrine, anche ragionamenti profondi."
(Anonymous introductory text, in *Catalogo 1*, Rome 1964, p. 1)

October 19: *Premio "La Tartaruga."* On display are works by: Carla Accardi, Franco Angeli, Gianfranco Baruchello, Umberto Bignardi, Tano Festa, Giosetta Fioroni, Sergio Lombardo, Jannis Kounellis, Renato Mambor, Titina Maselli, Fabio Mauri, Mimmo Rotella, Pasquale Santoro, Mario Schifano, Cesare Tacchi, Piero D'Orazio, Achille Perilli, Antonio Sanfilippo, Peter Saul, Cy Twombly. Vince Achille Perilli. [Invitation].

"Una notizia sul Premio Tartaruga che viene assegnato in questi giorni. [...] Una previsione? Amara: gli artisti giovani ci lasciano progetti sull'America, New York è la Parigi di cinquanta anni fa e non vi si muore neanche di fame. Troppo allettante quindi, ma certo è un peccato."
(Frosini Deanna, "Galleristi in galleria De Martiis," in *Nazione Sera*, October 30, 1964)

November 11: *Ceroli.* [Card].

"Le sue grandi sigle, i suoi immensi e armoniosi 'Sì', 'No', orologi e ricalchi rilevati o incisi – sempre nel legno – di immagini della reclame, dando l'idea di un mondo lilliput, aggirantesi in mezzo ai mass media giganteschi. Le lettere *zeta*, *o*, *a*, *esse*, [...] sono alte quasi una persona e si presentano davvero in modo impressionante: le lettere perdono la loro apparente innocuità, acquistando invece una vis di segreto e misterioso maleficio, di ingannevole perfettibilità."
(Venturoli Marcello, "Tre artisti cugini dei pop," in *Le Ore*, December 1964)

1965

January 11: *Pascali*. First solo show. [Card, with a text by Cesare Vivaldi].

"Nel 1964, con i 'rilievi' in parte ora esposti alla *Tartaruga*, è approdato a una terra tutta sua, [...] una nuova conferma delle possibilità europee, anzi italiane, di superare la *pop-art* per creare una pittura e una scultura più complesse, più attente alla molteplicità del reale, se mi è lecito dirlo più 'colte' [...]. Pascali ci restituisce un Colosseo, dei ruderi di colonne, un muro di tufo che sono sì una satira della romanità di cartapesta, ma anche un omaggio ironico-commosso a un passato, a una tradizione non tanto facilmente sopprimibili."
(Vivaldi Cesare, No Title, in the card of the exhibition, Rome 1965, n. pag.)

January 17: screening of three short films by Taylor Mead.

"'I AM A VEDETTE.' ripeteva queste parole, senza saper aggiungere altro, quando si è presentato a Plinio De Martiis che dirige la galleria 'La Tartaruga' [...] e porgeva un biglietto sul quale c'era scritto solo l'indirizzo della galleria, avuto a Parigi da Mimmo Rotella [...]. Alla 'Tartaruga.' l'altro giorno, per la prima presentazione romana delle sue pellicole, aveva invitato quindici persone. Riaccese le luci, nell'improvvisata saletta privata, c'erano una cinquantina di spettatori, tra cui Moravia, Elsa Morante, Michelangelo Antonioni, Barbara Steel, Dacia Maraini."
(Locatelli Luigi, "I cinematografi 'pop' hanno ripreso fiato," in *Il Giorno*, January 28, 1965)

January 30: *Giosetta Fioroni*. [Card].

"Benché impercettibilmente e talvolta col pericolo di subito raggelarsi in imprimiture più nette e polemiche, la tavolozza lavagna e grigiofumo della Fioroni [...] ammorbidisce le

sagome, le fa posare sulla superficie neutra [...] con una tenuità ed un'eleganza maestre: per cui si avverte in lei la lunga lezione italiana del tono, l'amore per la bella pittura, per le scadenze in cui nulla si ripeta con monotonia: un severo languore, una dolcezza senza smancerie, uno sguardo fermo ma non impietoso."
(Venturoli Marcello, "La dolcezza delle imprimiture," in *Le Ore*, February 1965)

February 18: *Una camera da letto di Balla*. [Card, with a text by Maurizio Calvesi].

"Rimane da constatare che, accanto ai triangoli, qui troviamo un nuovo motivo, non più ripetuto da Balla: quello della scacchiera, e anzi della scacchiera deformata, quasi fosse proiettata su una superficie ondulata [...] il proprietario stesso della fabbrica di mobili che Balla [...] trascinò con il suo entusiasmo in un'impresa commercialmente infelice. La camera non fu mai venduta e la produzione subì un arresto."
(Calvesi Maurizio, No Title, in the card of the exhibition, Rome 1965, n. pag.)

February 27: *Catalogo 2* is published, with texts and images of the activities held at La Tartaruga from 1964 to 1965 (texts by Cesare Vivaldi, Nanni Balestrini, Maurizio Calvesi, and anonymous write-up about the "Premio La Tartaruga").

March 27: *Cesare Tacchi*. First solo exhibition. [Card].

"Il segno scorre fluido a tracciare la figura di un giovane assiso in una poltrona delineato con tratto bianco sulla negativa del nero ed il fondo della superficie del quadro, intorno all'immagine, è tutta ricoperta di una sottile stoffa a fiorami, giallina, mentre l'altra poltrona che campeggia solitaria sul fondo di un diverso quadro è tutta di un rosso fiammante che dà al carminio. Il nudo di donna distesa, di spalle, in una successiva opera è chiuso nella patina aurea come la vittima di Goldfinger. Non si può negare a Tacchi una sua personale sensibilità e originalità inventiva di carattere lievemente ironico nella polemica che si cela sotto la sua opera e che affiora chiaramente dalle immagini."
(Bovi Arturo, "Mostre d'arte. Tacchi," in *Il Messaggero*, April 6, 1965)

April 21: *Renato Mambor*. First solo exhibition. [Card].

"Il suo disegno traccia i contorni degli oggetti a larghi piani e con colori chiari, ben netti e spaziati. Sia che evochi alla immaginazione la figura di un enorme cavallo verde zebrato dinanzi alle rovine di Roma, sia che profili l'immagine della guardia pontificia come un'ombra chiara accanto ad un fiorito ananas o che un gigantesco calabrone volteggi su una macchina in sosta o che una mano plani dal cielo su un rustico tavolo. Le sue opere fanno l'effetto di grandi decalcomanie portate su tono poetico."
(Bovi Arturo, "Mambor," in *Il Messaggero*, May 3, 1965)

May 6: *Achille Perilli*. On display are eleven paintings and four sculptures made between 1961 and 1964. [Invitation; Catalogue, with letters from Alfredo Giuliani and Elio Pagliarani to the artist, a biographical note, a list of the artist's exhibitions, publications about the artist, and a list of the works exhibited].

"Nelle sue opere dal '61 al '64 oggi esposte alla Tartaruga Perilli ci riporta le sue composizioni della penultima Biennale. [...] La sua continua impaginazione di gusto ritmico e filmico [...]

ha indubbiamente un certo vago sapore di carattere orientale nel succedersi e contrapporsi in misura lirica del segno pittorico sullo schermo della tela."
(Bovi Arturo, "Mostre d'Arte," in *Il Messaggero*, May 18, 1965)

June: *Angeli, Ceroli, Festa, Fioroni, Lombardo, Mambor, Kounellis, Schifano, Tacchi.*

June 10: *Catalogo 3* is published, with texts and images related to the exhibition activity starting in March 1965 (texts by Marisa Volpi, Maurizio Calvesi, Carla Lonzi, Gillo Dorfles, Guido Ballo).

October 22: *Festa*. [Card].

"I quadri odierni, vedono una grande immagine che occupa tutto il quadro (un cielo o un'opera di Michelangiolo) a cui si sovrappone una serie di piccole immagini inquadrate in zone, come lo scorrimento verticale di una pellicola. Giocano sul doppio piano grande-piccolo, intero-particolare: sono veri 'film a soggetto.' Festa viene così a criticare l'ingigantimento polemico dell'immagine, ma anche lo spezzettarsi del frammento, con una immagine che è insieme una e tante."
(Fagiolo dell'Arco Maurizio, "Un pittore-regista alla 'Tartaruga,'" in *L'Avanti*, November 1965)

November 12: *Castellani*. [Card].

December 10: *Mario Ceroli*. [Card].

"Ceroli, ai suoi inizi, ha ricorso ad immagini desunte dal mondo eroico della nostra storia figurativa [...]. Devo dire però che preferisco quest'ultime cose esposte alla 'Tartaruga' che tentano un più vivo inserto nel mondo delle immagini. C'è sempre qualcosa di sonoro, di fragrante, di grezzo, vorrei dire di umano e di antico nelle ben connesse costruzioni in legno grezzo. La sua 'Scala' sembra un pezzo della gradinata del teatro Farnese di Parma, la sua 'Casa' la vecchia e rozza biblioteca di un convento. E le invenzioni formali delle sagome delle figure non sono mai prive di una certa metafisica nobiltà nel loro stringato rigore. Ma è soprattutto nell'intelligente recupero di ancestrali e sane doti artigianesche che consiste il merito maggiore della carpenteria di Ceroli."
(Briganti Giulio, "Lo scultore con la sega elettrica," in *L'Espresso*, January 9, 1966)

1966

January 20: *Gerd Richter*. First solo show in Italy. [Poster].

"Il pittore tedesco Gerd Richter che espone alla Tartaruga, copia, con l'ausilio del proiettore, in bianco e nero con la più tradizionale tecnica ad olio, le fotografie desunte dalla cronaca aggiungendovi la sfocatura e l'incertezza tipica delle istantanee prese con il flash. Dopo quasi un secolo le cose si sono capovolte: non è più fotografia a rifare la pittura ma è la pittura ad ispirarsi con fedele minuziosità alla fotografia."
(Trucchi Lorenza, "Le mostre di Roma. Richter alla Tartaruga," in *Momento Sera*, February 19, 1966)

February 5: *Lombardo*. First solo show. [Poster].
"Alla Galleria 'La Tartaruga' in piazza del Popolo una mostra di Sergio Lombardo […]. Egli propone un racconto continuo, grafico ed esemplificato della immagine umana appiattita e ritagliata nel segno e nei moduli del colore che le danno un accento diverso di situazioni, non di approfondimento interiore; di situazioni di fatto che si rivelano sempre più meccanicistiche, statiche o dinamiche, di un'esistenza che tende a indicare l'uomo sotto un comune denominatore, come di essere sottoposto a una cronaca del fatto che lo determina, gli conferisce una tipologia, nulla più che una 'sagoma' fra 'tante.'"
(Bovi Arturo, "Mostre d'arte. Lombardo," in *Il Messaggero*, February 23, 1966)

March 2: *Capogrossi e Fontana*. [Card].

April 18: *Ceroli, Fioroni, Kounellis, Tacchi, Rotella, Twombly*.

April 27: *Rotella. Decollages - reportages 1954-1966*. [Poster].

May 13: *Müller-Brittnau*. [Invitation].

June 10: *Roma 1966 realtà dell'immagine*. On display are works by: Franco Angeli, Mario Ceroli, Tano Festa, Giosetta Fioroni, Ettore Innocente, Jannis Kounellis, Sergio Lombardo, Renato Mambor, Pino Pascali, Cesare Tacchi. [Poster].

June 10: *Catalogo 3* is published, with texts by Marisa Volpi and Giorgio De Marchis.

September: *Castellani, Ceroli, Festa, Kounellis, Rotella, Schifano, Twombly*.

November 3: *Jacquet, Lichtestein, Rauschenberg, Rosenquist, Rotella, Warhol*. [Invitation].

November 19: *Ceroli*. [Catalogue, with a text by Maurizio Calvesi, a letter from Goffredo Parise to the artist, and a biographical note about the artist].

"Caro Mario, […] sono molto contento di scriverti questa 'lettera – trattatello – conversazione su alcune forme di passione espressiva'; lettera di auguri in occasione della nuova mostra dovuta non soltanto al tuo quasi crudele accanimento espressivo, ma, bisogna dirlo (anche se vuole a tutti i costi che non si dica e se si dice protesta come un estroso volatile) alla bruciante passione 'visiva' di Plinio De Martiis che non si limita ad esporti, ma, da buon coreografo, soprattutto ti esibisce. Giusto, naturale, fatale show perché il vostro è l'incontro di due passioni: la sua appunto 'visiva' o se vogliamo scenica, coreografica, registica, la tua espressiva ed esibizionistica. Sì, proprio come un grande attore in mano ad un regista."
(Parise Goffredo, *Letterina su alcune passioni equivalenti nei lavori in legno*, in the exhibition catalogue, Rome 1967, n. pag.)

December 15: *Baruchello, Ceroli, Festa, Fioroni, Kounellis, Lombardo, Mambor, Pascali, Tacchi, Twombly*.

1967

January 9: *Piero Manzoni.* [Invitation].

January 21: *Mario Schifano.* [Invitation; Poster].

"Anche in quest'ultima mostra alla Tartaruga – la prima *après la déluge* – tornano gli alberi, il grande amore di Schifano. Alberi e alberelli visti dietro schermi di vetro o di rhodoid smerigliati. O intravisti con la morbida anima di un malato o di un prigioniero. E tornano i titoli infantili o gratuiti, da sillabario o da muraglia, da asilo o da latrina: 'Ossigeno, ossigeno,' 'Approssimativamente,' 'Fu vero amore.' Sovraesposte, o negative. Agli eroi del 'Futurismo rivisitato' Stefano ha lasciato soltanto i cappotti, li ha succhiati. Ecco i trucchi seducenti di uno studente svogliato! [...] Con la sua aria sorvegliata e assente Schifano gioca a sporcarsi, a sfregiarsi le mani. C'è un desiderio prepotente di mescolare vita e arte, diavoli e santi, cronaca rosa e nera."
(Sinisgalli Leonardo, "Le vetrofanie di Schifano," in *Il Tempo-Illustrato*, February 1963)

March 6: *Eliseo Mattiacci.* First solo show. [Invitation].

April 3: *Cy Twombly.* [Invitation].

April 8-28: *8 pittori romani. Angeli, Ceroli, Festa, Fioroni, Kounellis, Pascali, Schifano, Tacchi.* Exhibition held at the Galleria de' Foscherari, Bologna, and produced in collaboration with La Tartaruga. [Catalogue published by Galleria de' Foscherari, Bologna 1967, with a text by Maurizio Calvesi, a list of the works exhibited, a list of the exhibitions of each of the artists, and a newsletter edited by Pietro Bonfiglioli].

"Scuola di Piazza del Popolo, ovvero i Pop romani: sono infatti le due definizioni più frequenti anche se, ovviamente, la seconda odiosa agli interessati, come qualsiasi etichetta genericamente cumulativa e, in sostanza, impropria. [...] Raggruppare certi nomi oggi che ognuno ormai, come naturale, va sempre più per la sua strada, e sempre più è chiamato a rispondere come singolo del suo personale bilancio, è sempre più un omaggio alla 'Tartaruga' [...]. E raggruppare certi nomi non si può senza pensar anche ad altri, ad esempio all''antefatto' di Mimmo Rotella, [...] il gusto di certi materiali, legno o stoffa, la dimensione artigianale, tutto questo ha corrisposto non ad una traduzione, ma ad una tradizione, e soprattutto ad una condizione, autenticamente italiana."
(Calvesi Maurizio, *8 pittori romani*, in the exhibition catalogue, Galleria de' Foscherari, Bologna 1967, n. pag.)

May 2: *Ettore Innocente.*

"Ettore Innocente, trentaduenne romano, espone alla Tartaruga: è già una indicazione precisa di un gusto e di una situazione [...], quella di un'arte che, abbandonato il quadro di cavalletto e la scultura di piedistallo, costruisce oggetti con i più vari materiali e con i più vari simboli occupando lo spazio in un modo teatrale, in una sorta di spettacolo al quale partecipa anche il visitatore."
(No Author, "Ettore Innocente," in *L'Espresso Sera*, May 1967)

June 13: *Paolo Icaro*. [Invitation].

December 4: *Alberto Burri*. On display are works made between 1949 and 1956. [Invitation].

"LA TARTARUGA ha iniziato la propria stagione in bellezza, presentando uno scelto gruppo di opere di Burri, datate tra il 1949 e 1956. […] Burri ha voluto riproporre al pubblico romano, che è stato per anni così scettico sul suo nome, questi vecchi quadri di un'importanza ormai storica. E sono opere che avevamo negli occhi e nel cuore ma che a rivederle ci hanno ridato una intatta ed intensa emozione."
(Brandi Cesare, "Burri alla Tartaruga," in *Il Punto*, December 1967)

1968

February 10: *Un quadro e venti serigrafie di Andy Warhol per "Che" Guevara*. [Invitation; Poster].

"Warhol ha ricostruito questo processo di usura e assimilazione dell'immagine: ha ripetuto molte volte la stessa fotografia, accostando all'insieme il particolare ingrandito della testa del Che […]. Ha collegato il processo dell'usura tecnica (il cliclé sempre più logoro) con quello dell'usura psicologica (il dileguare della notizia, l'emergere di un significato profondo) e con quello della decomposizione della salma. Da questo triplice disgregarsi del documento visivo ha fatto nascere uno schema ritmico cadenzato come quello di una trenodia o di una laude […]. Prima ancora del mito dell'eroe è nato il mito del martire: così la sua immagine si collega automaticamente (possibile che gli esperti della C.I.A. non ci avessero pensato?) con quella, che tutti ci portiamo dentro dalla prima infanzia, del Cristo deposto. Ancora più pietosa perché intorno alla salma non v'è la Madonna e la Maddalena, ma gli aguzzini e i carnefici."
(Argan Giulio Carlo, "Cronache. Il sudario del 'che,'" in *L'astrolabio*, March 17, 1968)

March 16: *Franco Angeli*. [Invitation].

"Queste recenti opere […] sono la conferma di quel primitivo rifiuto della maniera 'pop' per l'accoglimento di quell'invito all'oggetto e alla vita di tutti che era un po' il messaggio e un po' la lezione dell'esperienza nordamericana. E credo che alla distanza il suo aver lasciato lievitare le idee e il giudizio storico-sociale nel bel mezzo dell'oggettivismo 'pop' qualifichi e renda più durevole la sua esperienza di italiano. […] Segnali, impronte e emblemi Franco Angeli li ha tratti dall'iconografia dell'ambiente americano come dell'ambiente romano. Li ha scelti, montati, messi in evidenza plastica come 'segni' del potere […]. L'efficacia di queste opere ultime di Angeli è grande. Resta un che di provvisorio nel velo di nailon che forse meriterebbe una soluzione pittorica più duratura come materiale e più organica la sutura dell'immagine."
(Micacchi Dario, "Nella nera terra bruciata l'impronta del dollaro," in *L'Unità*, March 1968)

March: *Cy Twombly*. Retrospective exhibition with works from 1954 to 1968. [Invitation].

"Ebbene se non ci fossero le date queste opere sembrerebbero tutte di una stessa stagione. Twombly è un artista senza progresso e senza decadenza: più fisso che coerente, immobile quasi per meglio registrare la febbre incessante delle proprie sensazioni. Da indefesso diarista egli scrive con un segno, incisivo come un bisturi e sensibile come l'ago di un sismografo, un privatissimo memoriale, per metà angelico e per metà luciferino."

(Trucchi Lorenza, "Twombly alla Tartaruga," in *Momento Sera*, March 22, 1968)

April 5: *Cesare Tacchi.*

"Tacchi dichiara che i suoi 'oggetto-quadri' sono delle idee (impossibili: sedia con l'acqua, letto ad acqua mossa, poltrona chiusa, cornice senza quadro, ecc.); poi dichiara che 'l'idea modifica la struttura,' cioè gli 'oggetto-quadri' modificano le strutture; infine dichiara che le strutture sono le idee assimilate ed elaborate; cioè, in ultima analisi, le idee modificano le idee, i quadri modificano se stessi. [...] 'Lo spettatore si troverà quindi a percepire questi oggetto-quadri sensitivamente e dovrà più avvertire che guardare, provare cioè sensazioni.'"
(Calvesi Maurizio, *Credimi, non viene dall'anima ...*, unpublished typescript, April 1968, n. pag.)

May 6-31: *Teatro delle Mostre*. Actions and installations by: Giosetta Fioroni, Ciro Ciriacono, Giulio Paolini, Ettore Innocente, Emilio Prini, Paolo Icaro, Pier Paolo Calzolari, Franco Angeli, Enrico Castellani, Paolo Scheggi, Mario Ceroli, Cesare Tacchi, Alighiero Boetti, Gino Marotta, Renato Mambor, Fabio Mauri, Laura Grisi, Sylvano Bussotti, Loreto Soro, Nanni Balestrini, Goffredo Parise. [Poster; Catalogue, published by Marcatré-Lerici editore, Rome 1968, with a text by Maurizio Calvesi and captions by Achille Bonito Oliva].

"Il carattere di oggettualità dell'opera, in quanto rinuncia al principio di rappresentazione della realtà, è sempre fuori discussione; invece l'oggettualità come presenza fisica, occupante, pregnante esaurita in se stessa, è controvertita da una ricerca di strutture o di processi. Il tempo non è recuperato come arresto o come flusso, ma come processo: l'opera, in quanto esperienza, porta insita in se stessa il tempo della propria processualità, la propria cadenza temporale, direi, ed è questa che è emersa come perno di una nuova struttura. [...] Un'esperienza quale è illustrata in questo libro non ambisce ad essere totale, abbracciante, e in quanto tale spettacolare, ma cerca un minimo denominatore comune con il teatro, nell'elemento dell'azione e nell'esplicita temporaneità dei suoi processi."
(Calvesi Maurizio, *Arte tempo*, in the exhibition catalogue, Marcatré-Lerici editore, Rome 1968, n. pag.)

June 5: *Gianfranco Fini: Il grande schermo.*

"Una parete e ventiquattro televisori. Audio spenti e accesi per due ore di seguito sullo stesso canale. Risultato: ossessione sincrona di immagini scorporate, frazioni di gesti, storie senza senso. Allucinazione visiva di un unico grande schermo."
(No Author, "Videopittura e arte quotidiana," in *Domina*, no. 5, July 1968)

June 11: *Gianfranco Baruchello: Finanziaria Artiflex.* [Invitation].

"*Finanziaria Artiflex* di Baruchello, ossia la vendita, con tanto di commessa e cassa automatica, di scatole sigillate contenenti monete da diecimila lire: le scatole erano vendute per cinquemila lire."
(Trucchi Lorenza, "Il festival della disobbedienza," in *Europa* 23, June 22, 1968)

June 12: *Gianfranco Baruchello: Sala d'attesa Artiflex.*

"L'effetto sul pubblico era di sorpresa, di evasione, di freschezza, finché si finiva con il partecipare al gioco, quasi ritornando all'infanzia."
(Trucchi Lorenza, "Il festival della disobbedienza," in *Europa* 23, June 22, 1968)

October: closing of the gallery's location in Piazza del Popolo no. 3.

1969

February 28: the gallery is relocated to Via Principessa Clotilde n. 1/A, Rome, and the new location is inaugurated with the exhibition *Archivio (1954-1969)*. On display are photographs from the Archivio La Tartatuga. [Invitation].

May: *Giulio Paolini*. [Invitation].

1970

February 28: *Cy Twombly*. [Card].

March 14: *Tano Festa. I quadri privati*. [Card].

April 15: *Enrico Castellani. Spartito*. [Invitation].

May 6: *M. Caio Garrubba*. [Invitation].

May 19: *Mario Ceroli*. [Card].

June 25: *Angeli, Castellani, Ceroli, Festa, Fioroni, Fontana, Rotella, Scheggi, Twombly*. [Card].

November 10: *Giosetta Fioroni. Laguna*. [Card].

December 4: *A. Burri. Litografie e serigrafie*. [Card].

December 18: *Rigore e utopia a Milano*. On display are works by: Getullio Alviani, Agostino Bonalumi, Enrico Castellani, Lucio Fontana, Piero Manzoni, Paolo Scheggi. [Card].

1971

February 15: *Jannis Kounellis. Lettere del 1960*. [Card].

March 5: *Gianfranco Notargiacomo. Le nostre divergenze*. [Card].

March 26: *Vincenzo Agnetti. Ritratti e Paesaggi*. [Card].

April 16: *Mario Ceroli*. [Card].

May 18: *Enea Ferrari*. At the end of the exhibition the gallery closes its location on Via Principessa Clotilde n. 1/A. [Card].

1974

April 9: the gallery moves to Via Ripetta n. 22, Rome, and it inaugurates its new location with the exhibition *Una favola di Alberto Boatto con musiche di Sylvano Bussotti e tavole di Giosetta Fioroni*. Voice: Paolo Bonacelli; Sound: Renato Marinelli. [Invitation].

April 10: *Enrico Castellani*.

May 5: *Tano Festa*.

May 21: *Paolo Cotani*. [Invitation].

June 11: *Gianfranco Notargiacomo*. At the end of the exhibition the gallery closes its location on Via Ripetta n. 22. [Invitation].

December 19: the gallery relocates to Pompeo Magno n. 6/b, Rome, and inaugurates its new location with the exhibition *Marcello Aste. Il posto dove tramonta il sole*. [Invitation].

1975

January 16: *Cesare Tacchi*. [Invitation].

February 10-13: *Quattro concerti. Akerman, Curran, Giammarco, Iannacone, Nebbiosi, Schiaffini*. [Foldout; Catalogue, with a text by Alvin Curran and with anonymous texts].

February 22: *Antonello Agliotti e Memè Perlini. Smettere di giocare nella strada*. Scenic-pictorial action. [Foldout].

February 26: *Ettore Spalletti*. [Foldout].

March 25: *Davide Mosconi*. Concert. [Foldout].

April 14-18: *Parlare e scrivere*. Exhibition curated by Renato Barilli, with debates, talks, screenings, reproductions of audiotapes, produced in collaboration with the Archivio Denza of Brescia. Participating artists: Vincenzo Accame, Vincenzo Agnetti, Arcelli & Comini, Ugo Carrega, Bruno Di Bello, Giuliano Giuliani, Ketty La Rocca, Lora, Matz, Plinio Mesciulam, Martino and Anna Oberto, Elio Pagliarani, Luca Patella, Edoardo Sanguineti, Tonino, Cesare Zavattini. [Foldout; Catalogue, with a text by Renato Barilli].

May 26: *Camera 3*. Super 8 mm by Luigi Barzini, Anna Carini, Annabella Miscuglio. [Foldout].

June 3-6: *Corpus Scripsit*. Reading of poetic texts, curated by Nanni Cagnone. [Foldout].

November 13: *Nove quadri e una scultura*. On display are works by: Franco Angeli, Enrico Castellani, Mario Ceroli, Tano Festa, Jannis Kounellis, Pino Pascali, Mimmo Rotella, Salvatore Scarpitta, Mario Schifano, Cy Twombly. [Invitation].

December 15: *Nuove forme sonore*. Concert with: Luciano Berio, Sylvano Bussotti, Marianne Eckstein, Michelle Jannacone, Michiko Hirayama, Gianfranco Pernaiachi, Stefano Renoso, Scelsi, Giancarlo Schiaffini, Frances Marie Uitti. [Poster].

1976

January 15: *Claudio Parmiggiani. Theatrum orbi*. [Invitation].

February 6: *Gianfranco Notargiacomo. Famiglia famiglia*. [Invitation].

March 12: *Mario Ceroli*. [Invitation].

April 7: *Kounellis 1960*. [Invitation].

April 29: *Pino Pascali*. On display are works from 1968. [Invitation].

June 4: *Scarpitta 1958*. [Invitation].

November 25: *Ennio Tamburi. Vernissage*. [Invitation].

December 10: *Franco Angeli*. [Invitation].

1977

February 2: *Andrea Barzini*. Screening of three Super 8s: *Un chant d'amour*, 1976; *Parco, 172-1976; Mente catta mente chiara (immagini Parco Lambro)*, 1976. [Poster].

February 15: *Cesare Tacchi. La didattica in galleria*. [Poster].

February 16: *Galluzzi, Bruno, Carneo*. Tre films. [Poster].

April 21: *Taylor Mead*. Screening of the film *Diaries of Taylor Mead*. [Poster].

December: *Laboratorio di poesia. Regole del ritmo e tecniche della versificazione*. Workshop curated by Elio Pagliarani, with: Rosario Romero, Antonio De Rose, Guido Galeno, Plateo Danilo, Chiara Scalesse, Edoardo Albinati, Emilio Villa. [Poster].

1978

January 26: *Marco Dolcetta. Sentieri interrotti*. Screening of Super 8 with music by Claudio Giusti and Tito Rinesi. [Poster].

February 1: *Andrea Barzini. Peggio di così*. Screening of Super 8. [Poster].

February 3: *Tre libri d'artista*. Presentation of the books: *Pantomima* by Marco Gastini, *Sei illustrazioni per gli scritti sull'Arte antica di J. J. Winckelmann* by Giulio Paolini, *L'arte è una scienza esatta* by Claudio Parmiggiani; all of them published in 1977 by Franco Mello and Giorgio Persano. [Poster].

April 13: *Jannis Kounellis*. [Invitation].

May 3: *Franco Piruca*. First solo show in Rome. [Invitation; Brochure, with texts by the artist].

June 22: *Laboratorio di poesia*. Reading workshop curated by Elio Pagliarani, to bring the year's activity to a conclusion. When the exhibition ends the gallery closes its location on Via Pompeo Magno no. 6/b. [Poster].

1980

March 3: the gallery relocates to Piazza Miglianelli no. 25, Rome, and inaugurates its new location with *Sei pittori*; the show is transferred from April to May of the same year to the Galleria de' Foscherari, Bologna. On display are works by: Alberto Abate, Stefano Di Stasio, Salvatore Marrone, Nino Panarello, Franco Piruca, Piero Pizzi Cannella. [Catalogue of the exhibition held in Rome, with an anonymous text; Catalogue of the exhibition held in Bologna, with a text by Maurizio Calvesi].

April 16: *Di Stasio*. Exhibition produced in collaboration with the Galleria Contini, Venice. [Invitation].

May 21: *Ligas*. Exhibition organized in collaboration with the Galleria Contini, Venice. [Invitation].

October 18: *Abate, Di Stasio, Marrone, Piruca*. Exhibition produced in collaboration with the Galleria Contini, Venice. [Invitation].

November 21: *Abate, Di Stasio, Marrone, Panarello, Piruca*. Exhibition produced in collaboration with the Galleria Contini, Venice. [Invitation].

1981

February 14: *Bulzatti, Gandolfi, Ligas*. Exhibition produced in collaboration with the Galleria Contini, Venice. [Invitation].

March 14: *Buscagli*. Exhibition produced in collaboration with the Galleria Contini, Venice. [Invitation].

April 6: *Franco Piruca*. Exhibition produced in collaboration with the Galleria Contini, Venice. [Invitation; Catalogue, with a text by the artist].

November 6: *6 poeti leggono 6 poeti*. Event produced in collaboration with the Galleria Contini, Venice. [Card; Catalogue, with an anonymous text and with poems by Milo de Angelis, Roberto

Mussapi, Amelia Rosselli, Maurizio Guercini, Alessandro Ceni, Ivano Fermini].

November 20: *Mario Schifano*. On display are paintings from 1961. Exhibition produced in collaboration with the Galleria Contini, Venice. [Card].

1982

January 15: *Mario Ceroli. Opere recenti*. Exhibition produced in collaboration with the Galleria Contini, Venice, and was then trasferred on January 19 to the Galleria de' Foscherari, Bologna, and on January 21 to the Studio Marconi, Milan. [Invitation; Catalogue, with a text by Maurizio Calvesi].

March 19: *Disegni: D'Argenta, Di Stasio, Gandolfi, Ligas, Piruca*. Exhibition produced in collaboration with the Galleria Contini, Venice [Catalogue, with a text by Maurizio Calvesi].

May 14: *Guido Ceronetti. L'impazienza di Giobbe*. A reading by Guido Ceronetti and a conversation about his Old Testament work. Exhibition held at the Galleria Contini, Venice, in collaboration with La Tartaruga. [Catalogue, with a text by Maurizio Guercini and with extracts from works by Guido Ceronetti].

1983

March 10: *Stefano Di Stasio*. [Invitation].

April 12: *La Scuola Romana (dal 1928 al 1933)*. Exhibition produced in collaboration with the Galleria Marino, Rome. On display are works by: Corrado Cagli, Emanuele Cavalli, Giampaolo Di Cocco, Stefano Ianni, Pericle Fazzini, Walter Lazzaro, Mario Mafai, Renato Marino Mazzacurati, Raphael, Scipione, Alberto Ziveri. [Invitation; Card; Catalogue, with the republication of texts by Dario Durbè, Libero de Libero, Roberto Longhi, and with a letter written by Scipione to Mazzacurati and poems by Giuseppe Ungaretti and by Scipione].

April 28: *Amelia Rosselli legge Sandro Penna*. Exhibition produced in collaboration with the Galleria Marino, Rome. [Invitation].

10 May: *Bulzatti, Ligas*. Exhibition produced in collaboration with the Galleria Marino, Rome. [Invitation].

June 9: *Roma 1960: la Scuola di Piazza del Popolo*. Exhibition produced in collaboration with the Galleria Marino, Rome. On display are works by: Franco Angeli, Mario Ceroli, Tano Festa, Giosetta Fioroni, Jannis Kounellis, Fabio Mauri, Pino Pascali, Mimmo Rotella, Salvatore Scarpitta, Mario Schifano, Cesare Tacchi. [Invitation; Catalogue, with a text by Plinio De Martiis].

July 30: *Bulzatti, Di Stasio, Gandolfi, Ligas, Piruca*. Exhibition held at the Galleria Monti, Macerata, and produced in collaboration with La Tartaruga. [Foldout].

October 16: *Stefano Di Stasio*. Exhibition held at the Galleria Monti, Macerata, and produced in collaboration with La Tartaruga. [Catalogue, with texts by Maurizio Calvesi and Italo Tomassoni].

1984

January: publication of *La Tartaruga. Quaderno 1*, edited by Plinio De Martiis, Rome 1984, with texts by Marisa Volpi, Maurizio Calvesi, Stefano Di Stasio, Franco Piruca, Roberto Vidali.

January 4: *5 quadri e una scultura*. On display are works by: Aurelio Bulzatti, Stefano Di Stasio, Paola Gandolfi, Marco Gozzi, Piero Ligas, Alessandro Marrone. Exhibition produced in collaboration with the Galleria Marino, Rome. [Invitation].

February 7: *Aurelio Bulzatti*. Exhibition produced in collaboration with the Galleria Marino, Rome. [Invitation; Catalogue published as *La Tartaruga. Quaderno 2*, with a text by Maria Silvia Farci].

March 9: *Franco Piruca*. Exhibition produced in collaboration with the Galleria Marino, Rome. [Invitation; Catalogue published as *La Tartaruga. Quaderno 3*, with texts by Maurizio Calvesi, Maurizio Guercini, Franco Piruca].

November 10: *Giorgio Morandi – 60 acqueforti*. Exhibition produced in collaboration with the Galleria Marino, Rome. When the exhibition comes to an end the gallery closes its location in Piazza Mignanelli no. 25. [Invitation].

1986

March 23: the gallery is relocated to Via Ripetta no. 19, Rome, and inaugurates its new location with the presentation, curated by Plinio De Martiis and Stefano De Luca, of the first issue of *La Tartaruga. Quaderni di arte e letteratura*, edited by Plinio De Martiis, De Luca Editore, Rome 1986, with texts by Bruno Barilli, Leonardo Sinisgalli, Giuliano Briganti, Guido Cernetti, Giosetta Fioroni, Curzio Malaparte, Marisa Volpi. [Invitation].

April 23: *Maurizio Ligas*. [Invitation; Catalogue, with a text by Marisa Volpi].

June: publication of *La Tartaruga. Quaderni di arte e letteratura*, no. 2, edited by Plinio De Martiis, De Luca Editore, Rome 1986.

1987

May 25: *Aurelio Bulzatti*. When the exhibition ends the gallery closes its location on Via Ripetta no. 19. [Invitation; Catalogue published as *La Tartaruga. Quaderni di arte e letteratura*, nos. 3-4, De Luca Editore, Rome 1988, with a text by Luigi Ficacci].

1988

22 February: the gallery relocates to Via S. Anna no. 18, Rome, and inaugurates its new location with the exhibition *Cartelli di artisti 1954-1962*. On display are signs (*cartelli*) by: Afro, Umberto Bignardi, Alberto Burri, Enrico Castellani, Antonio Corpora, Piero Dorazio, Giosetta Fioroni, Jannis Kounellis, Leoncillo, Mario Mafai, Piero Manzoni, Titina Maselli, Gastone Novelli, Achille Perilli,

Fausto Pirandello, Raphael, Piero Sadun, Salvatore Scarpitta, Mario Schifano, Toti Scialoja, Antonio Scordia, Giulio Turcato, Cy Twombly. [Invitation].

May 11: *Frangia*. [Invitation; Brochure].

June: publication of *La Tartaruga. Quaderni di arte e letteratura*, nos. 3-4, edited by Plinio De Martiis, De Luca Editore, Rome 1988.

1989

March: publication of *La Tartaruga. Quaderni di arte e letteratura*, nos. 5-6, edited by Plinio De Martiis, De Luca Editore, Rome 1989.

May 23: *ProMemoria*. Exhibition curated by Netta Vespignani, Plinio De Martiis and Giovanni Audoli produced at the Galleria Netta Vespignani. On display are works by: Jos Albert, Giacomo Balla, Alberto Burri, Felice Casorati, Enrico Castellani, Giorgio de Chirico, Otto Dix, Antonio Donghi, Piero Dorazio, Ferruccio Ferrazzi, Albert Heinrich, Jannis Kounellis, Mario Mafai, Piero Manzoni, Arturo Martini, Fausto Pirandello, Franz Radziwill, Antonietta Raphael De Simon, Mimmo Rotella, Alberto Savinio, Chistian Schad, Scipione, Gino Severini, Mario Sironi, Francesco Trombadori, Cy Twombly, Alberto Ziveri. [Invitation; Catalogue published by Umberto Allemandi & C., Turin 1989, with texts by Netta Vespignani, Plinio De Martiis, and Giovanni Audoli].

October 24: *I fiori di Mafai*. Exhibition, curated by Maurizio Fagiolo dell'Arco, produced at the Galleria Netta Vespignani, Rome, in collaboration with La Tartaruga. [Invitation; Catalogue, edited by Maurizio Fagiolo dell'Arco, Società editrice Umberto Allemandi & C., Turin 1989, with texts by Giulio Carlo Argan, Piero Dorazio, and Alberto Ziveri].

1990

February: *MillenovecentoSessanta*. Exhibition, curated by Plinio De Martiis, held at the Galleria Netta Vespignani. On display are works by: Enrico Castellani, Piero Dorazio, Tano Festa, Giosetta Fioroni, Jannis Kounellis, Francesco Lo Savio, Piero Manzoni, Fabio Mauri, Giulio Paolini, Mimmo Rotella, Salvatore Scarpitta, Mario Schifano, Giuseppe Uncini. [Catalogue published by the Società editrice Umberto Allemandi & C., Turin 1990, with texts by Maria Silvia Farci, Laura Cherubini, Maria D'Alesio, Giulio Carlo Argan, Guido Ballo, Alberto Boatto, William Demby, Mario Diacono, Piero Dorazio, Gillo Dorfles, Enrico Castellani, Enrico Crispolti, Will Grohmann, Ugo Kiltermann, Francesco Lo Savio, Piero Manzoni, Filiberto Menna, Leo Paolazzi, Pierre Restany, Mimmo Rotella, Cesare Vivaldi, Marisa Volpi].

May: *La Tartaruga. Quaderni di arte e letteratura*, no. 7, edited by Plinio De Martiis, De Luca Editore, Rome 1990.

October-November: *Giusetta Fioroni. Roma*. Exhibition held at the Galleria Netta Vespignani in collaboration with La Tartaruga. [Catalogue published by Netta Vespigani, Rome, with a text by Guido Ceronetti].

1991

February-March: *Enrico Castellani*. Exhibition curated by Netta Vespignani, Plinio De Martiis, and Giovanni Audoli held at the Galleria Netta Vespignani, Rome. [Catalogue published by Netta Vespignani, Rome 1991, with interviews with the artist and texts by Gillo Dorfles and Adachiara Zevi].

May: *La Tartaruga. Quaderni di arte e letteratura*, nos. 8-9, edited by Plinio De Martiis, De Luca Editore, Rome 1991.

1992

May-June: *Ruggero Savinio*. Exhibition held at the Galleria Netta Vespignani, Rome, in collaboration with La Tartaruga. [Catalogue published by Netta Vespignani, Rome 1992, with a text by Gianni Carchia].

December 16: *Appunti fotografici di Giosetta Fioroni*. Exhibition curated by Guido Ceronetti, Erri De Luca, Cesare Garboli, Andrea Zanzotto. [Invitation].

December: *Interior*. Exhibition curated by Plinio de Martiis held at the Galleria Netta Vespignani, Rome. On display are works by: Giuseppe Bergomi, Aurelio Bulzatti, Tom Corey, Lino Frongia, Paola Gandolfi, Alessandra Giovannoni, Dieter Koop, Maurizio Ligas, Franco Piruca, Franco Polizzi, Ruggero Savinio, Peter Schmersal. [Catalogue editedby Plinio de Martiis, published by Netta Vespignani, Rome 1992].

1993

May: "Umano-Disumano." *La Tartaruga. Quaderni di arte e letteratura*, no. 10, edited by Plinio De Martiis, De Luca Editore, Rome 1993.

June 14 – October 10: photographs by Plinio De Martiis are on display at the Italian Pavilion, curated by Achille Bonito Oliva, as part of the *XLV Biennale Internazionale d'Arte di Venezia. Punti Cardinali dell'arte*. [Catalogue, Marsilio Editore, Venice 1993].

November: *Archivio. Fotografie di Plinio De Martiis*. Exhibition curated by Plinio De Martiis held at the Galleria Netta Vespignani, Rome. [Catalogue published by Netta Vespignani, Rome 1993, with an interview by Duccio Trombadori with Plinio De Martiis, and with texts by Miriam Mafai and Achille Bonito Oliva].

No Exact Date: the gallery's location on Via S. Anna no. 18 closes.

1994

April-May: *Aurelio Bulzatti*. Exhibition held at the Galleria Netta Vespignani in Rome, in collaboration with La Tartaruga. [Catalogo, published by Netta Vespignani, Rome 1994, with texts by Maria Silvia Farci and Tullio Kezich].

October-November: *Giorgio Franchetti. Undici ritratti.* Exhibition held at the Galleria Netta Vespignani in Rome, in collaboration with La Tartaruga. [Catalogue published by Netta Vespignani, Rome 1994, edited by Maria Silvia Farci].

November: *Italia 1980. Povratak Slikarstvu.* Exhbition held in Kraljev Dvorac in collaboration with La Tartaruga. [Catalogue].

1995

February: *Italia '80. Ritorno alla pittura.* Exhibition held at the Monastero di Santa Croce, Bisceglie, in collaboration with La Tartaruga. [Catalogue].

April-May: *Realismo a Roma, 1938-1943.* Exhibition curated by Fabrizio D'Amico held at the Galleria Netta Vespignani, Rome, in collaboration with La Tartaruga. On display are works by: Renato Guttuso, Fausto Pirandello, Alberto Ziveri. [Catalogue published by Netta Vespignani, with texts by Fabrizio D'Amico, and chronology curated by Romana Morelli].

July 21: the gallery relocates to Castelluccio di Pienza (Siena) and in Foce it inagurates its new location with *Gli anni originali,* curated by Plinio De Martiis. On display are works by: Giuseppe Capogrossi, Lucio Fontana, Alberto Burri, Mimmo Rotella, Ettore Colla, Piero Dorazio, Salvatore Scarpitta, Enrico Castellani, Piero Manzoni, Mario Schifano, Francesco Lo Savio, Franco Angeli, Giosetta Fioroni, Fabio Mauri, Jannis Kounellis, Giuseppe Uncini, Tano Festa. [Catalogue, published by Editori del Grifo, Montepulciano 1995, edited by Plinio de Martiis, with an introduction by Maria Silvia Farci and a critical anthology by Maria D'Alesio, 1995].

September 29: *Cinque personali. Shemesh, Pintaldi, Frish Prei, Di Fabio, Cosentini.* [Catalogue, published by DonChisciotte, San Quirico d'Orcia 1995, edited by Plinio De Martiis, with an introduction by Maria Silvia Farci].

1996

September 20 – October 20: *Piero Manzoni.* Mostra, curated by Plinio De Martiis, with twenty-one works from the collection of Karsten Greve. Held at the same time as the exhibition is a series of documentaries titled *Il secolo del cinema.* [Catalogue, published by DonChisciotte, San Quirico d'Orcia 1996, with an introduction by Bruno Corà, a poem by Gianni Malabarba, and a text by Piero Manzoni].

June 29 – August 4: *La misura italiana.* [Invitation].

July 30: *Jannis Kounellis.* [Invitation].
December: *Antonio Donghi.* [Catalogue, published by Netta Vespigani, Rome 1996, edited by Valerio Rivosecchi].

1997

May-July: *La ceramica degli artisti (1910-1997)*. Exhibition curated by Luciano Caramel and held at the Galleria Netta Vespigni with the collaboration of La Tartuga. On display are works by: Duilio Cambellotti, Giovanni Prini, Alfredo Biagini, Felice Casorati, Fillia, Arturo Martini, Corrado Cagli, Mirko Basaldella, Salvatore Fancello, Leoncillo, Lucio Fontana, Alberto Savinio, Luigi Broggini, Fausto Melotti, Renato Birolli, Pietro Malandri, Emilio Scanavino, Lucio Fontana, Nanni Valentini, Luigi Mainolfi, Mirella Saluzzo, Pino Castagna, Valter Boy, Enzo Esposito, Mimmo Paladino, Emanuele de Reggi, Giuseppe Bergomi, Luigi Ontani, Giosetta Fioroni, Marino Mazzacurati. [Catalogue, published by Netta Vespignani, Rome 1997, with entries about the artists by Isabella Montesi].

July 5 – August 20: *6 personali. Khebrehzadeh, Maccari, Migone, Pfrang, Pizzingrilli, Ruspoli.* [Catalogue, published by DonChisciotte, San Quirico d'Orcia 1997].

1998

July 4: *Per il clima felice degli anni Sessanta*. Exhibition curated by Plinio De Martiis, and later transferred, on November 26, to the Archivio della Scuola Romana, Rome. On display are works by: Franco Angeli, Roberto Barni, Gianfranco Baruchello, Umberto Bignardi, Agostino Bonalumi, Caniaris, Mario Ceroli, Claudio Cintoli, Piero Dorazio, Tano Festa, Fioroni, Gaul, Domenico Gnoli, Paolo Icaro, Ettore Innocente, Jannis Kounellis, Sergio Lombardo, Francesco Lo Savio, Renato Mambor, Gino Marotta, Eliseo Mattiacci, Fabio Mauri, Gastone Novelli, Giulio Paolini, Pino Pascali, Mimmo Rotella, Salvatore Scarpitta, Mario Schifano, Cesare Tacchi, Cy Twombly, Giuseppe Uncini. Also on display are photographs, letters, reviews, poems, and posters related to La Tartaruga's activity in the 1960s. [Catalogue, published by DonChisciotte, San Quirico d'Orcia 1998, with a text by Maria Silvia Farci].

September 5 – October 11: *Fabio Mauri. Picnic o il buon soldato*. Exhibition curated by Plinio De Martiis. [Catalogue, published by DonChisciotte, San Quirico d'Orcia 1998, with texts by Fabio Mauri].

1999

April: *Giorgio De Chirico*. Exhibition of graphic works.

April-May: *Francesco Trombadori. I Paesaggi del silenzio 1945-1961*. Exhibition curated by Valerio Rivosecchi held at the Archivio della Scuola Romana, Rome, in collaboration with La Tartaruga. [Catalogue, published by Archivio della Scuola Romana, Rome 1999, edited by Valerio Rivosecchi, with texts by Maurizio Fagiolo dell'Arco, Valerio Rivosecchi, Duccio Trombadori].

June 12: *La scuola di via Cavour*. Exhibition curated by Plinio De Martiis.

July 10: *Franco Angeli*. Retrospective curated by Plinio De Martiis. [Foldout].

September 11: *Tano Festa*. Exhibition curated by Plinio De Martiis.

December 18, 1999 – March 6, 2000: *L'arte pop in Italia: pittura, design e grafica negli anni Sessanta*. Exhibition curated by Plinio De Martiis and held at the Galleria d'arte Niccoli, Parma. [Catalogue, published by Galleria d'arte Niccoli, Parla and Grafiche Aurora, Verona 1999, texts by Plinio De Martiis, Teresilla F. Giacobone, Alan Jones, Alessandro Riva, with a critical anthology by Daniela Lancioni].

2000

March: *Plinio De Martiis e la Tartaruga*. Photography exhibition of the works of Plinio De Martiis and documents from La Tartaruga, held at the Collegio Cairoli, Pavia.

July 1: *Scarpitta-Dell'Angelo Scarpella*. Exhibition curated by Plinio De Martiis.

No Exact Date: the location in Castelluccio di Pienza closes.

2003

June 3 – July 13, 2003: *Le collezioni: arte contemporanea per l'Istituto Nazionale per la grafica*. Exhibition curated by Luigi Ficacci and held at the Istituto Nazionale per la Grafica in Rome following the acquisition by the latter of La Tartaruga's complete collection of 'signs-posters' exhibited on this occasion. [Catalogo, published by Hopefulmonster, Torino 2003, with a text by Luigi Ficacci].

May 29 – June 22: *Piazza del Popolo - sessanta/settanta*. Exhibition curated by Monica De Bei Schifano, Gianni Mercurio, Luca Ronchi and held in various locations, in Piazza del Popolo and in some of the windows and galleries of the Tridente. On display are photographs by Plinio De Martiis. [Catalogue, published by Legenda Aurea, Rome 2003, with a text by Walter Veltroni].

June: *Americaniaroma. Fotografie di Plinio De Martiis*. Exhibition curated by Maria Silvia Farci and held at the Spazio Fendi, Rome. [Catalogue].

July 12 – September 30: *54° Premio Michetti*, Francavilla al Mare. The jury, presided over by Duccio Trombadori, awards Plinio De Martiis the *Premio Michetti alla Carriera*.

2004

July 2: Plinio De Martiis passes away in Bagno Vignoni, San Quirico d'Orcia (Siena).

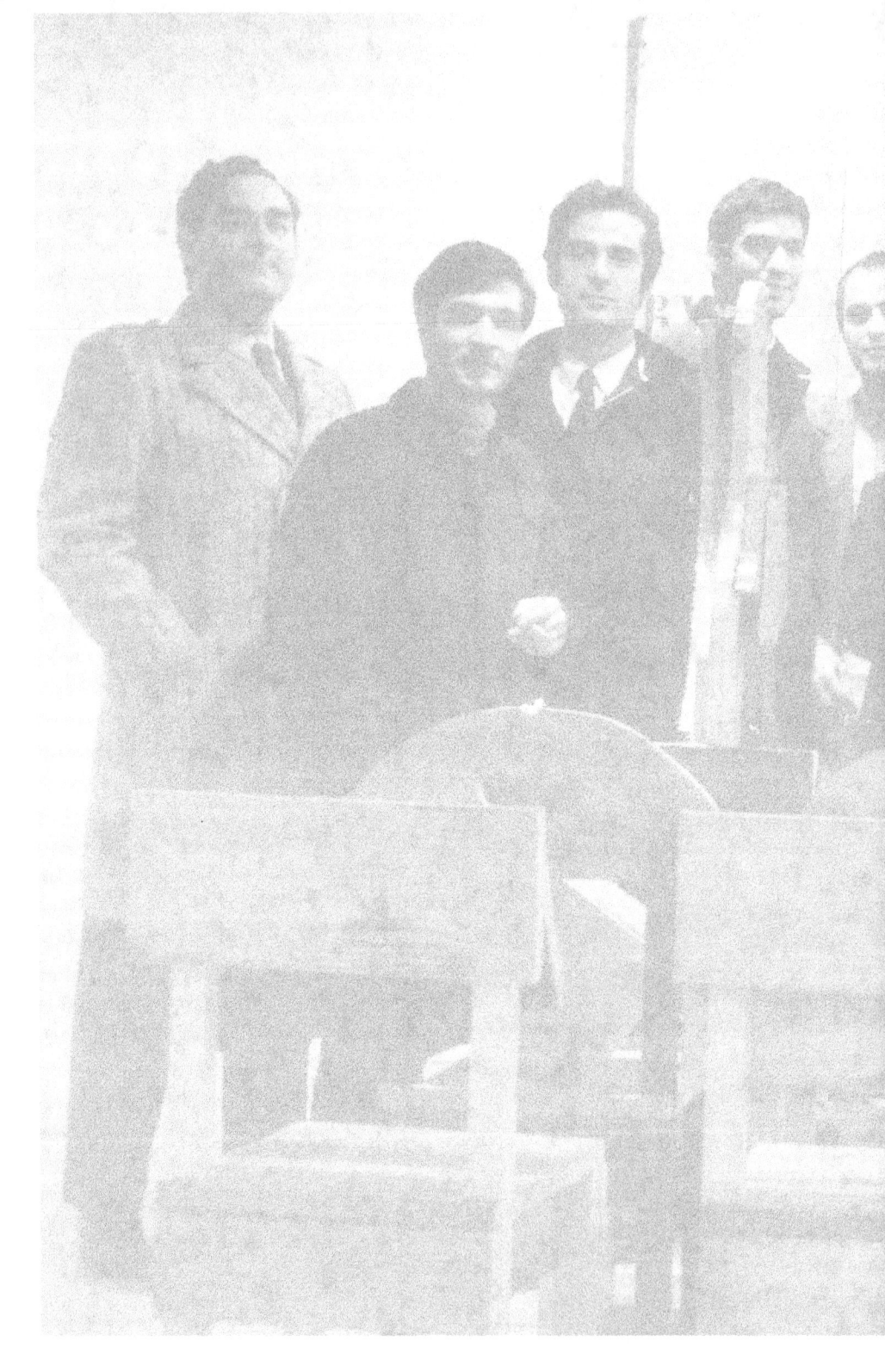

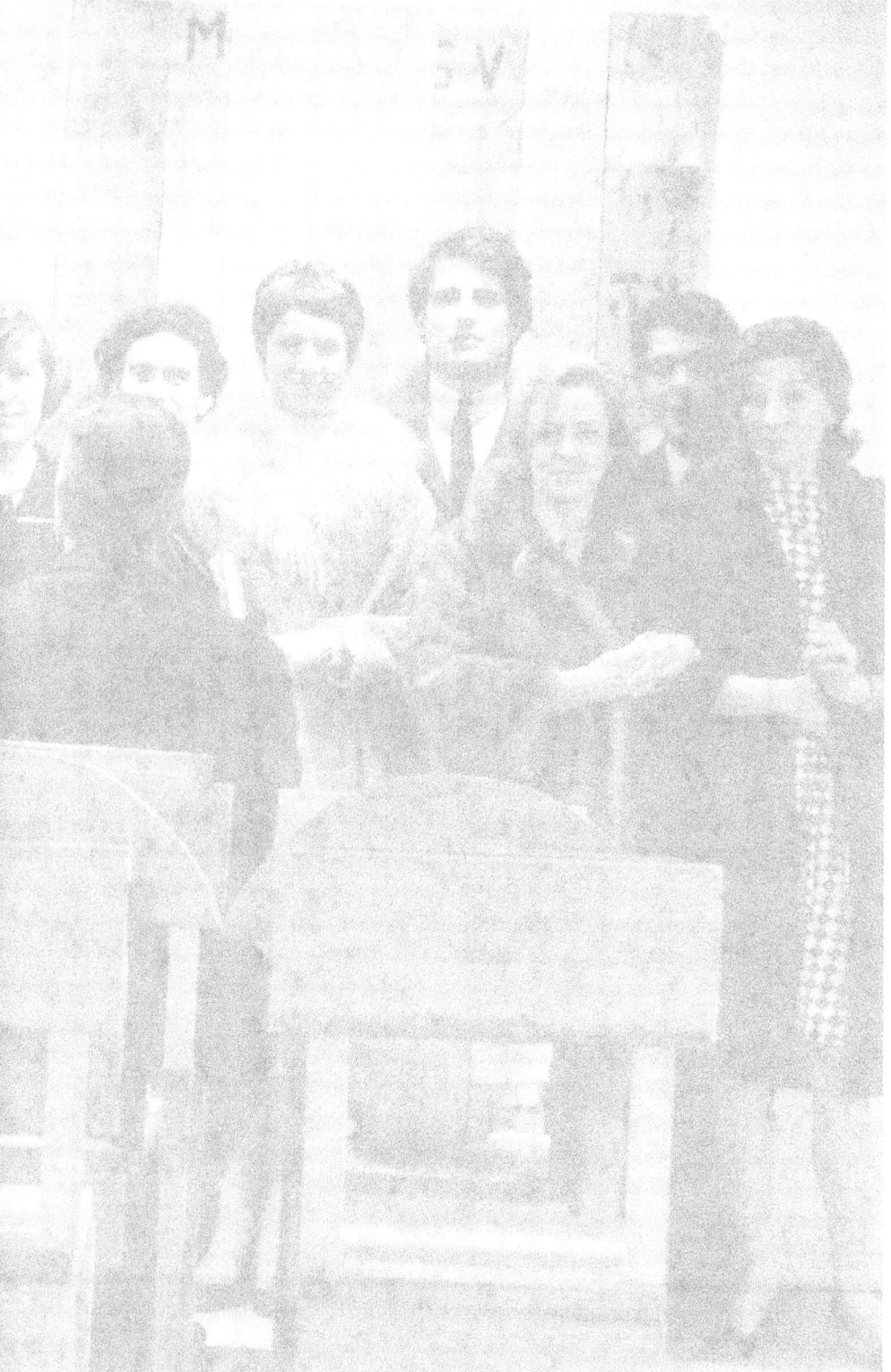

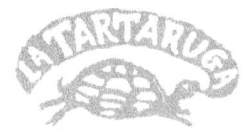

all rights reserved

All rights reserved. No part of this book may be reproduced
or transmitted in any form or by any means, electronic or mechanical,
without permission in writing from the Publisher.

Postmedia Srl
www.postmediabooks.it

www.ingramcontent.com/pod-product-compliance
Lightning Source LLC
Chambersburg PA
CBHW071410210526
45465CB00001B/327